THE COTSWOLDS

Landscapes of the Imagination

THE COTSWOLDS

A CULTURAL HISTORY

Jane Bingham

OXFORD
UNIVERSITY PRESS

2009

OXFORD
UNIVERSITY PRESS

Oxford University Press, Inc., publishes works that further
Oxford University's objective of excellence
in research, scholarship, and education.

Oxford   New York
Auckland   Cape Town   Dar es Salaam   Hong Kong   Karachi
Kuala Lumpur   Madrid   Melbourne   Mexico City   Nairobi
New Delhi   Shanghai   Taipei   Toronto

With offices in
Argentina   Austria   Brazil   Chile   Czech Republic   France   Greece
Guatemala   Hungary   Italy   Japan   Poland   Portugal   Singapore
South Korea   Switzerland   Thailand   Turkey   Ukraine   Vietnam

Published by Oxford University Press, Inc.
198 Madison Avenue, New York, New York 10016

www.oup.com

Oxford is a registered trademark of Oxford University Press.

Co-published in Great Britain by Signal Books

Library of Congress Cataloging-in-Publication Data
Bingham, Jane
    The Cotswolds : a cultural history / Jane Bingham.
    p.   cm.—(Landscapes of imagination)
    Includes bibliographical references and index.
    ISBN 978-0-19-539876-2; 978-0-19-539875-5 (pbk.)
    1. Cotswold Hills (England)—History.   2. Cotswold Hills (England)—Social life and customs.
3. Cotswold Hills (England)—Social conditions.   I. Title.
DA670.C83B45 2009
942.4'17—dc22   2009038286

Illustrations: alamy.com: 2, 23, 50, 144, 151; dreamstime.com: xii, 16, 32, 69, 78, 153;
istockphoto.com: i, 71, 111, 184, 197, 207; Jane Bingham: 105, 163, 193; David Vines: 57, 189;
Sam Vines: 47, 89, 127, 180; © Cheltenham Art Gallery & Museum: 118, 196, 210;
adderburyvillagemorrismen.co.uk: 222

9 8 7 6 5 4 3 2 1

Printed in the United States of America

Contents

Preface & Acknowledgements

One hot day in the summer of 1976 my partner and I took a break from house-hunting in Oxford and headed for the Cotswolds. The plan was to find a riverbank and relax, but it didn't work out like that. Driving past a village lane, we saw an intriguing sign and found ourselves investigating Tewer Cottage, a stone labourer's home with four small windows, a fireplace you could stand up in and a lean-to kitchen converted from a privy. There was an apple tree in the garden, honeysuckle round the porch and a prospect of Wychwood country from the upstairs rooms.

The following day we cancelled our plans for a city mid-terrace and put down a deposit on a dream. Three months later, with winter approaching fast, we began our initiation into life in the Cotswolds. Living in Tewer Cottage I discovered that anything you drop on a stone-flagged floor shatters instantly, that field-mice love warm kitchens (or, better still, warm beds) and that winters in a stone-built cottage can be bleak—even with the back-up of oil-fired heaters. I also discovered the pleasures of gathering logs in the woods, meeting the locals in the pub and having a choice of country walks minutes from my door. Intrigued by the lives of the families who had lived in our cottage, I visited the excellent Oxfordshire Studies Library and read about the Stonesfield slate industry that had lasted into the early years of the twentieth century. At the same time I began to collect novels and poems by writers who had known and loved the area.

Three years on, it was time to move back to Oxford, but I have continued to explore the Cotswolds—a pleasure that has intensified as I researched this book. In my explorations I have been accompanied by Luke, Tom, Peter and Elsie Ashby, Mary Ayres, Penny Bingham, Denise Cullington, Clive Fewins, Sandra Soper and David Vines. Mary, Denise, Clive and David have read parts of my text and offered valuable advice. Countless friends and acquaintances have shared their knowledge with me and I am especially grateful to Sarah and Daryl Cockings, Ann Fewins, Maggie Hartford and George Wormald. James Ferguson of Signal Books has been an excellent editor, making many thoughtful suggestions, but all errors and omissions are of course my own. Finally, I would like to say a special thank you to my husband David for living patiently with someone whose mind has often been elsewhere, wandering somewhere in the Cotswolds.

A book of this scope inevitably draws on the knowledge of others, and I am indebted to the painstaking Cotswold researches of Edith Brill, Josceline Finberg, Mary Greensted, Allan Jones and Alan Sutton. The work of two biographers has proved particularly helpful: Fiona MacCarthy's lives of William Morris and C. R. Ashbee provided a wealth of information and anecdotes for the chapters on Arts and Crafts; Valerie Grove's biography of Laurie Lee includes a fascinating account of the writer's youth and later life in the Cotswolds.

One of my favourite Cotswold places is the Woolpack Inn in Slad, where Laurie Lee used to drink. After he returned to his childhood village, Lee gave several interviews, usually conducted in the Woolpack garden overlooking the valley where he grew up. Speaking to a reporter from *The Independent* in 1966, he explained why the Slad valley had such a hold on him: "I used to think the whole world was like my valley. But when I went out into the world to try my fortune I realised there was only one place like this."

I hope that this book conveys something of the special nature of the Cotswolds—a place like no other in the world.

Introduction

"A COUNTRY MADE OF MEN'S VISIONS"

In the autumn of 1933 the playwright and novelist J. B. Priestley motored through the Cotswolds as part of his *English Journey*, a book that would become a classic of travel writing. The weather was fine but misty as he drove from Burford to Chipping Campden, following roads that "climbed and vanished into dripping space" and entering "little valleys as remote as Avallon." Immersed in this timeless scene, Priestley was enchanted: "we might have been journeying through the England of the poets, a country made of men's visions."

This book approaches the Cotswolds as a country of visions, but it is also rooted in a real place: a roughly lozenge-shaped region of hilly country extending for approximately eighty miles from Chipping Campden in the north-east to Bath in the south-west. The region known as "Cotsall" was already recognized by Shakespeare's time, but it was not until the 1960s that some precise boundaries were established. In 1966 the Cotswolds were designated an Area of Outstanding Natural Beauty with the aim of protecting the landscape from over-development, and in 1990 this area was extended to cover 790 square miles, making it the largest protected landscape in Britain. This unique region is marked on maps as an enticing patch of pale green between the capital and the West Country, and staked out on the ground by a set of roadside stones guarding the entrance to the Cotswolds.

The Cotswold AONB straddles six counties of southern England, with most of its bulk in Gloucestershire, although the Oxfordshire Cotswolds contain such well-known places as Burford and Charlbury. To the north, some of the outlying Cotswold hills extend into Warwickshire and Worcestershire, and the region's southern tip dips into Wiltshire and Somerset. Predominantly rural in character, it is a landscape of hamlets, villages and market towns (such as Northleach, Cirencester and Chipping Campden), with the more industrial towns of Stroud, Dursley and Chipping Norton on its margins. The borders of the AONB skirt the cities of Cheltenham and Bath, and this book does the same, referring to these cities only when they affect life in the Cotswolds.

Conspicuously excluded from the AONB are two iconic Cotswold

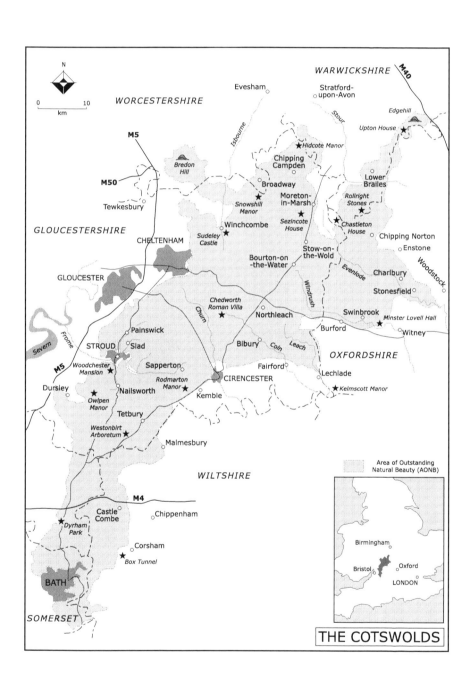

places: William Morris' beloved Kelmscott Manor lies close to the River Thames, a few miles south of the region's border. The ancient town of Woodstock, along with its grander neighbour Blenheim Palace, also stands just outside the AONB. These two places are so central to the Cotswold story that they have been included in this book, while a few other marginal locations (such as Witney, Fairford and Enstone) make brief appearances in the text.

LOOKING AT THE LAND

Of course, the real boundaries of the Cotswolds are carved in stone. Underlying the region is a band of limestone: part of a long diagonal strip crossing England from Dorset in the west to Lincolnshire in the east, and reaching its widest and highest points in the Cotswolds. Originally laid down in the Jurassic era when the region was a gigantic lake, the limestone provided a bulwark against the polar ice cap of the last Ice Age, forming the northernmost cliff of British land before the vast northern sea of ice began. By the end of the Ice Age, around 10,000 years ago, pressure from the ice cap had caused the limestone to buckle, resulting in the creation of the high escarpment known as the "Cotswold Edge". In the western Cotswolds the Edge takes the form of an undulating cliff of land, running from Bath to Cheltenham and offering spectacular views over the Severn to Wales. In the north the line of the ridge is less well defined, with long fingers of limestone extending northwards. At the time of the Ice Age the Cotswold promontories of Bredon Hill and Edgehill would have both been stranded in a sea of ice. Today they command a stunning prospect of the English Midlands.

From its highest point at the Cotswold Edge the land slopes slowly downwards towards the south and east. (It has been compared to a wedge of cheese, with the rind representing the Edge.) Lying behind the escarpment are the bare Cotswold uplands, often simply known as the "wolds". Occupying the lower ground are the river valleys where most of the towns and villages are found. In the central and eastern Cotswolds a leisurely group of streams meander gently south and east towards the Thames valley. These clear-watered streams include the infant Thames and its Cotswold tributaries: the Coln, the Churn, the Leach, the Windrush and the Evenlode. In the north and west the fast-flowing Stour, Isbourne and Frome rise in the Cotswold Edge and race downhill to join the Avon and Severn, carving steep gorges through the valleys.

The distinctive landscape of the Cotswolds has helped to determine the region's history. On the high wolds the bare, well-drained hills have provided excellent pasture for sheep since the Middle Ages. In the north and west, energy from fast-flowing rivers was used for driving water mills, and some thriving industries developed along the steep-sided valleys. The gentler river valleys of the central and eastern Cotswolds have always been more suited to farming.

Cotswold limestone has also given the area its instantly recognizable character. Ever since Neolithic times locally quarried stone has been used for buildings of all types, and the harmony between Cotswold buildings and their landscape has often been admired. (William Morris observed that traditional Cotswold houses seem to grow out of the land in which they stand.) Varying in tone from silvery grey in the west to buttery gold in the north, Cotswold limestone is easy to carve when it is dug out of the ground, but later becomes hard and durable. Its structure is oolitic (or "egglike")—made up of millions of prehistoric fossils—and this organic texture gives it an unusual capacity to reflect sunlight. The apparently luminous nature of Cotswold stone is especially noticeable in the early evening, when the sun is low. Wandering round the village of Lower Slaughter at dusk, J. B. Priestley saw this effect as a kind of magic: "these walls were still faintly warm and luminous, as if they knew the trick of keeping the lost sunlight of centuries glimmering about them. This lovely trick is at the very heart of the Cotswold mystery."

THE HISTORY OF THE COTSWOLDS

The human history of the Cotswolds began around ten thousand years ago with the arrival of Mesolithic hunters in the densely forested valleys of southern England. These primitive hunter-gatherers were succeeded around 4000BCE by Neolithic people, who began to clear land for grazing and built impressive tombs on the Cotswold Edge. The Neolithic Age lasted until around 2000BCE, when Bronze-Age settlers established small farming communities and created the mysterious stone circle known as the Rollright Stones. By 500BCE the Iron Age had begun, as waves of Celtic tribes invaded the Cotswolds, setting up rival territories in the region. A string of Iron-Age forts survives from this warlike period, but the Celtic warriors proved no match for the Roman army, who arrived in

Britain in 43CE and rapidly made their mark on the Cotswolds.

The Roman occupation of Britain lasted for almost four hundred years, bringing peace and prosperity to the Cotswolds. Roman Corinium (modern-day Cirencester) was the largest city after London. Wealthy villa farms were established in the Cotswold valleys, and the region became a busy trading hub sited at the junction of three major Roman roads. Following the departure of the Romans, communities in the Cotswolds gradually returned to a tribal way of life until a new order was imposed by the Anglo-Saxons. In the eighth century Winchcombe was the capital of the powerful Saxon kingdom of Mercia, and some remarkable abbeys and churches date from this time.

With the Norman Conquest in 1066 a new era of prosperity began in the Cotswolds. The Normans built castles, churches, abbeys and manor houses, and introduced sheep rearing on a massive scale. By the fifteenth century the fame of Cotswold wool had spread throughout Europe as market towns flourished and wealthy wool merchants paid for spectacular churches. For a few turbulent years in the 1640s the Cotswolds were devastated by civil war, but the seventeenth century also saw the flourishing of the cloth-making industry based around small mills and weavers' cottages. In the last decades of the following century the Industrial Revolution arrived in the Cotswolds, encouraging the building of factories, canals and railways. Prosperity did not last in the region, however, and by the 1850s many factories were standing empty. Farming also suffered at this time and the Cotswold countryside gradually sank into a state of picturesque decay.

In 1871 the artist and socialist William Morris discovered Kelmscott Manor and fell in love with the Cotswolds. Inspired by his example, craft communities were established in the Frome valley around Sapperton (led by Ernest Gimson and Ernest and Sidney Barnsley) and at Chipping Campden (led by C. R. Ashbee). These pioneers soon generated a flourishing Arts and Crafts movement whose impact can still be seen in the region today. Meanwhile, the mass-production of motorcars made the countryside accessible to tourists, and by the 1930s the Cotswold leisure industry was born. The exodus of young men to fight in two world wars helped to accelerate a decline in farming, and new social patterns emerged as a flood of newcomers arrived, many of them retirees and country-weekenders.

Over the past fifty years many native Cotswolders have moved away in search of new employment and cheaper housing. Others have found jobs in tourism, which is now the Cotswolds' leading industry. An influx of celebrities has recently put the region in the media spotlight. Yet despite these changes, the basic character of the Cotswolds has survived. Away from the crowded tourist spots and gastro-pubs it can still be seen as "a country made of men's visions."

CHANGING VIEWS: COMMENTATORS ON THE COTSWOLDS

Priestley's lyrical view of the Cotswolds would not have been recognized by early commentators on the region. When Shakespeare's Earl of Northumberland travels across the Cotswolds in the play of *Richard II*, his report is anything but romantic:

> These high wild hills and rough uneven ways
> Draw out our miles, and make them wearisome.

Other travellers had kinder things to say. Sir Richard Colt Hoare, riding around the region in the 1790s, wrote appreciatively of its rich vales and woods. Yet the Cotswolds were still perceived by many as a charmless, in-between land. In the 1820s, William Cobbett visited the region as part of his *Rural Rides* around England and was not impressed. Driving "between stone walls" across the wolds from Cheltenham to Oxford, he reported on "A very poor, dull and uninteresting country all the way to Oxford" and his account of the countryside around Cirencester is even more damning:

> In leaving Cirencester... I came up hill into a country, apparently formerly a down or common, but now divided into large fields by stone walls. Anything so ugly I have never seen before... Anything quite so cheerless as this I do not recollect to have seen.

Cobbett's impressions were bleak, but there was worse to come. In the 1830s the Rev. Sidney Smith saw nothing but "stone and sorrow" when he jolted over the wolds:

You travel for… twenty miles over one of the most unfortunate, deso-
late counties under heaven, divided by stone walls and abandoned to
the screaming kites and the larcenous crows: after travelling really twenty
and to appearance ninety miles over this region of stone and sorrow, life
begins to be a burden and you wish to perish. At the very moment when
you are taking this melancholy view of human affairs and hating the
postilion and blaming the horses, there bursts upon your view, with all
its towers, forests and streams, the deep and shaded Vale of Severn.

Less than forty years after Sidney Smith made his dismal journey
William Morris decided to rent the Cotswold manor house that he would
later immortalize in *News from Nowhere.* The land around Kelmscott
Manor is much gentler than the open wolds, but by the 1870s attitudes
to the countryside were changing fast. Wordsworth's *Prelude* had been published in 1850, and the Romantic Movement was soon well established in
Britain, bringing with it a new appreciation of nature. While the Cotswold
landscape could never inspire the wonder and awe of the Lake District,
people had become more responsive to its unspoilt charms.

An important factor in changing attitudes to the countryside was the
rapid industrialization of Britain. As the nation's towns and cities became
increasingly crowded and polluted, so the pleasures of the countryside
grew in comparison. Wealthy city dwellers longed to escape to the
country—at least for a long weekend—and the arrival of the railways made
this dream a reality. In the opening chapter of *A Cotswold Village* (published in 1898) J. Arthur Gibbs invites his readers to take the train from
London and flee with him to the Cotswolds:

London is becoming miserably hot and dusty; everyone who can away
is rushing off… Who will fly with me to the land of golden sunshine and
silvery trout streams, the land of breezy uplands and valleys nestling
under limestone hills, where the smoke of the factory darkens not the
long summer days?

Gibbs' account of his life as the gentleman squire of Ablington (near
Cirencester) unfolds in a string of lyrical chapters on picturesque villages,
amusing local characters and country sports. At moments in his eulogy
there are acknowledgements that the Cotswolds is in the grip of a severe

agricultural depression, but from the outset Gibbs makes plain his intention to present a rural arcadia: "let us endeavour to depict a state of existence as far as possible approaching the Utopian ideal… let us gaze at the evening brightening in the west."

To the fanciful Arthur Gibbs the Cotswolds offered a living embodiment of an Elizabethan "Merrie England". Emphasizing the region's (rather tenuous) links to William Shakespeare, he scatters quotations throughout his text, even going so far as to create an imagined scene featuring Master Shakespeare in the village of Bibury. Gibbs' approach can be seen as perversely whimsical in the face of real deprivation, but he was not alone in his romanticizing. Over the following fifty years, identification with an imagined Tudor past was to become a recurrent theme in writing on the Cotswolds. In his introduction to *The Footpath Way in Gloucestershire* (1924), Algernon Gissing (brother of the more famous George) described arriving in the Cotswolds as a boy: "To a bookish and impressionable lad, from north-country industrial surroundings, it was nothing less than stepping into Elizabethan England… The local language, the whole life and landscape, the very atmosphere itself was nothing but Shakespearean."

While the Cotswold eulogists constructed a Shakespearian fantasy land, Arts and Crafts practitioners in the region went in active search of the past, as they attempted to revive the ancient crafts and even built new houses in a consciously medieval style. Writer-craftsmen such as Morris, Ashbee and Norman Jewson praised the old-fashioned charms of the region and some members of the Movement even tried to adopt a medieval way of life with some unintentionally comic effects (described in Chapter Nine). By the 1930s the deliberate medievalism of the Arts and Craft Movement had fallen out of fashion (although crafts of all kinds still flourished in the Cotswolds). Nevertheless, an antiquarian image of the Cotswolds stubbornly persisted in the public imagination and in much of the writing of the period.

Nostalgia for a Cotswold arcadia reached its peak in the 1930s as writers made their escape to the region under the shadow of economic depression and impending war. Between the years 1932 and 1939 C. Henry Warren, H. J. Massingham and R. P. Beckinsale all produced loving evocations of the region. Also dating from this time is the account of John Moore, who snatched a brief journey through the land of his youth as war approached in 1937. Moore's view of the Cotswolds is refreshingly clear-eyed (he is ruthless in his contempt for what he sees as arty-crafty nonsense), but his book also contains a powerful assertion of the eternal values of the Cotswolds in the face of imminent destruction.

> As I topped the rise and looked down at the bright welcoming windows of Burford in the hollow below me, I began to feel like a man who has come to say goodbye… When the guns began, when the world came toppling about our ears and we that were young started to build a new world there would be no time for country contentments… The Cotswolds were the old world; and I had come back to them to say my farewell, and to set down in a little book my love of them, and of the… things which I should have no leisure for later; the rivers, the birds, the village churches, the talk at evening in the pubs. I should set it all down and count the time not wasted, for soon it might be too late and I might be too busy.

J. B. Priestley belongs firmly inside the magic circle of nostalgic commentators on the Cotswolds. On his *English Journey* towards the depressed North, he deliberately turns to the Cotswolds as "the most English and the least spoiled of all our countrysides" and within a few miles of approaching Burford he has allowed himself to fall under the spell "of a mysterious hollow land". For much of his chapter on the Cotswolds Priestley's trademark northern bluntness is abandoned as he adopts a semi-mystical tone:

> … you have only to take a turn or two from a main road into one of these enchanted little valleys, these misty cups of verdure and grey walls, and you are gone and lost, somewhere at the end of space and dubiously situated even in time… This, then, was one of these valleys… looking as if it had decided to detach itself form the rest of England about the time of the civil war…

LIVING LANDSCAPE OR HERITAGE PARK?
By the end of his stay in the Cotswolds Priestley had reached a radical conclusion. Recognizing that the region was "a land apart", he suggested that steps should be taken so that is could be preserved as:

a sort of national park, and by that, of course, I do not mean a playground or mere picnicking place… but a district that, regarded as a national heritage of great value, is controlled by a commonwealth… It may be necessary to banish from these hills the grimmer realities of our economic life, to make it artificially secure in its fairy tale of grey old stone and misty valleys, but… the move will be worth making.

In fact, Priestley's "national park" could be a description of the Cotswold AONB today. Thanks to a series of conservation measures, the Cotswolds still retain much of the "fairy tale" aspect that Priestley so admired in the 1930s. Yet with such preservation have come drawbacks. The region's timeless good looks have allowed Cotswolders to create a thriving "heritage park" filled with tearooms, antique shops and other tourist attractions. Even back in the 1930s Priestley recognized—and hated—this activity, which he christened "Ye Olde Game". Visiting Broadway, he found it "loud with bright young people who had just arrived from town and the *Tatler* in gamboge and vermillion sports cars." At Bourton-on-the-Water, Priestley faced more disappointments, finding the place "very conscious of itself". Drinking tea in a café adorned with "antique knick-knacks", he considered how the building's history accurately reflected the story of the Cotswolds: "Once, I imagine, it had some concern with agriculture or industry; then it was turned into [an artist's] studio; and now it is a picturesque tea-room: a sequence of some significance."

Nowadays the Cotswolds attracts thousands of visitors every year, but there are some positive aspects to the tourist trade. English Heritage and the National Trust have led the way in opening up the region's monuments, homes and gardens; visitors can learn about country life in centres such as the Cotswold Farm Park; and the area is especially welcoming to walkers, with a choice of long distance paths including the Cotswold Way, which runs along the Cotswold Edge from Chipping Campden to Bath. Walkers on the Way hike through Cotswold history as they encounter monuments from Neolithic, Bronze-Age and Roman times as well as churches, abbeys and manor houses.

RECENT VIEWS: BEHIND THE PRETTY PICTURES

The Cotswolds still inspire much whimsical writing. Guides to the region tend to lapse into eulogies to "honey-coloured stone", "nestling villages"

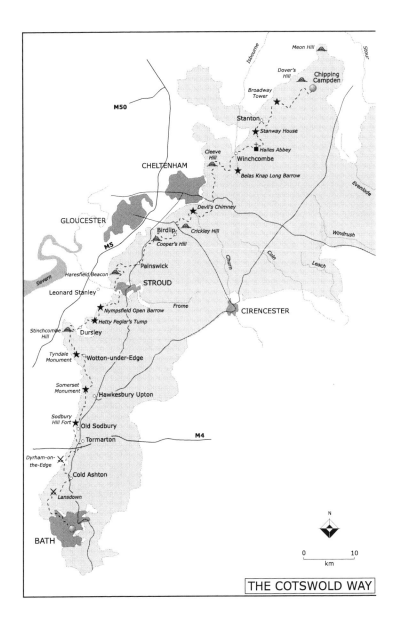

THE COTSWOLD WAY

and "quintessential Englishness". But a few observers have dared to take a less golden-hued view. Bill Bryson is far too good-natured to attack the Cotswolds although he does complain, in *Notes from a Small Island* (1993), of a surfeit of "Chippings and Slaughters and various Tweeness upon the Waters". Ian Walthew's discovery of the harsh realities of a Cotswold village is movingly related in *A Place in My Country: In Search of a Rural Dream* (2007), while A. A. Gill pulls no punches. In *The Angry Island: Hunting the English* (2005) Gill gives the Cotswolds a chapter of its own—the only English region to be singled out for sustained abuse. To Gill, Stow-on-the-Wold is quite simply "the worst place in the world". In his view, the "pale-yellow stone [which] is endlessly referred to as honey-coloured… could easily be piss-stained or nicotine-smoked," and the antique shops that line its streets have turned the town into a ghoulish "Vale of Curios".

While Gill despises Stow and the heritage industry it represents, he reserves his fiercest criticism for what he sees as the real Cotswold racket:

> The antique, novelty shops and tea rooms of Stow are really just a front for the true business of the Cotswolds, which is selling off lumps of itself. Property, second-homes and country life dreams are the staple money crop of the Cotswolds.

Gill goes on to paint an all too recognizable picture of the "new ruralists" of the Cotswolds: a noisy, self-conscious tribe with Agas in their kitchens and ponies in their paddocks. He is equally scathing about the incomers' enthusiasm for organics, which "has allowed 28-year-old former models and cosmetics PRs married to reality-television producers to know more about the countryside than fifth-generation farmers." Surveying a countryside invaded by new ruralists, he notes an unnatural neatness and trimness and "very little sign of dirty farming and nature". The Cotswolds according to Gill is a relentlessly depressing place, yet behind the caricature are some uncomfortable truths.

THE INSIDERS' VIEW

The views of commentators are all very well, but what of the true Cotswolders? Some of the clearest insights into Cotswold life have been provided by people who have spent their childhood in the region—and the best observer of all was Laurie Lee. Lee's *Cider with Rosie* looks back on his childhood in the Slad valley in the decade following the First World War. Recognized as a masterpiece of poetic rural writing, it stands in a class of its own and has been given a separate chapter in this book. Sid Knight's *A Cotswold Lad* describes a Broadway childhood in the opening years of the twentieth century, recalling details of school, work and leisure. Montague Abbot lived in the village of Enstone (near Charlbury) for 87 years, accumulating a wealth of stories, which he dictated to Sheila Stewart in *Lifting the Latch: A Life on the Land*. Most recently, Xandra Bingley has added to this group of Cotswold memoirs with *Bertie, May and Mrs Fish: Country Memories of Wartime*, a vivid account of a young girl's life on an isolated farm near Cirencester.

IMAGINATION AND IMAGES

One other significant group has helped to form our perception of the Cotswolds. Ever since Shakespeare's time, the region has inspired a range of writers, artists and musicians to create their own particular vision of Cotswold life. Writers who have produced Cotswold poems include (in chronological order): A. E. Housman, Hilaire Belloc, W. H. Davies, Edward Thomas, John Masefield, James Elroy Flecker, Ivor Gurney, T. S. Eliot, Laurie Lee and U. A. Fanthorpe. William Shakespeare made his Justice Shallow a Cotswold man, and novelists as varied as E. F. Benson, Nancy Mitford, John Buchan, J. B. Priestley, Barbara Pym and Jilly Cooper have given their stories a Cotswold setting. The paintings of Sir William Rothenstein capture the spirit of the landscape, while Stanley Spencer's Cotswold images show everyday country scenes filtered through a unique imagination. Probably the best-known artistic products of the region are the works of members of the Arts and Crafts Movement, whose work was guided by local craft traditions, and Cotswold traditions also informed the music of Ralph Vaughan Williams and Gustav Holst. All these varied responses to the Cotswold scene are described in Chapter Eleven and are often referred to in the course of this book.

RESPONSES TO THE LANDSCAPE

Responses to a landscape can take many forms. Ever since Neolithic times people have used the local stone to create homes and places of worship. For many Cotswolders, the land has been their livelihood, either through farming or working with stone. Wealthy landowners have moulded the landscape into sweeping estates, solitary eccentrics have hidden away in valleys, and bold industrialists have left their imprint, building mills, canals and railways. At times in the region's history it has been a battlefield, but it has also provided a playground for both rich and poor. Cotswold houses and villages have been a source of inspiration for many, most notably William Morris and his followers, while generations of gardeners have established their own particular landscapes within a Cotswold setting.

In constructing this book I have taken a thematic approach, using a series of chapters to consider a range of responses to the Cotswold landscape. Each chapter examines a different "vision of the landscape" and can be read independently. I have supplied some essential historical background, but my focus has always been on the people, stories and writings that make a place come alive. Above all, I have aimed to demonstrate how a very particular English landscape can take hold of the imagination.

THE COTSWOLDS

Chapter One
ANCIENT ECHOES
FROM PREHISTORY TO THE COMING OF THE
ANGLO-SAXONS

"To anybody who loves to glance into the very source of things, these bare uplands offer romantic interest in their abundant traces of prehistoric times. All our history begins here… the old camps and burial-places; the flints and stone implements which the ploughed fields have supplied, and still supply, so plentifully; the British, Roman, or earlier roads and trackways which traverse the lonely wolds."

Algernon Gissing, *The Footpath Way in Gloucestershire* (1924)

"One comes across the strangest things in walks…"

Ivor Gurney, *Cotswold Ways* (c.1920)

One of the finest walks in the western Cotswolds is the climb through Humblebee Wood up to Belas Knap (three miles south of Winchcombe). Leaving the road behind, the walker has a sense of moving back through time as the prospect of Sudeley Castle appears, framed by woods. The castle dates from the fifteenth century, but a much older building stands on the crest of the hill. Beyond the last stone stile is a whale-shape mound of earth—the Stone-Age burial chamber known as Belas Knap.

EXPLORING BELAS KNAP

Belas Knap was built as a communal tomb by Neolithic people around 2000 BCE. (Its name is probably derived from a corruption of the Latin for beautiful, and the old English "knap", meaning a crest of a hill.) Now mainly covered with grass, its structure is still easy to make out and its spectacular entrance porch seems hardly to have weathered in four millennia. The tomb measures some 180 feet long by 70 feet wide, gradually rising to a height of sixteen feet at its highest end, where an imposing entranceway is formed by a pair of gently curving dry-stone walls. These grand entrance walls have been the subject of much admiration. Algernon

The Rollright Stones: "The greatest Antiquity we have yet seen… corroded like wormeaten wood by the harsh Jaws of Time" (William Stukeley)

Gissing delighted in their "exquisite" gradual inward curve "faultlessly constructed in Hogarth's line of beauty, known to architects as ogee". For H. J. Massingham the wonder of the walls lay in their construction:

> [They] are built up of thin, close-fitting, superimposed wafers of stone whose perfect workmanship is proven not merely by their appearance but by the fact that parts of the walls have remained without a loose slate to this day... This ceremonial forecourt is the unacknowledged prototype of all the stone walls of field, bridge and street that are fundamental to the Cotswold scene... The only difference between any Cotswold stone wall and these horns of 2000B.C. is that, with some exceptions, the prehistoric technique is superior.

When the tomb was first uncovered in the 1860s, the remains of 38 skeletons of both sexes and all ages were found inside its chambers. It was also discovered that the grand entrance porch was a false portal, with a true entrance formed by a smaller doorway at the opposite end. The porch at Belas Knap has become one of the best-known images of Stone-Age Britain, but its real purpose remains a mystery. Was it merely intended as a decoy to distract tomb-raiders, or did it once provide a "ceremonial forecourt", where ancient rituals were enacted?

TOMBS FROM THE STONE AGE

Belas Knap is the largest and most recent of a series of Stone-Age tombs that survive along the Cotswold Edge. Known as long barrows because of their rectangular shape, they all follow the same basic pattern, with a long central corridor and a set of box-like chambers on each side. Giant stone slabs were used to form the walls and ceilings of the chambers, and a massive mound of stones was piled above them, making a monument that dominated the surrounding landscape. Inside the chambers there was room for up to thirty corpses, probably buried over several generations, and interred with animals, weapons, pots and ornaments—all in readiness for the afterlife.

At Nympsfield open barrow on Coaley Peak (six miles south-west of Stroud) the covering mound of stones has been lost, providing an excellent chance to appreciate the skill of the Neolithic builders. It has been estimated that each barrow required as much stone as a church, and the

Belas Knap, the grandest but not the earliest of the Cotswold long barrows

structures would have taken five thousand hours to build using basic tools made from stone and antlers. Stripped of its covering, the Nympsfield barrow has lost most of its mystery but it is still possible to admire its magnificent setting on one of the most spectacular sites in the Cotswolds, with a view across the Severn valley to the Welsh hills.

Visiting Nympsfield barrow is a fascinating experience but those in search of atmosphere should head for Hetty Pegler's Tump, two miles further down the Uley road. Back in the seventeenth century the "tump" was found in a field belonging to Hetty Pegler, a local landowner, and it still stands on farming land today. Approached by a path through the fields, the barrow resembles a small, grass-covered mound—until you notice the low stone entrance in its side, rather like a portal into Middle Earth. Inside, the tomb is dark and cramped, with only enough room to enter on hands and knees. Visitors today can explore the tomb by torchlight, but back in the 1930s, R. P. Beckinsale took a candle and experienced some distinctly queasy sensations.

> A dank, sepulchral smell comes from the darkness… and as the candle burns brighter we find ourselves in a stone gallery over 20 feet long… Two chambers, formed of huge blocks of stone, may be entered on the left, but the two similar chambers that probably stood on the right have been lost. A weird feeling of trespass, of indescribable watchful resentment at our intrusion, enhances the musty, earthy smell of this burial vault of forty centuries ago.

AT THE ROLLRIGHT STONES

Less than 500 years after the construction of the Belas Knap barrow, another great monument was erected in the Cotswolds. This was the "Rollright Stones", a circle of standing stones in the northern wolds, two miles north of Chipping Norton. The Rollright circle was constructed in the early Bronze Age, some time between 2500 and 2000 BCE. More accessible than Belas Knap, it became a popular place to visit and attracted some colourful local legends.

One of the earliest visitors was William Stukeley, who made a special journey to see the stones in 1743. As the leading antiquarian of his age he had already written a famous book on Stonehenge and Avebury, and now he was anxious to see a third stone circle. What he saw did not disappoint him. He reported that the Rollright Stones were "the greatest Antiquity we have yet seen... corroded like wormeaten wood by the harsh Jaws of Time" and observed that this "noble, rustic sight" was enough to "strike an odd terror upon the spectators." Today the Rollright circle is even more eroded than in Stukeley's time. Reduced to a set of stumps, the stones form a ragged circle roughly a hundred feet in diameter.

At certain times of day, when the light is dim, the Rollright circle resembles a group of men, leaning and crouching together, and by the Middle Ages they had gained the popular name of the "King's Men". Standing fifty yards south-east of the King's Men is a single monolith, called the King Stone, while 400 yards to the south-west are the "Whispering Knights", five tall stones leaning together. This scattered pattern of boulders is known collectively as the Rollright Stones, and several poetic legends have grown up to explain them. In 1610 the historian William Camden recorded a rhyming cautionary tale about an ambitious king, a witch and some soldiers, all immortalized by features in the landscape.

Camden's story reads like a Cotswold *Macbeth*. As a king and his army were marching through the hills they met a witch with a tantalizing message for the king:

> Seven long strides shalt thou take, says she,
> If Long Compton thou canst see,
> King of England thou shalt be.

Excited by the prospect of gaining the crown, the king set off eastwards, but on his seventh stride he found his view blocked by a hill, and the witch revealed the rest of her tragic prophecy:

As Long Compton thou canst not see
King of England thou shalt not be.
Rise up stick and stand still stone
For King of England thou shalt be none;
Thou and thy men hoar stones shall be
And I myself an eldern tree.

The prophecy came true as the king was turned to stone where he stood, while his petrified army became a ring of boulders. The witch was transformed into an elder tree, and the Whispering Knights, busy plotting the death of their king, changed forever into a group of leaning stones.

The story of the king, his men and the knights is just one of many attached to the Rollright Stones. Over the centuries there have been rumours of fairies dancing around the circle, and tales of the stones walking down to a stream to take a midnight drink. Until the nineteenth century, some young women would visit the King Stone at night to touch it with their breasts in the hope that they would be rewarded with a baby, and anyone who dared to meddle with the stones was reputed to suffer a horrible death. More recently there have been other explanations for the monuments—some of them quite outlandish. (One theory even suggests that the stones were used for extra-terrestrial communication.) But most archaeologists agree that the Rollright circle would have provided some kind of arena for religious rituals. It is possible that the stones were used for some kind of sun worship, and it has been posited that the circle could have functioned as a giant astronomical calculator, allowing early people to chart the movements of the sun and stars.

Although the Rollright Stones are grouped together by legend, they were never intended to form a cohesive unit. The circle known as the King's Men was probably constructed between 2500 and 2000 BCE. The Whispering Knights are part of a much earlier Stone-Age long barrow, and the King Stone dates from around 1500 BCE. The closeness of the three monuments is probably best explained by a continuous tradition of worship on a sacred stretch of ground.

BRONZE-AGE SURVIVALS

The Rollright circle is one of the first great monuments of the Bronze Age, a period lasting in Britain from around 2000 to 650 BCE. During this time, people began to adopt a settled way of life, living in small communities surrounded by farming land and producing fine metalwork and pottery. Organized religion appears to have played an important role in community life and several monuments dating from the Bronze Age survive in the Cotswolds. Two miles south of Rollright, a smaller stone circle has been found in a farmer's field at Cornwell, and there are single standing stones all over the region. (The Tinglestone at Gatcombe Park, the Longstone on Minchinhampton Common and the Thor Stone at Taston are just a few examples.) The significance of these monoliths has been much debated. Some of them, like the King Stone at Rollright, provided markers for cemeteries, and they must have created a dramatic focus for religious ceremonies.

The most common monuments surviving from the Bronze Age are round barrows. These were circular stone tombs for individual leaders, usually containing a jar of cremated remains, accompanied by weapons and ornaments. Today most round barrows have been reduced to grassy mounds in the landscape, but a larger structure survives near Little Sodbury, where a small hill is topped by trees. Known as Nan Tow's Tump, the barrow attracted a legend that it was the grave of a local witch, who had been buried standing upright.

CLUES FROM THE CELTS

Around 500 BCE a new surge of settlers began to arrive in Britain. They were Celtic people, who had come originally from Eastern Europe, bringing the new skill of iron smelting. Within a few centuries, the British Iron Age had begun as the Celts took over most of the country. Celtic metalworkers used iron to make tools and weapons, as well as fashioning jewellery from bronze, silver and gold. They survived by farming and hunting, and also introduced a more warlike way of life into Britain, waging battles against neighbouring tribes.

The most dramatic surviving Iron-Age remains in the Cotswolds can be seen on the high western escarpment north of Bath. Here, Celtic warriors built a series of forts to protect themselves against attacks from the Severn valley, and the ruins of these structures survive at Sodbury, Leckhampton, Cleeve, Crickley and Shenberrow. Excavations at Crickley Hill have revealed a complete fortified town, with rubble and timber walls, an imposing double gateway and a paved central street flanked by long houses. At Kemerton Fort on Bredon Hill archaeologists unearthed the mutilated bodies of about fifty young men whose remains were left un-buried, strewn over a battleground.

At some time during the first century CE, the powerful Celtic tribe of the Dobunni became the dominant group in the Cotswolds, building a large encampment at Bagendon (near Cirencester). Like most large Celtic settlements, Bagendon was defended by a series of ditches and walls and some of these earthworks survive as ridges in the landscape. The smiths of Bagendon were highly skilled, and they were probably responsible for the treasures found in a grave at Birdlip, where a Celtic princess was buried with a set of fine bronze bowls, bracelets, rings, beads and brooches. Among the Birdlip treasures was a round bronze mirror ornamented with delicate swirling patterns and inlaid with red enamel. Now displayed in the Gloucester City Museum and Art Gallery, the Birdlip Mirror is one of the best-known examples of Celtic art in Britain.

Remembering the Romans

In 43CE news reached the Cotswolds of a new invasion from the south. Following the orders of the Emperor Claudius, an army of 40,000 Romans had landed in Kent and had begun to gain control of southern England. Faced with the might of the Roman army, King Bodvoc of the Dobunni decided not to put up a fight, sending envoys to Kent to offer his sub-mission. By 47CE the Romans had set up camp at Chesterton, close to Bagendon and their soldiers and engineers were hard at work, building a network of roads across the Cotswolds.

By the start of the second century the Cotswold kingdom of the Dobunni had been incorporated into Roman Britain. At the heart of the region was the city of Corinium (present-day Cirencester), linked by road to the military colony at Glevum (Gloucester) and the spa at Aquae Sulis (Bath). Corinium grew rapidly and by 300 CE it was Britain's second largest city, providing the capital for Britannia Prima, one of the four sub-provinces of the British Isles.

Corinium was a model Roman city. Built from Cotswold stone and surrounded by a high perimeter wall, it covered 240 acres and contained an impressive set of public buildings including a basilica, public baths and a theatre. Just outside the city walls stood a large amphitheatre, whose remains can still be seen in a hilly public park on the outskirts of the modern town. In Roman times the amphitheatre would have drawn massive crowds with a spectacular programme that featured animal hunts, religious festivals and public executions. Nowadays you can just make out the outlines of the oval arena, while rising up on all sides are grassy banks that once provided seating for over eight thousand spectators.

Very few Roman remains survive in Cirencester itself, but a good way to visualize the ancient city is to visit the Corinium Museum. Through an award-winning set of displays, visitors are introduced to Corinium in its Roman heyday (and are also shown the history of the town through the ages). The Museum provides a showcase for Roman finds from all over the region, including some intriguing religious carvings and several fine mosaics unearthed from Cotswold villas. Corinium was a centre for mosaic making, and the city's workshops produced high-quality pavements with a delicate palette of pinks, ochres, white and grey. The Corinium masters often depicted animals and hunters, but their trademark theme was the legend of Orpheus. The story of the man who lived in a forest, charming all the animals with his music, must have had a special appeal for the Cotswold people in their deeply wooded valleys.

As well as building cities the Romans made their mark on the countryside, importing sheep and grain and establishing farms all over the Cotswolds. Over a hundred farmhouses have been discovered in the region, most of them modest buildings, but at least a dozen were substantial villas, which must have belonged to very wealthy landowners. A magnificent pavement at Woodchester (now only rarely open to the public) may have formed part of the palace of a regional governor, and the remains of important farmhouses can be seen at Great Witcombe and North Leigh. The most complete Cotswold villa is at Chedworth, eight miles north of Corinium. It was discovered in 1864, when a local gamekeeper digging in the woods for his lost ferret noticed some unusual fragments of pottery—a chance find that led to the uncovering of a magnificent 32-room home.

The Roman villa at Chedworth began as a modest farmhouse in the second century, but was greatly enlarged two centuries later, making the focus of the house a set of grand reception rooms arranged around a central courtyard. Many of these rooms still have the remains of painted walls and mosaic pavements, and an ingenious 'hypocaust' system of under-floor heating. A small shrine dedicated to a water goddess stands on the high ground in the north-west corner of the site, and just below the shrine are the ruins of a private spa, equipped with hot steam bath, cold plunge, sauna and exercise room.

The Romans had a genius for choosing wonderful sites, and Chedworth is one of the best. Sited at the head of a steep-sided valley, the villa commands astonishing views down the valley to the water meadows. Di-

rectly behind the house rise thickly wooded hills where the master and his guests would have hunted for game. In Roman times these woods supplied most of the game for the banqueting table, as well as a more unusual delicacy. Walking through the Chedworth woods today, you can still find descendants of the giant snails that the Romans imported to the Cotswolds eighteen centuries ago.

At Chedworth Roman Villa everything is orderly and explained, according to the best modern principles (although the original Victorian museum has been preserved on site). But searchers for ancient mystery should seek out the remains hidden in Spoonley Wood (close to Winchcombe). Bill Bryson knew the way, but wisely did not divulge it, and neither shall I. Arriving in a clearing he found low walls and the remains of a complete Roman pavement, and felt a sense of disorientated delight: "I cannot tell you how odd it felt to be standing in a forgotten wood in what had once been, in an inconceivably distant past, the home of a Roman family, looking at a mosaic laid at least 1,600 years ago when this was an open sunny space, long before this ancient wood grew up around it."

Tracing the Ancient Ways

Modern travellers from Cirencester to Chedworth can chose between two routes, both originally built by the Romans. The minor road from Cirencester to Chedworth was once the Roman White Way, connecting Corinium with several large villas in the northern Cotswolds. The A429 was part of the famous Fosse Way, passing through Bath and Cirencester on its bold diagonal course from Exeter to Lincoln. Fosse Way was one of three major routes that met at Corinium. Akeman Street ran due east to St. Albans, while Ermin Street headed west to Gloucester and Wales.

The best way to appreciate the lines of the Roman roads is from the air. John Moore flew his biplane over Cirencester in the 1930s, and saw the marks the Romans made two thousand years before:

> And now for the first time I saw, not Cirencester, but Roman Corinium. Our pusillanimous modern roads, twisting, winding, criss-crossing each other, were hardly distinguishable at three thousand feet; as if they had been rubbed out of the landscape... But the Roman roads endured. Incredibly straight, incredibly purposeful, sweeping majestically over the hills to their meeting-place at Corinium, ran the three straight tracks hammered out by the feet of the legions nearly two thousand years ago: Ermine Street, Akeman Street, Fosse Way. The Roman roads dwarfed [our modern routes] and so dominated the landscape I realized with a something of a shock that I was looking down on Roman Britain. A high-flying eagle hovering over Corinium in the time of the Emperor Claudius would have seen.... exactly what I saw two thousand years later.

The Roman roads are not the oldest routes to survive in the Cotswolds. Running the length of the Cotswold Edge, just below the escarpment, is an ancient walking track that probably dates from the Palaeolithic period. Known today as the Jurassic Way, the track was probably first established by nomadic people in search of new hunting grounds. In the Neolithic period it was used for trade with neighbouring tribes, and by Roman times farmers with horses and carts were riding along the track. Signs of other ancient tracks have been uncovered in the Cotswolds. At Lower Slaughter, Ryknield Street crossed the Roman Fosse Way; Buckle (or Buggilde) Street ran through the north-east Cotswolds; and Icknield Street crossed the valleys in the south. Some of the most important routes through the Cotswolds were the Saltways, which were used to transport essential supplies of salt from Droitwich Spa, in Worcestershire, to the southeast of England. The Saltways traced diagonal paths across the region, ending up at Lechlade, where the salt was loaded onto barges. Dating from pre-Roman times, they were in constant use until the sixteenth century, as trains of packhorses crossed the Cotswolds bringing salt to towns, villages and farms along the way.

After the Romans

For almost 400 years the Cotswolds enjoyed peace and prosperity, as the Romano-Britons reaped the benefits of belonging to a great empire. But this peaceful period did not last. By the 370s the Romans were under threat from warlike tribes, and in 410 the last of the Roman legions withdrew from Britain, leaving the natives to look after their own defence.

By the time Rome fell, in 476, life had already changed for the worse in the Cotswolds. Farmers no longer had a ready-made market for their produce, and without the restraining presence of the Roman army violent feuds broke out between rival tribes. Over the next two centuries the British people gradually reverted to a tribal way of life. Cities and villas fell into ruins as Britain became an easy target for the next wave of invaders.

Even before the Roman legions left Britain, tribes of Angles and Saxons had already begun to arrive on Britain's southern shores. Originating from Denmark and northern Germany, they were tough warriors who fought in small, well-organized groups. The invaders advanced steadily across the country and by the 550s a tribe called the West Saxons had established the kingdom of Wessex in the Thames Valley. Over the next twenty years the Cotswolds were invaded on two fronts. West Saxon conquerors made steady progress through the southern valleys, while Angles took control of the north-west. Faced with danger on both sides, the Dobunni leaders retreated to the cities of Gloucester, Cirencester and Bath, where they drew up their armies and prepared to fight to defend their ancient Celtic territory.

In 577 the assault arrived. Led by their chieftains Ceawlin and Cuthwine, a Saxon army stormed through the southern Cotswolds, marching west towards Bath, while the Celtic kings led their forces to meet the Saxons. The two sides met at Dyrham-on-the-Edge, eight miles north of Bath, where a historic battle was fought on the escarpment (close to the spot where the Civil War Battle of Lansdown was waged). The Saxons gained a resounding victory, moving on to seize Bath, Cirencester and Gloucester, while the Dobunni chiefs retreated, heading west to join their fellow Celts in Wales. The Battle of Dyrham marked a major turning point in British history. From that time on, England belonged to the Anglo-Saxons.

ANGLO-SAXON ECHOES

The Anglo-Saxons brought major changes to the Cotswolds, as the region was gradually transformed into a landscape of villages grouped around manors and churches. A feudal pattern of farming evolved, with fields shared by villagers, and some small towns, such as Winchcombe, were established as centres for trade. Around the year 600 the Cotswolds became part of Mercia, the largest of the seven kingdoms that made up Anglo-Saxon England. Mercia covered most of central England, and had several capitals during its history, but in the eighth century Winchcombe became the seat of the powerful Mercian kings, who established an important abbey in the town.

Within the kingdom of Mercia a smaller tribal group, known as the Hwicce, lived in the Cotswold region and Worcestershire. This tribe gave their name to Wychwood Forest, a densely wooded area extending over most of west Oxfordshire, which provided a favourite hunting ground for the Saxon kings. Sometime during the Anglo-Saxon period the Cotswold region also gained its name. According to one theory, a chieftain named Cod owned some high land or "wold" close to the source of the River Windrush, and the local name of "Cod's wold" gradually expanded until it covered a much larger area. The Cotswolds are hence sometimes known as "King Cod's land". A more mundane theory suggests that the first part of Cotswold is derived from the Saxon word "Cote", meaning a hollow in the ground or an animal pen.

Chapter Two

FINDING GOD IN GLOUCESTERSHIRE

SAINTS, CHURCHES AND CLERICS

"As sure as God's in Gloucestershire…"

Old country saying

Walkers on the Cotswold Way heading west from Winchcombe may be surprised to find some ancient paving stones underfoot—signs that they are following one of the busiest pilgrim routes of the Middle Ages. Back in the fifteenth century people flocked to this remote corner of the Cotswolds to visit the famous abbeys of Winchcombe and Hailes. At Winchcombe they prayed at the shrine of St. Kenelm and drank the healing waters of his well. A couple of miles along the pilgrim way they queued to view the precious relic of Hailes, claimed to be the True Blood of Christ. Hailes Abbey was famous all over England; Geoffrey Chaucer even made one of his characters in the *Canterbury Tales* swear a solemn oath "by the blode of Christ that is in Hailes", and Christians were convinced that just one sight of its Holy Blood could guarantee salvation. Of all the shires in England, Christians felt, God was surely to be found in Gloucestershire, and the early history of the region is intimately linked to its churches and abbeys.

EARLY ABBEYS AND THE BOY SAINT OF WINCHCOMBE

Christianity came slowly to the Cotswolds. There is some evidence of Christian worship in Roman Britain (at Chedworth Villa the Christian Chi-Ro symbol has been found scratched on the stones of a water shrine), but it was not until the sixth century that the Christian message was widely accepted in the Cotswold valleys. In the following century work began on the building of abbeys, and by the 800s the region had eight major foundations, two of them famous throughout England. Malmesbury Abbey, in the south-west, was founded by a scholar-poet in the seventh century and rapidly gained a reputation for learning, acquiring the second largest library in Europe. In the northern Cotswolds Winchcombe Abbey was es-

Chipping Campden church, one of the Cotswolds' "Woolgothic wonders"

tablished in 811 by Kenulf, King of the Mercians. When Kenulf's heir died young (probably in a hunting accident in a forest), an elaborate legend grew up to explain his death and Winchcombe rose to fame as the site of the remarkable miracle of the boy-martyr known as St. Kenelm.

> Lo in the Life of Saint Kenelm I read –
> That was Kenwulph's son, the noble King
> Of Mercia - how Kenelm met a thing;
> A little ere he was murdered on a day
> His murder in a vision he saw…
>
> Geoffrey Chaucer, *The Nun's Priest's Tale*

By the time Chaucer recorded the story of St.Kenelm in his *Canterbury Tales*, the brief life of an obscure Mercian prince had been transformed into a popular tale of piety and magic. According to the legend, Kenelm was just seven years old when he inherited the throne from his father, but he had scarcely had time to enjoy his kingdom before he was murdered in a distant forest. Fortunately, however, Kenelm was no ordinary murder victim. The marvellous boy had already foreseen his death "in a vision" and knew the exact spot where it would take place. No sooner had the deed been done, than the boy's spirit was transformed into a dove that flew to the Pope in Rome and back, bringing news of where his body lay to the grieving monks of Winchcombe. With the miraculous dove as their guide, the monks set off for northern Mercia, where they found Kenelm's body in a forest, and carried it back to Winchcombe to be buried. The journey from Romsley in Worcestershire covered some sixty miles, a route that can now be followed on the St. Kenelm's Walking Trail, and is said to have featured several miracles. Each time the monks laid down the coffin to rest, a crystal spring gushed up, with the last and most important fountain bursting out of the ground less than a mile from Winchcombe Abbey.

Within a century of his mysterious death Kenelm had been recognized as a saint. His feast day was celebrated on 17 July (the day his body was said to have arrived in Winchcombe) and churches all over the Cotswolds were dedicated to him (there are churches of St Kenelm at Alderley, Minster Lovell, Enstone and Sapperton). At Winchcombe, the cult of the boy martyr was especially strong. The waters of St Kenelm's Well became renowned for their healing powers, attracting hordes of pilgrims who also stopped at the abbey to say prayers at the saint's tomb. Writing in the early twelfth century, William of Malmesbury could claim "there was no place in England to which more pilgrims travelled than to Winchcombe on Kenelm's feast day." Today Kenulf and Kenelm are commemorated in Winchcombe Church, while the site of St. Kenelm's Well can still be found, neglected and overgrown, half a mile down the road leading from Sudeley Castle to Guiting Power.

SACRED SITES AND SAXON SCULPTURES

By the start of the tenth century Christians in the Cotswolds had begun to build simple churches from stone. These tall, box-like structures were often constructed on the sites of older sacred shrines. At Bisley a set of pagan altars has been discovered under the church tower, and the church at Ozleworth stands in a circular churchyard, which may once have been a Bronze-Age stone circle. The most intriguing evidence for a pagan past survives at Daglingworth, where a carved stone panel was built into the structure of a Saxon wall. Inscribed with the words DEA MATRES (a trio of mother goddesses worshipped in Romano-British times), the panel provides a hint of the pagan ceremonies that were probably celebrated on the site of the present church.

No complete Saxon church survives in the Cotswolds, but some churches have substantial Saxon features. At Coln Rogers the Saxon nave and chancel are almost intact, with thick stone walls and narrow slits for windows. North Leigh church has kept its solid Saxon tower, with alternate long and short stones at each corner, and the simple field church at Duntisbourne Rouse has a narrow Saxon nave, with a crypt dug into the hillside. The church at Duntisbourne Rouse dates almost entirely from the eleventh and twelfth centuries, and is one of the hidden treasures of the Cotswolds. Reached by an overgrown lychgate, it stands in a tiny valley of its own. "Everything here is diminutive," Alec Clifton-Taylor writes, "except one's pleasure."

A mile south-east of Duntisbourne Rouse is the Saxon church at Daglingworth (mentioned above). It was heavily restored in the 1840s, but a Saxon doorway has survived with a sundial scratched above it. Inside the church three carved stone panels date from the early years of the eleventh century. The panels show the Crucifixion, St. Peter with his key and Christ in Judgment, all very simply carved with large, staring eyes.

For David Verey, these "moving archaic sculptures" make Daglingworth "one of the shrines of art in England".

NORMAN CHURCHES AND CARVINGS

Church building in the Cotswolds really took off in the 1100s, with the arrival of the Normans. For the next 200 years Norman masons worked all over the region, adding to Saxon structures and building churches of their own. Today there is hardly a church in the Cotswolds without a few surviving Romanesque features, and many of the smaller village churches have kept the massive pillars, rounded arches and sturdy central towers that are so characteristic of the Norman period.

The most outstanding Norman church in the Cotswolds stands on a windy escarpment at Elkstone, just off the A417 from Cirencester to Gloucester. John Moore found Elkstone church "curious" and "haunted-looking" and saw it as a symbol of the eternal values of the Cotswolds: "I felt, as I stood here in the dusk, that I had found one certainty among a confusion of uncertainties; and that if in the next few years we make a shambles of the world, and if I survive it, I shall be able to come back here knowing surely that I shall see the tall, square tower on the windy hill…" To Massingham, Elkstone was "stalwart, grand and grim". He was intrigued by the gallery of carvings on its outer walls (depicting animals and birds and signs of the zodiac). "Nowhere is the figure-work of the corbels more fantastic and ribald and Freudian than at Elkstone." Stepping inside the church, under a carved Christ in Majesty, Massingham was surprised (as all visitors to Elkstone are) by the golden light of the chancel, and admired the deeply incised Norman arches with their zig-zag patterning and fierce dragonheads.

Elkstone is one of many Cotswold churches with dramatic Norman carvings. There are striking porch carvings at Quenington, Salford and Harnhill; fonts at Rendcomb, Southrop and Hook Norton; and carved capitals at Leonard Stanley. But these are all outclassed by the remarkable carvings at Malmesbury Abbey. Here the great south door is surrounded by eight bands of ornament, while facing each other across the porch are a pair of monumental scenes showing a group of apostles visited by a flying angel. The Malmesbury apostles have been described as the most outstanding Romanesque sculptures in Britain. They are also surprisingly modern in their power to move and surprise.

STORIES ON WALLS

Every parish church in the Middle Ages would have had its own set of wall paintings, providing a handy teaching aid for a largely illiterate congregation. Only a tiny proportion of these paintings have survived today, but some fine examples can be seen in the small field church at Ampney St. Mary, just beside the busy A417. Opening the church door, the visitor is confronted by the giant figure of St. Christopher crossing a river with the Christ child on his shoulders. Christopher is the patron saint of journeys and his comforting image was usually painted facing the south door, where it could be seen by passing travellers. Next to him are scenes from the life of St. George, a popular subject in medieval England, and across the aisle is an intriguing teaching diagram, known as Christ of the Trades. The mural of Christ of the Trades shows a giant figure of a bleeding Christ surrounded by medieval tradesmen's tools. In the Middle Ages (and for several centuries afterwards) it was strictly forbidden for people to work on the Sabbath, and the painting demonstrates in vivid detail how the wicked tradesmen who use their tools on a Sunday are in fact inflicting wounds on their Saviour's body.

There are excellent wall paintings at Stowell, Baunton and Hailes, but the best place for atmosphere is the church at Lower Oddington, where the whole of the north wall is covered with images. Close to the pulpit a pair of medieval teaching aids depicts the popular subjects of the Seven Acts of Mercy and the Seven Deadly Sins, while the rest of the wall is covered by scenes from the Day of Doom, showing Christ in Judgment at the end of the world. At the painting's centre a pair of angels blow on their trumpets to summon the dead from their tombs. On either side angels and demons claim the saved and the damned, leading them off to their eternal fates. The painting is packed with incidents, but a few vivid scenes stand out. In the regions of hell a striped demon uses a pair of bellows to fan the flames beneath a cauldron of souls and a thief hangs from a gallows, while in the heavenly city an angel leans over a parapet to offer a lucky soul a helping hand to eternal bliss.

WOOLGOTHIC WONDERS

The architectural superstars of the Cotswolds are the great wool churches. In the fifteenth century wealthy wool merchants lavished large fortunes on their local churches, in the hope of gaining admiration on earth and reward in heaven. Using the finest craftsmen, they financed major renovations as Norman pillars and arches were demolished to make way for slender columns and enormous windows. Porches and side chapels were added, and soaring towers were built in the Perpendicular style. At the same time, the churches were adorned with statues, brasses and stained glass. The result was an exuberant form of Perpendicular Gothic, sometimes known in the Cotswolds as "Woolgothic".

At Chipping Campden the church dominates the town, and its elegant tower can be seen for miles, topped by twelve pinnacles. The nave was rebuilt in 1488, creating two storeys of generous windows, and a large new window was inserted above the chancel arch (a feature sometimes known as a Cotswold window). The Campden master mason also rebuilt the nave at Northleach, where the proportions of hexagonal columns and wide, flat-arched windows are even more perfect. Northleach's greatest glories are its giant east window, which floods the church with light, and a generous "Cotswold window" over the chancel arch. The church also has an exquisite fifteenth-century porch, with a priest's chamber overhead, but this is a tiny structure compared with the massive addition to Cirencester church, where the three-storey porch was used as a town hall for hundreds of years. Cirencester is the largest and grandest of the Cotswold wool churches and its many improvements and alterations took more than a century to complete. Between 1400 and 1521 the nave was remodelled, new chapels were added, and the completed building was given a handsome set of pierced battlements. The original plan was for an impressive spire, but when the tower showed signs of movement it was quickly shored up with buttresses.

St. John's church in Burford was also remodelled using money from wool, but it has a distinctive character of its own. Originally built as a Norman parish church, it was slowly added to over the next five centuries as the town grew in size and wealth. The result of this gradual enlargement is, in Jennifer Sherwood's words, "a cluster of aisles and chapels and a complex labyrinthine interior with the parts at odd angles and on different levels." Some uniformity was imposed in the fifteenth century, when arcades and windows were added in the Perpendicular style, along with a slender spire and a handsome porch, but the church remains a fascinating jumble of styles. As Simon Jenkins puts it, "Burford is queen of Oxfordshire, a paragon and museum of the English parish church."

In contrast to Burford's eclectic charms, Fairford presents a textbook example of the Perpendicular style. In the 1480s John Tame of Cirencester gave orders for the old parish church to be razed to the ground, making way for his state-of-the-art new building. The resulting structure provided the perfect showcase for a stunning collection of church furnishings, including a set of misericords in the choir, and a series of 28 stained glass windows—the only complete medieval glazing scheme to survive in England.

Walking into Fairford church is like entering a luminous picture gallery. The glass is top quality—the work of the royal glazier, Barnard Flower, who also designed the windows for Kings' College, Cambridge—and his designs are bold and graceful. All the windows contribute to a scheme that tells the Christian story, from the creation to the end of the world. At the heart of the scheme, in the great east window, is the Crucifixion, and leading up to this image are the stories of Christ and his mother Mary. The main aisle provides a Biblical portrait gallery on two levels: in the lower windows, apostles on the south side face prophets on the north; in the clerestorey, the company of saints are lined-up opposite a set of villains, including Judas and Herod. The end of the story comes in a vision of the Last Day filling the huge west window, with Christ seated in Judgement while the saved ascend to heaven and the damned tumble into hell. John Moore loved these hell scenes and lingered long at Fairford, studying the "red and blue devils, all obscenely grinning... dog-faced, lion-faced, monkey-faced, evil beyond words, and yet with a smack of very human mischief in their make-up too."

The End of the Abbeys

Fairford Church was consecrated in 1497, but by then the great age of church building was almost over. In 1531 King Henry VIII made his final break with the Pope, establishing an independent Church of England. Five years later he embarked on his project of "dissolving" the religious houses and seizing their treasures for the crown. In five tumultuous years, from 1536 to 1541, Thomas Cromwell supervised a programme of systematic looting and destruction, as abbeys and convents all over England were emptied of their contents while their beautiful buildings were left to fall into ruins.

In the Cotswolds, a set of wealthy abbeys provided prime targets for

Cromwell's destruction. Almost nothing remains today of the abbeys at Eynsham, Bruern and Cirencester, while at Malmesbury and Bath only the abbey churches have survived, with the church at Malmesbury partly in ruins. The attack on Winchcombe came on 23 December 1539, and the following day Cromwell moved on to Hailes, one of richest abbeys in England and the subject of the king's special displeasure.

FAME AND FRAUD AT HAILES ABBEY

The Cistercian abbey at Hailes had been founded in 1242 by Richard, Earl of Cornwall, in an act of piety after he had been saved from a storm at sea. Deliberately sited in a remote valley, like most Cistercian houses, it was nevertheless an important foundation, and its consecration was attended by King Henry III and his queen, as well as thirteen bishops. The service was splendid affair, but the most significant event in the abbey's history came 25 years later when Richard's son presented the monks with a phial from Jerusalem, believed to contain the true blood of Christ. The phial was placed in a glass and gold container at the eastern end of the abbey church, and the message soon got out that anyone who gazed on it was guaranteed salvation.

By the 1400s Hailes had become a major centre of pilgrimage, and the abbey's wealth and fame grew steadily. Yet there were a few who dared to question the authenticity of the relic, and in the weeks leading up to Cromwell's raid a sample of the abbey's "holy blood" was seized and taken to London, where it was exposed as a shocking fraud. It appeared that the famous blood was in fact nothing more than honey coloured with saffron. Worse than this, it was revealed that the monks were operating an elaborate confidence trick. The glass container for the blood was transparent on one side and opaque on the other. When it was first shown to the pilgrims the monks presented its opaque side, explaining that people in mortal sin could not see the blood. Only after the pilgrims had paid sufficient money would the container be reversed, and a "miracle" took place, allowing the grateful pilgrims to see the blood.

Once the fraud at Hailes had been exposed, Cromwell's men were ruthless. Descending on the abbey on Christmas Eve (one of the holiest days in the Church's calendar), they stripped it of all its treasures. It is even said that Cromwell settled himself in a special seat on Hailes hill so that he could thoroughly enjoy the destruction. Cromwell left behind an empty

"The small cluster of ruins at Hailes forms a striking picture rising in lonely majesty from a flat green plain" (R. P. Beckinsale)

shell at Hailes, which was gradually raided over the following years as the local people claimed its valuable stones, slates and lead. Within a century all that was left of the once famous abbey was the jumble of tumbledown walls and arches that remain in the valley today.

Visitors at the Rectory: Jane Austen and John Wesley

By the 1700s the passionate upheavals of the sixteenth century were long forgotten, as the Anglican Church settled comfortably into its role inside the English establishment. In most country parishes a system of patronage ensured that the rector was a man of good social connections, who lived in a spacious rectory, combining the roles of parson and country squire. All over the Cotswolds elegant rectory buildings stand close to the parish church, providing a reminder of a vanished way of life when the village "squarson" could afford to live in genteel comfort. There are fine examples of grand country rectories at Elkstone, Rodmarton and Upper Slaughter (now The Lords of the Manor hotel). In the village of Adlestrop the handsome redbrick mansion opposite the church was once the home of the Rev. Thomas Leigh, the maternal uncle of Jane Austen. Between the years 1794 and 1806 Jane paid several visits to Adlestrop, first staying there with her mother and sister when she was nineteen years old, and her observations of life in the rectory must have supplied some interesting material for her novels.

Jane Austen was not the only famous person to experience life in a Cotswold rectory. In the early eighteenth century, the young John Wesley was a frequent visitor to the rectories at Broadway and Stanton, just below the brow of the northern escarpment. As a student at Oxford, the man who would later found the Methodist Church was already convinced of his mission as a preacher. Nevertheless he was lively and sociable, and when his Cotswold friends invited him to join them at home, he was delighted.

The group of young people that Wesley joined in the Cotswolds included several students of theology, but also a number of intelligent young women. Friends since childhood, they had established a pleasant routine of walking in the hills and spending long afternoons in country gardens, reading poetry, plays and sermons. In the evenings the group enjoyed dancing and playing cards. There were merry games at Christmas, and picnics in the summer, but among these activities there was always time for regular visits to church. Wesley often preached in the church at Stanton, where he was assured of an appreciative audience of friends among the local congregation. Some of the young women in his circle were a little in love with him, and his diaries reveal that he was also charmed by them, but he was not prepared to be deflected from his serious purpose in life.

For eight years Wesley enjoyed his sojourns in Broadway and Stanton, but, as the years went by he found less time for relaxation. In 1729 he formed the Holy Club with his brother Charles, a group that gained the nickname of "Methodists" because of their strict rules for living. Wesley was also keen to spread the Christian message to other parts of the world, and in 1734 he formed a plan to travel to Georgia, in North America. In this year he made a farewell visit to the Cotswolds before setting sail across the Atlantic. Wesley's American adventure lasted three years, and on his return to England he began an evangelical campaign that would take him all over the country. For the rest of his life he travelled through England, holding open-air meetings that attracted enormous crowds of converts. Some of his preaching tours took him through the Cotswolds, but he never returned to the villages he had loved, and his "dear, delightful Stanton" became a distant memory of his youth.

JOHN KEBLE AT EASTLEACH

Less than a century after Wesley made his break with the Anglican Church, the Cotswolds produced a very different church reformer. John Keble (1792-1866) was the son of the rector of Fairford, one of the region's most spectacular Gothic churches. Growing up surrounded by the Fairford windows must have had a profound effect on Keble, giving him a love of beauty and ritual that would later shape his approach to Christian worship.

Keble's Cotswold childhood was spent quietly at home, enjoying country life with his brother and two sisters. There were long periods of study with his father and many hours in church, but he also witnessed the chronic problems of poverty and disease among the local people. He was an excellent student, and at the age of fourteen (the usual age for students to enter the university) he won a scholarship to Oxford. Keble proved himself to be a brilliant Biblical scholar, and he soon embarked on a successful career in the university. During these years he developed an admiration for Catholicism, and began to dream of an Anglican Church that was closely linked to Rome.

At the age of 23 Keble was ordained into the Church of England and volunteered for a curacy in the parishes of Eastleach and Burthrop (now Eastleach Turville and Eastleach Martin). It was the perfect position for a young scholar with an active social conscience. Eastleach was an easy ride from Oxford. There was important work to be done in educating and helping the congregation, and the twin churches stood just a few paces apart, sharing the same beautiful valley. Keble was delighted with his new situation, and his initial six-week engagement soon became a permanent post as he devoted himself to his clerical duties.

In 1818 Keble became a tutor at Oxford, and was forced to rely on his brother's help at Eastleach, but he longed to spend more time in his parish. In 1821 he wrote to a friend: "I always feel more at home in my parish in two hours than in my College in two weeks." The situation was finally resolved in 1823, when he took up a full-time post at Southrop church, less than two miles south of Eastleach. As parish priest of Southrop, Keble had a large vicarage, which was often filled with visiting Oxford friends, and it was there that the Oxford Movement to reform the Church had its origins.

The next three years at Southrop were busy and fulfilling. Keble held lively reading parties for his Oxford friends, composed hymns and poems and wrote tracts to educate the public about his views. He also busied himself with practical work in his parishes (of Southrop, Eastleach and Burthrop), reporting to a friend, "…the poor places are in a most pitiable condition, the farmer quarrelling, the labourer oppressed and starved, and typhus fever prevalent among them: a resident curate could not expect to do much, but it would at least be giving them one chance more of a partial reformation."

In 1825 Keble's years in the Cotswolds came to an end when he was offered a new position at Hursley, near Winchester. This was his permanent home for the rest of his life, although he often returned to the Cotswolds, staying in the rectory at Fairford, where he helped his father with parish duties, and riding over to Bisley, where his brother Thomas was vicar for forty years. In his later years John Keble devoted most of his energies to the Oxford Movement and its attempts to introduce Anglo-Catholic practices into English churches. The Movement has left its legacy in the elaborate rituals of the Anglican High Church, yet in the Cotswolds Keble is remembered in the simple churches at Eastleach, linked by a stone clapper bridge over a shallow stream.

NON-CONFORMISM: A DIFFERENT WAY OF WORSHIP

By the 1850s the once-unified English Church had dispersed into many movements. Among the Anglicans one faction followed the practices of the "high church" Anglo-Catholics, while another group was resolutely "low church". At the same time Non-Conformism was flourishing, with Methodists, Baptists and Congregationalists all attracting their own loyal followers. With their emphasis on singing and sermonizing in place of the ancient rituals, Non-Conformist preachers held a special appeal for the new industrial working class. Most of the workers in the Cotswolds' factories and mills had severed their ties with the old parish churches, and found a warm welcome in the new chapels with their promise of salvation for all.

Non-Conformist chapels can be found all over the Cotswolds today, but they are especially numerous in the areas where the cloth-making industry was based. Just a short walk through the centre of Stroud takes you past the octagonal stone Wesleyan chapel built in 1763, a handsome Georgian-fronted Baptist chapel dating from 1824, and a vast Congregationalist church, constructed in the classical style in 1835, all reflecting the popularity of these vital new Christian movements.

SELSEY CHURCH: PRE-RAPHAELITE SHOWCASE

The Non-Conformists were not the only church builders of the Industrial Age. During the nineteenth century dozens of Anglican churches were constructed in the growing towns and suburbs of the Cotswolds. Most of their buildings follow a standard neo-Gothic template, but the Church of All Saints at Selsey, perched on a ridge above Stroud, is unique. Selsey's church was funded by Sir Samuel Marling, a local cloth manufacturer, who chose the talented G. F. Bodley as his architect. Apparently Marling instructed Bodley to base his design on Marling church in the Austrian Tyrol, and the church has a distinctly alpine feel, with its tall bell tower and steeply pitched roof.

Bodley was a friend of William Morris, and he decided to give the keen young man the task of making all the stained glass for the Church of all Saints. It was Morris' first contract for glass and he turned the work into a team project, assigning different windows to each of his friends. The result is a Pre-Raphaelite gallery in glass, with designs by Morris, Dante Gabriel Rossetti, Edward Burne-Jones and Ford Maddox Brown.

The scenes by Rossetti and Burne-Jones are especially striking, and a giant rose, showing God's Creation, dominates the church.

WHAT NEXT?

By the early years of the twentieth century the flood of church building in the Cotswolds had slowed to a trickle, and a century later it has almost stopped entirely. In the twenty-first century growing numbers of redundant churches have been given new uses as homes or studios. Hundreds of churches and chapels in the Cotswolds are at risk as congregations shrink and clergy spread themselves between multiple parishes. While the famous tourist gems are certain to survive, many Cotswold churches face an uncertain future. Most of the parish churches have lasted for over a thousand years, but how will they survive in the new millennium?

Chapter Three

LIVING OFF THE LAND

SHEEP, CROPS AND STONE

"In these woulds there feed in great numbers flockes of sheepe... whose wool being most fine and soft, is had in passing great account among nations."

William Camden, *Brittania* (1586)

"I've scratched old England on the back and her's gived me wealth untold."

Old Mont of Enstone, *Lifting the Latch* (1987)

When William Cobbett crossed the Cotswolds in 1826 he reported on a stony, barren country, observing gloomily: "anything quite so cheerless as this I do not recollect to have seen." Later, he painted an altogether more cheerful picture, reporting on an acquaintance who "has taken up his quarters on the healthy and I say beautiful Cotswold of Gloucestershire." These contradictory reports may possibly refer first to the high wolds and second to the gentler river valleys. But whatever the reason for Cobbett's opposing views, they both ring true. Anyone who has spent some time in the Cotswolds knows that they can feel both cheerless and beautiful. It is a land that can be both harsh and fertile—and the region's farmers know this best of all. Throughout the history of farming in the Cotswolds some have struggled to survive, while a lucky few have grown rich.

WEALTH FROM WOOL

The early history of farming in the Cotswolds is a story of gradual evolution from hunting and gathering in the Mesolithic period to herding and growing crops in the Bronze Age. With the arrival of the Romans came a settled pattern of farming in the valleys and sheep grazing on the wolds. Roman villa farms were large-scale operations, supervised by a farm manager who relied on slaves to keep things running. A typical villa farm,

such as Chedworth, would have been highly profitable, selling its surplus produce in markets throughout southern Britain, and probably exporting grain and wool to other parts of the Empire.

The Romans are usually credited with bringing sheep to the Cotswolds, but sheep rearing really took off in Norman times. By the twelfth century vast flocks of sheep were grazing the high wolds, owned by powerful abbots who could earn a generous income from wool. All the local abbeys had their own sheep-walks in the Cotswolds. The Abbot of Evesham grazed his flocks around Stow-on-the-Wold. The lands around Northleach were claimed by the Abbot of Gloucester, and the Abbot of Tewkesbury built a splendid wool barn at Stanway, still in use today as a village hall. Even distant abbeys sometimes claimed Cotswold rights, with the Abbot of Westminster keeping his flocks around Bourton-on-the-Water.

Sheep thrived on the well-drained Cotswold uplands, but they needed constant herding to new pastures. This was the job of the shepherds, who lived a lonely, nomadic life driving their flocks across the wolds. By the early summer the sheep were all delivered to their traditional shearing places: villages with wide, fast-flowing streams. Here the sheep were washed and shorn by villagers, who bundled the valuable fleeces into sacks ready for market. In the northern Cotswolds the village of Blockley was used by the Abbot of Worcester for his annual shearing, while the Abbot of Winchcombe's flocks, which grazed around Snowshill, were driven south to the wide and shallow stream at Sherborne, near Burford.

The village of Sherborne gained its name from its role as a shearing place ("sher" comes from the Anglo-Saxon word for shearing, and "borne" means stream). There are places linked to sheep all over the Cotswolds (Shipton, Sheepscombe and Washbrook to name just a few) and sheep rearing has also left its mark on the landscape. During the twelfth century large areas of woodland were cleared from the high wolds and even villages were removed to make room for the all-important sheep-walks. It has been estimated that sheep outnumbered people by four to one in medieval England. This was the situation that prompted the Cotswold cleric William Tyndale to protest "God gave the earth to men to inhabit and not unto sheep."

While the ordinary Cotswold folk did the herding and shearing, the abbots claimed the profits, driving hard bargains with merchants from Flanders and Italy. English wool was in great demand in the weaving towns of Europe, with Cotswold wool fetching particularly high prices. Novices to the business were introduced to the heavy white fleeces of the Cotswold sheep and taught to recite the ditty: "In Europe the best wool is English, In England the best wool is Cotswolds." The sheep that produced this wonderful wool were known as Cotswold Lions: a large, long-necked breed with a heavy wool coat falling in a forelock over a narrow face. (Descendants of the Cotswold Lion and other local breeds can be seen today at the Cotswold Farm Park in Guiting Power.) These distinctive sheep were still grazing on the wolds in the 1600s when Michael Drayton described them lovingly in his verse epic *Poly-olbion*:

... Cotswold wisely fills
Her with the whitest kind: whose browes so woolly be,
As men in her sheepe no emptiness should see.
A body long and large, the buttocks equal broad;
As fit to undergo the full and weightie load...
The faire and goodly flock, the shepeards onely pride
As white as winters snowe, when from the winters side
He drives his new-washt sheepe...

By the fourteenth century wool was very big business in the Cotswolds. Regular markets were held in the region's towns, such as Tetbury, Northleach and Stow-on-the-Wold, and a class of wealthy middlemen had emerged. These were the wool merchants who took the role of brokers between the clergy and the cloth merchants, making a handsome profit on the side. The rise of the Cotswold wool merchants was spectacular. Within a single lifetime a man could accumulate enough wealth to buy a large flock of his own, and even purchase a ship to transport his wool across the English Channel. The merchants were the superrich of their day, funding lavish building projects in the local towns. At Northleach, John Fortey added a brand new storey to his parish church. William Grevel of Chipping Campden built himself a stylish new house as well as paying for the restoration of the parish church. Most spectacular of all, John Tame and his son Edmund funded a complete new church at Fairford.

A memorial brass to William Grevel in Chipping Campden Church proclaims him (in Latin) to be "the flower of the wool merchants of all

England" and he certainly had the funds to build himself a very fine home. Grevel's House still stands in the High Street. Built from local stone around 1380, it is a handsome, wide-fronted structure with tall bay windows, one of them topped by a flamboyant pair of gargoyles. Today Grevel's House takes its place alongside other houses, but in the fourteenth century it would have stood alone, its substantial rooms arranged around a courtyard. Anyone wanting to imagine the life of William Grevel should read *The Woolpack*, a vivid recreation of life in a Cotswold wool town. In her classic children's novel Cynthia Hartnett describes a world of merchants and shepherds, in which young Nicholas Fetterlock manages to save his father's wool from a band of unscrupulous double-crossers. The text is accompanied by the author's exquisite line drawings, based on Burford and its surroundings, and provides a vivid evocation of Cotswold life in the 1400s.

The best memorial brasses in the Cotswolds can be found in Northleach church, where the local merchants are portrayed with their wealth at their feet—in the form of Cotswold sheep and woolsacks. In the fourteenth century, fifty per cent of England's wealth was gained from wool, and the woolsack was such a powerful symbol of prosperity that it was presented to the Lord Chancellor, to be used as his seat. The "woolsack" still remains in Parliament to this day, providing a reminder of a distant time when high-quality wool could guarantee the country's financial stability.

The good times lasted for the merchants into the sixteenth century, but by the 1550s things had begun to change. The English were facing tough competition from abroad as Spanish merino fleeces replaced Cotswold wool as the new top-quality product. Meanwhile foreign merchants started to demand woven cloth instead of wool, and the emphasis in the Cotswolds gradually changed to manufacturing. During the sixteenth and seventeenth centuries English wool yielded everdecreasing returns, and by the 1660s the situation had become so desperate that parliament was forced to intervene. Between 1666 and 1680 three Burial in Woollen Acts were passed, requiring that all burial shrouds should be made from pure English wool. But even these measures were not enough to stop the sharp decline of the wool industry of the Cotswolds.

FIELDS, COMMONS AND WALLS

While the high wolds were dominated by sheep, there was plenty of other farming in the Cotswolds. Beginning in Anglo-Saxon times, a feudal way of life had evolved in England in which the lord of the manor owned a set of fields that were farmed by all the peasants living on his land. Most villages had three or four communal fields, divided into strips the width of a plough, which were assigned to individual families. Apart from growing crops for themselves and their lord, peasant families also had small kitchen gardens for vegetables, chickens and pigs, while their sheep, horses and cows were kept on the village commons. Medieval fields were ploughed in a manner known as "ridge and furrow", with a single plough board throwing up earth to one side only and gradually building up a series of parallel ridges.

Evidence of ridge and furrow ploughing is visible in the land around Dumbleton, near Broadway, while the commons at Rodborough and Minchinhampton are surviving examples of land once used for village live-stock. A different kind of memorial to the trials and pleasures of agrarian life in the Cotswolds survives in a traditional turnip-hoer's song, recorded in the eighteenth century but probably current for centuries before:

I be a turmut hower
Vram Gloucestershire I came;
My parents be hard-working volk,
Giles Wapshaw be my name.

The vly, the vly
The vly be on the turmut,
An 'it be aal me eye, and no use to try
To keep um off the turmut.

Zum be vond o' haymakin',
An' zum be vond o' mowin',
But of aal the trades thet I likes best
Gie I the turmut howin'
The vly, the vly etc.

By the sixteenth century the feudal system had broken down. Some villagers still worked for local landowners, but many were freeholders, jealously guarding their own strips of land. The practice of farming on large, open fields continued long after the Middle Ages, but these fields were divided into a complicated patchwork of smallholdings. At the same time, woods were cleared to create more farming land, and the sheep-walks of the high wolds began to be "enclosed" by dry-stone walls to form fields. The process of enclosure began in the sixteenth century and continued for the next four hundred years, reaching a peak in the eighteenth century, with the rise of the great agricultural estates. Under the direction of some very wealthy landowners the Cotswold uplands were gradually transformed into the ordered landscape that we see today, with its large rectangular fields, bordered by dry-stone walls, and its elegantly scattered beech plantations.

One of the leading landowners of the eighteenth century was Allen 1st Earl Bathurst, whose home at Cirencester Park sat at the heart of a large estate covering woods and wolds. The earl's enthusiastic approach to agriculture was praised by his friend the poet Alexander Pope, who wrote approvingly of the landlord:

Whose cheerful tenants bless their yearly toil
Yet to their Lord owe more then to the soil;
Whose ample lawns are not ashamed to feed
The milky heifer and deserving steed.

Pope was less admiring, however, of his friend's passion for "enclosing" the landscape to create more farming land. When Bathurst gave orders for some buildings in the village of Sapperton to be demolished, the poet protested against the plans in verse:

Alas, my Bathurst! What will they avail?
Join Cotswold hills to Sapperton's fair daile,
Enclose whole downs in walls—'tis all a joke!
Inexorable Death shall level all,
And trees, and stones, and farms, and farmers fall!

Two centuries on, Algernon Gissing was still bemoaning the destruction of small rural communities in the name of more efficient farming. Recounting the history of the village of Saintbury (near Broadway) he reported that no fewer than 23 houses had disappeared in the space of sixty years during the eighteenth century. He also observed that the same processes were still at work in the 1920s, and railed against the farmers who cause "trees to be felled, hedges stubbed up, little homesteads obliterated, for the purpose of instituting open ranch life on our English soil, so that the latest development in machinery may hum over the hundred acres at a time without any petty hindrances."

Good and Bad Times for Farmers

For some fortunate landowners in the Cotswolds, the early nineteenth century was a highly profitable period. Economies of scale, coupled with innovations in planting, machinery and livestock breeding, all led to dramatic increases in yields. Technological progress was accompanied by a rapid growth in the British population and a rising demand for food. In the Cotswolds, farmers practised new methods of crop rotation and created model farms stocked with the latest breeds of sheep and cattle. An outstanding estate of this period was Great Tew (near Chipping Norton) whose owners improved their farmland, rebuilt barns and renovated tenants' cottages, earning praise as "one of the best farmed parishes in the Midland Counties". (After this highpoint, very little changed at Great Tew, and the village is now preserved as a "time capsule" with its grand manor house set apart from the village and its row of estate cottages beside the village inn.) In the southern Cotswolds, Henry, 4th Earl Bathurst, inherited his great-grandfather's enthusiasm for agricultural reform, and in 1845 became the founding president of the Royal College of Agriculture in Cirencester, the first agricultural college in the English-speaking world. The college was founded to train young farmers in the best methods and to lead the way with innovations, roles that it still fulfils today.

By the 1870s, however, fortunes were changing for most Cotswold farmers, as Britain entered a severe agricultural depression. A series of bad harvests coincided with intense competition from the New World, and the farmers' problems were exacerbated by the drift of labour away from the countryside. The depressed conditions in the southern Cotswolds are vividly described by J. Arthur Gibbs in his memoir, *A Cotswold Village*. Writing in 1898, Gibbs paints a dismal picture of deserted farms, demoralized workers and absentee landlords. He remembers a time when "the uplands of Gloucestershire were almost entirely under the plough" but notes that "now, alas! the country is rapidly going back to its uncultivated state... In many parts of the country we see buildings falling out of repair and deserted mansions. Would that we knew the remedy for agricultural depression!" Arthur Gibbs was a gentleman-scholar who enjoyed playing the country squire, but a real farmer's view is provided by John Simpson Calvert of Leafield (near Charlbury). Farmer Calvert's diaries run from 1875 to 1900 and make grim reading, with their records of daily struggles with poor soil, terrible weather and disastrous harvests. They were later published under the fitting title of *Rain and Ruin*.

Times were hard for farmers in this period, but the plight of the labourers was far worse. Sid Knight grew up in Broadway in the years before the First World War, surrounded by men who had spent their lives on the land. In *A Cotswold Lad* he writes: "I can remember seeing many of them, long before old age, crippled with rheumatic complaints, with only the workhouse infirmary as a dubious refuge." Sid describes the back-breaking labour of flailing corn, a much-sought indoor job in the harsh winter weather. He recounts how his grandfather had to walk fourteen miles to find work, until he was injured falling off a hayrick, and he retells the family story of how his great-grandfather "once went off to work with pies filled with cooked rats' meat enclosed in ground-acorn pastry."

Experiments and Communities: Charterville and Whiteway

In the harsh conditions of the nineteenth century thousands of Cotswold-ers left the countryside in search of new employment in the towns. Two movements, however, went against this tide. In 1847 a group of city dwellers were relocated to Charterville, a newly created rural community just outside the picturesque village of Minster Lovell. Fifty years later, a band of Londoners set out for the Cotswolds to found a self-sufficient colony in Whiteway, near Stroud.

The community at Charterville was the brainchild of Feargus O'Connor, a fiery Irishman and member of the working-class Chartist movement. In the course of his campaigns he had been horrified by the living conditions of the urban slum-dwellers and had resolved to return them to the land that he saw as their birthright. O'Connor's scheme involved the buying up of agricultural land and the building of cottages, to be held in common by the new tenants. By the 1840s he had already established two trial communities, but Charterville in the Cotswolds was to be his model scheme. In 1847, O'Connor purchased 300 acres of land in the Windrush valley, and less than ten months later his community was ready. The land had been divided into 78 allotments, each with its own one-storey cottage and shed, and there was also an elegant schoolhouse to serve as a meeting house and school.

The first settlers arrived in Charterville in the spring of 1848. Most of the families came from factory towns in the Midlands and the North, and after the bustle of Birmingham and Manchester the quiet Cotswold countryside must have come as quite a shock. O'Connor had provided forty oxen and eighteen pigs for the community, along with generous supplies of manure, firewood and seed for planting, but there was still much work to be done.

A few of the settlers took to country life with enthusiasm, singing rousing songs while they harvested their crops and holding cheerful open-air picnics, but the majority found the task of farming their land impossibly hard. The land was dry and stony, and filled with tree-roots, and the crops needed constant weeding and watering. People missed the company and life of the towns and failed to make new friends among the suspicious locals. Over their first winter most of the families struggled with failing crops, and by the following spring many were defaulting on their rent, claiming poverty and destitution. In November 1849 a desperate O'Connor announced that anyone not paying their rent would be evicted. When the tenants refused to respond to his threats, the bailiffs were sent in. Two months later, in January 1850, the original owners reclaimed the estate, and Charterville collapsed, with most of the families returning to the cities they had left. Less than two years after its hopeful beginnings O'Connor's dream had ended in recriminations and anger.

All that remains of Charterville today is a scattering of three-roomed cottages among the modern bungalows flanking the B4477 from Minster Lovell to Brize Norton. Some of the houses have extra-large gardens, occupying the sites of the original allotments, but most of the land has been taken over by a modern housing estate. The only reminders of O'Connor's endeavours are provided by a set of street names: Charterville Close leads into Drylands Road and finally reaches a cul-de-sac with a faded nameplate—O'Connor's Road.

Charterville was the product of one man's vision, but the Whiteway community was a strictly communal affair. Inspired by Tolstoyan ideals of common ownership, a group of free-thinkers set off on their bicycles from Croydon in 1898, intent on creating a new way of life in the Cotswolds. Their destination was Whiteway House, a tall stone farmhouse surrounded by open fields six miles north-east of Stroud. In a dramatic ceremony the deeds of the house and land were burnt on the end of the pitchfork, much to the alarm of the surrounding landowners.

From its earliest days the community at Whiteway was run on uncompromisingly radical lines. The colonists were anti-property and anti-marriage, and aimed to live entirely off the land, surviving without using money at all. Each family was given an acre of land on which to build a home and scrape a living, but with almost no experience of farming (most of them had been clerks, shop assistants and teachers) they struggled to survive. For the first few years people lived mainly on a diet of cornmeal, but they gradually learned new skills and in 1904, when C. R. Ashbee visited the colony, he saw "little home-built cabins of wood and brick, dotted about among their allotment patches." Ashbee also noted that the children looked happy and healthy, but he found Whiteway distressingly uncouth compared with his own utopia at Chipping Campden (described in Chapter Eight).

Against all the odds, the Whiteway colony thrived, attracting an assortment of pacifists, communists and refugees. When Laurie Lee visited in 1930, he found a central meeting hall and a well-planned programme of activities. In 1998 the community celebrated its centenary, and it survives today as a loose cooperative of some sixty households linked by a maze of lanes. None of the present colonists aims to be entirely self-sufficient, although the spirit of enterprise can still be seen in a variety of eco-projects.

OLD MONT OF ENSTONE: A LIFE ON THE LAND

By the start of the twentieth century the lean years of the Great Agricultural Depression were over. On his walks in the wolds in the 1920s Algernon Gissing observed that "nearly all here is cultivated—barley, mangels, sanfoin or clover." But life continued to be very hard for anyone working on the land. In 1915, thirteen-year-old Mont Abbott rose at five for his first day's work at a local farm. It was the start of a lifetime's labouring, described in detail in *Lifting the Latch*:

> From half past five in the morning to half-past five at night I were lifting the latch of cowshed, stable, barn to help with the milking, the feeding, the mucking-out, the ploughing and drilling too. At the end of my seven-day week, I'd line with my little candle-lantern alongside Franky and Polly a stamping and snorting in their stalls… There Mr Lennox always paid us our wages of a Friday night.

Lifting the Latch records the details of a Cotswold farm labourer's life over a period of over eighty years. Through Sheila Stewart's expert transcription it presents the memories of "Old Mont" who spent his entire life in the village of Enstone (near Charlbury). The book is full of first-hand accounts of work on the land. Starting with Mont's early years as a farm "dogsbody", it moves on to his later work as a carter, caring for the horses, guiding the plough and carting vegetables to market. In his middle years Mont turned to shepherding, and he recalls the annual rituals of lambing, tailing, dipping and shearing, and the daily work of tending feet, coats, udders and mouths. There are accounts of building hayricks by hand and of ploughing the fields in the years before tractors, when ploughing a single acre of land involved fourteen miles of exhausting walking. Old Mont also describes other country jobs: the work of the stonemasons and farriers and the unusual toil of the "oak barkers", whose task was to strip the bark from the trees of Wychwood Forest to supply flotation for ships. At the end of his memoirs Mont surveys his life and pronounces himself "well content" at his "careering on the land": "I 'udn't say I've enjoyed every minute of it… but, ploughing, penning, planting, I've scratched old England on the back and her's gived me wealth untold."

Farming Today: Super-stars and Strugglers

By the time he died in 1989, Old Mont had seen farming change dramatically. Machinery played a vital role and new patterns of land-use had emerged, as the old meadows were ploughed up for crops. On the high wolds grazing sheep were replaced by fields of cereals, while cattle were reared more intensively than before, housed in large-scale parlours and feeding sheds. Nowadays the Cotswolds are mainly arable, with only two per cent of land devoted to pasture. Small, mixed farms are rare, and most farmers operate on a massive scale. Even the colour palette of the Cotswolds has changed, with rape and linseed proliferating, encouraged by government incentives and subsidies.

A few high-profile farmers have taken a stand against these trends. For the past twenty years HRH the Prince of Wales has run Home Farm on the Highgrove Estate as an organic enterprise. The 1,000-acre property is a traditional mixed farm, growing wheat, oats, and rye, and keeping sheep, pigs and cows. Traditional breeds are favoured, including Gloucester cattle and Cotswold sheep, and the farm incorporates a large kitchen garden for fruit and vegetables. Produce from Home Farm is sold in the Highgrove shop in Tetbury ("Britain's poshest greengrocer") or delivered in boxes to local families. Meat is supplied to restaurants in the Cotswolds and beyond. A recent project is organic mutton (meat from two-year-old sheep), and the Prince has launched a Mutton Renaissance campaign.

In the twenty-first century two celebrities have taken up farming in the Cotswolds. At Kingham, near Chipping Norton, Alex James, the bassist from the band Blur, runs a small sheep farm that makes specialist cheeses, while at Barnsley, near Cirencester, model Liz Hurley has a livestock farm. Hurley keeps cows and sheep and Gloucester Old Spot pigs, producing a sausage called "Hurley Old Spot".

Such farms are special cases. But what of the ordinary farmer today? In 2007 the plight of a Cotswold farmer was examined in an unusual book. Ian Walthew's *A Place in My Country* chronicles the author's move to a Cotswold village, but also focuses on the fate of his neighbour, as he struggles to run a small family farm. In a remarkably clear-eyed account, Walthew shows Norman (whose name was changed for the book) working sixteen hours a days, seven days a week, as prices for his produce keep on falling. While Norman copes with rundown machinery and broken fences, he is surrounded on all sides by giant agribusinesses, country weekenders and well-meaning ramblers. Sometimes comic and sometimes heart-breaking, it is the story of one man's attempt against the odds to maintain a dying way of life.

THE STONE AND THE MAGICIAN: QUARRIES AND QUARRYMEN

When the Rev. Sidney Smith crossed the Cotswolds in the 1830s he saw only "a region of stone and sorrow". But others have looked deeper. For H. J. Massingham, writing a century later, the stony Cotswold landscape provided as a semi-mystical arena for "the shapes of power summoned from the limestone by the magician, man". Like many other writers of his age, Massingham was incurably romantic, but he recognized in the Cotswold landscape a unique resource that people have been exploiting for thousands of years.

Ever since Neolithic times, people have been digging up Cotswold stone. There are remains of quarries close to towns and villages all over the region, and the Cotswold Edge is honeycombed with ancient excavations. Most of the quarries simply provided stone for local houses, but others were a valuable source of income and employment. On the southern margins of the region the massive quarries at Corsham supplied the famous Bath stone used in that city. Stone from Minchinhampton was used for the Houses of Parliament, while Leckhampton Hill was quarried to build regency Cheltenham. In the Oxfordshire Cotswolds the quarry at Taynton, near Burford, enjoyed nine centuries of productive activity (from the time of the Domesday Book until the 1990s) gaining a reputation for exceptionally high-quality stone. In the thirteenth century vast quantities of creamy Taynton stone were transported to Oxford for use in its colleges, and it was later used at Eton College, Windsor Castle and Blenheim Palace.

The stone at Taynton was extracted from an open amphitheatre, which is still visible today. But other quarrymen had to cope with harder working conditions. During the nineteenth century miners at Corsham Down worked in a cavern a hundred feet underground, while at Leckhampton work was carried out on a steep cliff face, with wagonloads of stone hauled by ropes to the top of the hill. The quarry workers at Leckhampton have left a lasting monument to their labours. The strangely contorted tower of stone known as the Devil's Chimney dates from around the end of the seventeenth century, and is a remnant of unusable rock left untouched by the quarrymen.

The landscape of the Cotswolds does not only yield excellent building stone. It also contains a fissile variety of limestone that can be split for use as roofing slates. Cotswold stone slates have been used on local buildings since Roman times, forming the perfect complement to limestone walls. William Morris famously compared the arrangement of tiles on a Cotswold roof to the feathers on a bird's wing and Laurie Lee wrote that the cottage tiles in his village "grew a kind of golden moss which sparkled like crystallized honey."

One of the most important centres for roofing slates was the appropriately named village of Stonesfield, in the eastern Cotswolds. Until the twentieth century, the Stonesfield quarries provided roofing slates for the Oxford colleges and for towns and villages far beyond the Cotswolds. The industry of splitting the slates was shared by all the villagers, who kept damp blocks of stone ready for winter. With the coming of the sharp winter frosts, the sleeping villagers were woken by church bells, summoning them to lay out their stone to be split into tiles by the fingers of frost.

USING THE STONE: STONEMASONS AND DRY-STONE WALLERS

J.B. Priestley encountered several Cotswold characters on his visit of 1933, but the one who impressed him most was "old George". George had worked as a stonemason all his life and had "a dusty puckered face" and "bits of stone all over him". Still hard at work in his seventies, he was rebuilding a dry-stone wall when the author was introduced to him. Priestley watched as George handled the stones "at once easily and lovingly, as women handle their babies," and expressed his admiration for the skills of the Cotswold builders. "In their hands," he wrote, "the stone flowers naturally into those mullions. They can see Cotswold houses already stirring in the very quarries."

The craft of the Cotswold masons is evident throughout the region. Many simple cottages have delicate door and window mouldings, while grander buildings are decorated with spectacular carvings. Over the centuries Cotswold masons have produced beautiful churches and stately homes—described in other chapters of this book—but perhaps their finest creations are the manor houses, such as William Morris' beloved Kelmscott Manor. Some of most exciting masons' work appears in unexpected places: a gallery of gargoyles under a church roof (as at Winchcombe, Aldsworth and Chedworth) or a collection of tombs in a country churchyard (at

Swinbrook and Brimpsfield). In the churchyard at Painswick (famous for its 99 yews) a family of masons carved over thirty ornamental tombs. Some of the tombs are shaped like tabletops. Others look like tea caddies complete with lids, and a bold stone pyramid marks the resting place of John Bryan, "carver".

The work of an outstanding Jacobean mason can be seen in the elegant gatehouse to Stanway House, near Winchcombe. It was probably carved by Timothy Strong, the first of a famous family of Cotswold masons who owned the Taynton quarry. Timothy's grandson, Thomas Strong, worked for the young Sir Christopher Wren on the Sheldonian Theatre in Oxford, later becoming Wren's master mason for St. Paul's Cathedral. Back in Gloucestershire, Thomas Strong built a bridge at Great Barrington and also helped his father, Valentine Strong, in the construction of Fairford Park (now sadly demolished).

An important part of the Cotswold mason's craft is the careful choosing and positioning of stones—a skill seen at its purest in the region's dry-stone walls. The art of dry-stone walling in the Cotswolds dates back to the Stone Age, when it was used for constructing the sides of burial chambers, but most of the Cotswold walls were built in the last three hundred years. By the 1900s much of the open wold had been enclosed by a network of low stone walls, and in the following century many wealthy landowners built high boundary walls around the perimeters of their estates. Travelling round the Cotswolds in the 1930s, Massingham admired the walls he saw in fields, bridges and streets, seeing them as an essential part of the landscape's distinctive character: "The stone hedges, dry-walled with copings of flat stones ("cock-ups") set edgewise, are integral to the landscape and likewise diversify it by following and stressing the wide undulations of the plateau."

One of the most remarkable characteristics of the Cotswold buildings is their continuity, both in style and materials, stretching back to before the Middle Ages. Looking at the main street of Chipping Campden, J. B. Priestley marvelled that a line of buildings which appeared to have come "from one particular mind", had in fact been pieced together over hundreds of years. Priestley loved the thought that generations of masons had maintained the same traditions: "If you told a Cotswold man to build you a house, this is how he built it. He knew—thank God—no other way."

When Priestley visited the Cotswolds, a team of local masons had re-

"When I met Old George he was engaged in the almost lost art of drystone walling. The stones fitted squarely and smoothly and were a delight to the eye and a great contentment to the mind, so weary of shoddy and rubbish. I have never done anything in my life so thoroughly as that old mason did his building" (J. B. Priestley)

cently been set an unusual challenge. In the 1930s the multi-millionaire Henry Ford paid for a seventeenth-century Cotswold cottage to be demolished, and all the stones shipped over to the United States. Along with the Cotswold stones went three local masons, who used their traditional skills to reconstruct the cottage exactly as it would have been built three centuries before. The cottage is now part of Ford's famous Greenfield Village in Dearborn, Michigan. Uprooted from its gentle Cotswold valley, it looks strangely denuded, but all its building details are perfectly correct.

BUILDING TODAY: THE TRADITION CONTINUES
The ancient building traditions of the Cotswolds have not died out. In the early years of the twentieth century the Arts and Crafts movement inspired by William Morris helped to keep the old crafts alive, as architects copied Cotswold styles and worked with local masons. The most outstanding example of this deliberate revival can be seen at Rodmarton Manor (described in Chapter Nine) where Ernest Barnsley employed a generation of Cotswold craft workers and educated the locals in traditional skills.

By the 1950s planning restrictions had been put in place to prevent the use of inappropriate building styles in the Cotswolds. At the same time, the growth of the tourist industry encouraged the preservation of anything old and picturesque. Incomers to the Cotswolds have continued to seek out traditional craftsmen and materials in an attempt to conserve their ancient properties. Working quarries still produce high-quality local stone and skilled Cotswold masons are in great demand, both for restoration work and new projects. The practices that began with the great Neolithic structures are still alive and well in the twenty-first century.

Chapter Four

THE COTSWOLDS AT WAR

BATTLEFIELDS, MEMORIES AND MEMORIALS

"The path turned sharp left and catapulted me into a large clearing, where I found myself surrounded by a scurrying throng of waistcoats and wooden carts and pikestaffs. Not to mention clanging armor and whinnying horses… What the bloody hell was going on here?"
Richard Hayward (describing an encounter with a Civil War battle re-enactment), *The Cotswold Way: A Walk though Middle Earth* (1992)

For several turbulent years in the 1640s the Cotswolds were devastated by war. Three major battles in the English Civil War were fought on Cotswold soil and most of the region's towns were violently contested. It was a time of turmoil throughout England, as families and friends were torn apart by conflicting loyalties to King or Parliament, but the conflict was especially fierce in the Cotswolds. From the opening battle of the war, held at Edgehill in 1642, to the last armed encounter in 1646 at Stow-on-the-Wold, troops from both sides marched across the wolds; houses, inns and farms were taken over as billets; and towns and cities were placed under siege. Today, many Cotswold places still bear battle scars.

THE CIVIL WAR BEGINS: THE BATTLE OF EDGEHILL

The English Civil War had its origins in a protracted power struggle between King Charles I and Parliament, which finally erupted into violence in 1642. In August, Charles rallied his Royalist troops in Nottingham, while supporters of Parliament, commonly known as Roundheads, gathered under the lead of Oliver Cromwell and others. Skirmishes broke out in the north of England, but war did not begin in earnest for another two months. By mid-October, Charles and his nephew, Prince Rupert, were leading their army south towards London, while a Roundhead force, led by the Earl of Essex, was also advancing south from Coventry. With both sides intent on capturing the capital for their base, Charles decided

FIGHT FOR THE STANDARD AT THE BATTLE OF EDGEHILL. 1642.

it was time to take a stand.

Early in the morning of 23 October 1642, the Royalists assembled at Edgehill and lined up along the top of the escarpment. Essex had been leading a march to Banbury, but he quickly marched to Kineton, where he assembled his forces in the valley just north of the Edge, relying on hedges for cover. Sometime after midday the Royalists began to descend the slope towards their opponents, and around 2 p.m., the king made an appearance, riding amongst his troops to offer encouragement. The sight of Charles I, resplendent in shining armour, finally spurred the Roundheads into opening fire and the battle began with a flurry of charges and returning salvoes. Fighting continued throughout the afternoon, but the conflict was marked by inexperience on both sides. Most of the king's artillery missed their targets and the Royalist cavalry lacked discipline. On the opposite side, many Parliamentarians were poorly trained and a substantial group fled the battlefield, hotly pursued by Cavaliers. Arriving late on the scene, Oliver Cromwell surveyed the Roundhead troops with despair, later writing to one of the battle commanders, "Your troopers are most of them old decayed servingmen and tapsters; and their [the Royalists] troopers are gentlemen's sons, younger sons and persons of quality..." By nightfall no clear outcome had emerged and both sides retreated to tend their wounded. (Total casualties were approximately one thousand dead and three thousand wounded, with the losses roughly equal on both sides.) The following day both armies formed ranks again, but neither had the heart to resume fighting and the battle came to an inconclusive end.

Edgehill is a famous name, but the battlefield cannot be visited today. In an ironic twist of history the Ministry of Defence took over the area for a military depot in the 1940s. Visitors to the site today have to make do with Edgehill Tower, now part of the Castle Inn. The sham castle, with its squat hexagonal tower, was built in 1742 in the centenary year of the battle and is believed to mark the spot where the king raised his standard at the start of the fighting. From the terraced gardens of the Castle Inn there are excellent views over the battlefield and a helpful guide identifies the territory where the fighting took place.

The days immediately following the Battle of Edgehill were to prove decisive for the rest of the war. Ignoring advice to head straight for London, Charles took a roundabout route, marching first to Banbury and then to Oxford and Reading. Meanwhile, Essex seized the initiative and led his troops directly to the capital. By the end of November, London was in the hands of the Parliamentarians, while Charles was forced to make his base in Oxford, where he was to remain for the rest of the war. For the next four years, the Royalists waged their campaign from Oxford, leading frequent forays over the Cotswolds in an attempt to gain control of key cities in the west and north.

FIGHTING ON THE EDGE: THE BATTLE OF LANSDOWN

After Edgehill, the next major encounter on Cotswold soil was the Battle of Lansdown, fought on 5 July 1643. The battle represented a desperate attempt by the Royalists to seize control of Bath, which was held by the Parliamentarians. Once again, fighting took place on the Cotswold escarpment, but this time the battleground lay five miles west of Bath, on the edge of a plateau known as Lansdown Hill. Here the Roundheads, under the command of Sir William Waller, established their stand against the Royalists, led by Waller's childhood friend, Sir Ralph Hopton.

Over the course of the summer Hopton had worked his way through the West Country, steadily winning support for the king, and by the start of July he was preparing for the next push eastwards. With his army swelled by a force of Cornish pikemen, Hopton was confident that he could seize Bath and then move on to the Cotswolds, but the reality proved much more challenging. Waller had used the Edge to great advantage, deploying his heavy artillery along the brow of the escarpment, thus forcing his opponents to attack uphill, Waller's canon were hidden behind some ancient Celtic earthworks while extra bands of musketeers were posted in the woods on either side of the hill. Even though Hopton's troops outnumbered the Roundheads by 6,000 to 4,000, Waller had a clear tactical advantage.

Right from the start of the battle Waller's strategy paid off, and he easily repulsed the Cavaliers' first cavalry charge. Meanwhile Hopton struggled to make any progress up the steep sides of the escarpment and around noon he gave orders for his troops to retreat. This would have been the end of the battle had not his loyal infantry persuaded Hopton to order a second charge. In the late afternoon an exhausted cavalry force rode up Lansdown Hill into a hail of gunfire. Confused and terrified, many riders fled from the battleground, but the Royalist infantry was made of sterner stuff. A determined force of Cornish pikemen stormed straight ahead, while bands of musketeers sneaked up through the woods to attack the enemy from the side. By this time Waller's men were scattered and exhausted, and he gave the order to retreat to a safer position behind a dry-stone wall. From their new position the Roundheads kept up their musket fire until long after dark, but both sides lacked the strength to bring the battle to a decisive end.

At dawn the following morning the Royalists discovered that Waller had withdrawn during the night. Hopton had won the battle for his king, but it was a Pyrrhic victory. The Roundhead force had suffered barely thirty casualties while most of the Royalist cavalry had been wiped out, and Hopton's army was left too weak to launch an attack on Bath. The Royalists had also lost one of their greatest heroes. In the late afternoon, Sir Bevil Grenville, leader of the Cornish pikemen, had been mortally wounded and had been carried to nearby Cold Aston house, where he had died later that night.

The site of the Battle of Lansdown can be seen today beside the country road from Bath to Wick (look out for the sign to Sir Bevil Grenville's monument), but the most exciting approach to the battlefield is via the Cotswold Way walking track. Walkers approaching Hanging Hill encounter a set of colourful metal pennants staking out the battle site, from the point where Hopton assembled his troops to the plateau where Waller took his stand. Standing on the brow of the escarpment is Grenville's monument, crowned by a griffon, marking the spot where the hero is believed to have fallen.

A REGION AT WAR

Between the years 1642 and 1646 the Cotswolds were in the thick of the conflict as soldiers from both armies marched across the landscape, waging battles for control of its towns. Soldiers—and their leaders—were often in need of places to stay the night, and there are many stories of overnight visitors. Three Cotswold inns can claim important guests. Charles I is said to have spent a night at the Kings Arms in Stow-on-the-Wold in 1645, just before the Battle of Naseby (in Northamptonshire). At the Lygon Arms in Broadway guests can stay in the room where Oliver Cromwell is believed to have slept. In the White Hart in Moreton-in-Marsh people still tell the story of how King Charles spent the night—but left in the morning without paying his bill. Another royal story is linked to the town of Painswick, where Charles marched with his army in 1643. The story goes that the king was resting on Painswick Hill when one of his sons asked him when they were going home. When Charles replied, "I have no home to go to," a kind-hearted local offered his monarch a bed on the outskirts of town. Charles is said to have been so overwhelmed with gratitude that he called the place "Paradise"—a name that it keeps today.

Some Cotswold places saw fighting in the streets, as Royalists and Parliamentarians battled for control of strategic centres. Malmesbury is said to have changed hands seven times, and its abbey walls are pitted with bullet marks. The church towers at Painswick and Winchcombe both bear the scars of skirmishes, and Cirencester endured a major siege. As a walled town, Cirencester had provided a secure arsenal for the Roundheads in the opening year of the war, and its citizens were vocal in their support for the Parliamentary cause. (On one occasion, a Royalist recruiter was chased out of town by an angry mob.) In January 1643 Prince Rupert led an unsuccessful attack on the town, and this was followed by a second attempt in the following month. The battle for Cirencester lasted for seven hours, with over 300 casualties, but eventually the Royalists prevailed. It is recorded that Prince Rupert took more than a thousand prisoners, locking them in the church overnight without food or water. A contemporary report from the thick of the battle records the horror and confusion of the day as men "were at their wits end and stood… amazed, feare bereft them of understanding and memory, beget confusion in the minde within, and [they] could bring forth nothing."

DAMAGE AND CONFUSION

Several grand houses were damaged in the war, as their owners became embroiled in the conflict. In the southern Cotswolds Sudeley Castle was an important royal base, providing one of Prince Rupert's key command posts in his assaults on Bristol and Gloucester. Charles I stayed at the castle several times, and on one occasion made himself a little too much at home, settling down to a game of cards when he was meant to be leading a cavalry charge. In 1644 Sudeley was captured by Parliamentary forces (its Octagon Tower still bears the marks of the besiegers' cannon balls), and at the end of the war the castle was despoiled in punishment for its owner's loyalty to the crown. When Sudeley was restored in the nineteenth century, the ruined banqueting hall was left untouched, as a reminder of troubled times in the Civil War.

At Chipping Campden the magnificent Campden Manor (home of the super-rich Sir Baptist Hicks) was used as a garrison by the king's troops. Before the Royalists withdrew to fight the Battle of Naseby they are said to have set the house on fire rather than let it fall into enemy hands. The fall of Beverstone Castle has a more comic side. It was bravely defended by the Royalists until their commander, Colonel Ogilvy, made a fatal mistake. Leaving only six men in charge for the night, Ogilvy slipped out for a romantic meeting, but his tryst was discovered and the castle was seized. Now a tumbledown tower is the only remnant of the castle.

Not all Cotswold gentry took the side of the king. Colonel Nathaniel Stephens of Chavenage House raised a small regiment to fight with the Roundheads, and later became a member of Cromwell's parliament. When Parliament decided that Charles should be executed, Cromwell visited the colonel at home, bringing with him the death warrant to be signed. Stephens put his name to the execution, but is said to have died of remorse very soon afterwards. There is a story told at Chavenage House that on the day of the colonel's death his ghost was driven away from the house by a headless coachman dressed like the king. The house is now open to the public, and the room where Cromwell stayed is filled with relics from the Civil War. In the centuries since the war Chavenage House has gained a reputation as one of England's most haunted homes.

Most Civil War stories concern the fate of powerful individuals, but the war also had a devastating effect on the lives of ordinary people. Often frightened and in danger, the people of the Cotswolds had to pay heavy contributions to both sides. Early in the conflict the king commandeered cloth from the Cotswold mills to clothe his soldiers, and mill owners were banned by royal mandate from trading with the treacherous people of London. Some consignments of cloth, sent by cart for dyeing, were seized by military commanders, and tolls on all the roads were raised. In the countryside, meanwhile, farms, houses and barns were used as billets, and soldiers demanded food and requisitioned animals.

THE BATTLE OF STOW-ON-THE-WOLD: THE END OF THE FIGHTING

By the opening months of 1646 there were signs that the war was coming to an end. Oliver Cromwell's New Model Army was proving unbeatable, and the Royalist troops were exhausted and demoralized. Yet King Charles was still not prepared to give up. Issuing orders to Sir Jacob Astley to gather all the men he could, the king prepared in Oxford for a renewed attack. In mid-March 1646 Astley set off from the Midlands towards Oxford with a force of around 3,000 men, but it was not long before he realized that he was being followed. Anxious to avoid attack while he on the move, he made the decision to turn and fight one mile north of Stow-on-the-Wold.

That night Astley drew up his troops on the side of a hill and waited anxiously for dawn. As soon as it was light on the morning of 21 March, the Roundhead army attacked, led by General Brereton. At first the Royalists managed to push the enemy back, but Brereton's forces gradually gained the upper hand. Faced with the prospect of imminent defeat, Astley ordered a fighting retreat into the town, and the last of the action took place in the market square. After the battle was over a thousand Royalists were imprisoned in the church, and the wounded were laid out along Digbeth Street, which, it was recorded, ran red with blood. The Royalist Hotel still stands on Digbeth Street, and the battle victims are commemorated by a modern memorial in the churchyard.

IMAGES OF CAVALIERS: STOW-ON-THE-WOLD AND SWINBROOK

Inside the church at Stow-on-the-Wold a slate in the chancel floor is etched with a portrait of Hastings Keyt, one of the Royalist troops who fought at the battle. It is a simple image of a Cavalier dressed in a lace-edged sash and framed by helmet, pike and gauntlets, with an ominous pair of skulls added for good measure. For a more lifelike Royalist effigy, the place to visit is the parish church at Swinbrook, ancestral home of the Fettiplace family. Here, six stone effigies of Fettiplace knights recline on a set of shelves, one above the other. (Alan Bennett has compared them to sleeping passengers in a "sepulchral couchette".) Three of the Fettiplace figures date from the years before the Civil War and are formal and plain in style. The later trio were completed in 1686 and are dressed in the elegant robes of the Cavaliers. The upper figure of these three is the staunch royalist Edmund Fettiplace. Edmund fought so loyally for the crown that he was made a Knight of the Royal Oak by King Charles II, following the monarch's restoration to the throne. Like many Cotswold families, however, the Fettiplaces had divided loyalties. Another Fettiplace was a

colonel in the Roundhead force who defended Cirencester against Prince Rupert's cavaliers.

THE BURFORD LEVELLERS

The Battle of Stow-on-the-Wold was the last pitched battle of the Civil War, but the conflict dragged on until 1649, when Charles I was executed and England became a Commonwealth. Under Oliver Cromwell's new regime people in the Cotswolds began to look forward to a more peaceful way of life. In the town of Burford, however, there was a violent epilogue to the war, as Cromwell's army turned against a group of "Levellers" in its ranks.

The grassroots group known as the Levellers has been described as an early prototype for the Civil Rights movement. Formed in the 1640s in protest against the abuses of the ruling class, the Levellers campaigned for equality before the law, religious toleration and an extended franchise. The group had originally placed their trust in Cromwell, joining in the struggle against the king, but by the end of the war many of them viewed him as a dictator.

In May 1649 Cromwell's army in Salisbury was disbanded without any pay and with little prospect of achieving the aims the Levellers had fought for. Among these troops were 800 angry Levellers, who elected new officers and marched north to Burford, with Cromwell in hot pursuit. In spite of his promise of peaceful negotiations, Cromwell charged into the town at midnight with 2,000 horsemen, rounding up over 300 Levellers and imprisoning them in the church overnight. On the following morning three of the leaders were led outside, lined up against the church wall and shot.

After the Burford incident the Levellers never achieved a voice in politics, but their beliefs have not been forgotten. Every May hundreds of people gather in Burford to mark the anniversary of the churchyard shooting. On Levellers' Day radical politicians, protest singers and trade-unionists join forces with Morris dancers in an anarchic celebration of the spirit of the Levellers. For the rest of the year the town reverts to its usual gentility, but the Levellers are remembered in the church. A rough carving on the rim of the font records the presence of "Anthony Sedley 1649 Prisner". Outside, on the church wall, a simple plaque recalls the fate of three brave men who dared to stand up for what they believed was right.

The Levellers, still remembered every year in the Cotswolds

Two World Wars

After the Civil War there was no more fighting on Cotswold soil. Over the next two centuries some local men fought in foreign wars, and the mills worked overtime to produce army uniforms. But it was not until the twentieth century that people in the Cotswolds really felt the impact of war once again.

By the end of 1914 Cotswold towns and villages had begun to empty out, as thousands of men and boys signed up to fight in the First World War. The Cotswold regiments were in the thick of the fighting, and the young men of Gloucestershire and Oxfordshire soon found themselves in a hell of mud, longing for home. One of these young soldiers was the Gloucestershire poet and composer Ivor Gurney, who wrote two collections of poems about his experiences on the Western Front. In *Severn and Somme* and *War's Embers* descriptions of the misery of life in the trenches are interspersed with memories of the woods and hills around Crickley, Cranham and Birdlip. Gurney's letters home are filled with nostalgia for the "the joy of life in those homely and friendly-seeming houses of grey stone" and he writes longingly of the "golden-pathed" Cotswold woods, where "the leaves must be flying on Cranham." Ivor Gurney survived the war, although he suffered from mental illness for the rest of his life, but thousands of young men never came home.

Today almost every village in the Cotswolds has its own memorial honouring the dead of two world wars. In even the smallest places there is a long list of names, often featuring the same families who experienced losses over two generations. The memorial at Stanway is especially striking. Standing on guard as you enter the village from the south is a bronze figure of St. George slaying a dragon. An inscription carved by Eric Gill is dedicated to the Men of Stanway and reads: "For Your Tomorrow we gave our To-day."

The First World War left its mark on the Cotswold landscape, as the open wolds were ploughed up to grow extra food and the woods were plundered for timber. But it was the Second World War that brought real changes to the region. Large areas of farmland were cleared for airfields—by 1942 there was an airfield roughly every ten miles in the Cotswolds — and anti-aircraft gun-emplacements were sited on the hills close to the towns. After centuries of rural isolation the Cotswold villagers were brought into frequent contact with foreign airmen, prisoners of war, and refugees. A Polish refugee camp was set up on the hills above Broadway, and evacuees from London and Birmingham arrived by the trainload, to be re-housed in villages and farms. Meanwhile some of the region's grand country houses were taken over for war work. Ditchley Park, close to Winston Churchill's family seat at Blenheim, became the prime minister's country retreat for the first four years of the war. Stowell Park, near Northleach, was turned into a camp for prisoners-of-war, and even parts of Sudeley Castle were used as accommodation for prisoners. In 1944 Chavenage House and Toddington Manor both housed American troops preparing for the D-Day landings, and in the same year RAF Fairford was hastily constructed to provide a base for British and American troop-carriers gathering for the Normandy invasions.

BERTIE, MAY AND MRS. FISH IN WARTIME

The experience of wartime in the Cotswolds is brought into sharp focus by Xandra Bingley. *Bertie, May and Mrs Fish: Country Memories of Wartime* describes a childhood in the 1940s through a series of anecdotes and snatches of dialogue. Xandra lived on a thousand-acre farm near Cirencester with her father and mother (Bertie and May) and a visiting cast of local village characters (such as Mrs. Fish), and she describes her mother's struggle to run the farm while her father is off fighting in the war.

> Joe Rumming and Mr Griff and Mr Munday are farm labourers too old for call-up. Landgirls are seconded from their work at the Wills Tobacco factory in Birmingham. A lorry load of Italian prisoners of war is driven for daily threshing and hoeing and fencing and stone collecting... The prisoners of war are forbidden to speak. Lined-up in the yard in dark-blue jackets and trousers, they call out to me... *Che bella bambina... cara... io te adoro... veni... veni qui.* A man in dark-blue uniform has a gun in a holster and shouts... No talky... allez... skeddadle... go-go... follow lady on horsey. My mother rides into Homefield leading the line. Each prisoner carries a long-handled hoe over his shoulder. They walk to fields of kale and mangolds and turnips and swedes to hoe out weeds along the rows... American airmen are billeted at Guiting Grange. Our landgirls walk down the lane to the pub at Kilkenny in the evenings in gumboots and flowered cotton dresses and mackintoshes. They carry high-heeled shoes and get picked up by US jeeps.

The war brings many incidents to puzzle young Xandra. German bombers roar overhead en route to Birmingham and foreign-sounding names crackle on the wireless. One night a German plane crashes in a field and catches fire. On another day a small plane flies overhead and "a shower of silver tinsel falls from the sky," an incident which remains unexplained. There are also chilling stories of the First World War—a time when "bread was black" for the poor in the Cotswolds, and babies died of starvation.

MODERN TIMES

After the Second World War Fairford continued to provide a base for the American Air Force. During the Cold War years it was home to US bomber operations, and for an anxious period in 1953 the peaceful southern Cotswolds contained a deadly force of B-47s, held at a permanent heightened state of alert. In the 1970s Fairford airbase was used as a test centre for Concorde's supersonic flights, but by the 1980s it was once again a potential launch pad for war. In 1986 US Stratotankers flew out of Fairford to launch attacks on Libya, and in the First Gulf War of 1991 B-52s hurtled down its runways. More recently, Fairford was a base for the US Air Force in the 2003 Iraq War, and became the focus of some impassioned peace protests. Nowadays the airbase is kept on standby, but it roars into life every summer when it is host to the Royal International Air Tattoo, one of the world's largest military air shows.

Ten miles east of Fairford, another Second World War airfield is in daily use. Built in 1937 as a training base, RAF Brize Norton is now the largest airbase in Britain and home for the country's air-transport operations. From this southern corner of the Cotswolds British troops fly out to war, and it is here that they are brought home again—alive or dead.

Fairford and Brize Norton are both giant complexes, but Kemble Airport still looks very much the same as it did in the 1940s. Kemble is home to a collection of flying veterans and once a year some of them take to the air. The annual Kemble Air Show attracts huge crowds to see the modern jets and to enjoy the sight of Dakotas, Hurricanes and Spitfires thundering once again over the Cotswolds.

Chapter Five

POSH COTSWOLDS

ROYALTY, ARISTOCRACY AND CELEBRITIES

"The electric gates had not yet been installed, so Ricky was able to open the iron ones. Deer and sheep blinked in the headlights as he drove up an avenue of chestnut trees. As he rattled over the second sheep grid, where the drive opened up into a big sweep of gravel, the beautiful seventeenth-century manor house, with its ruff of lavender and white roses clambering to the roof was suddenly floodlit… Ricky got out of the car, [made his way through a pack of dogs] and rung the doorbell.

A security guard answered. His shoulders seemed to fill the door.

"Mrs France-Lynch?" said Ricky."

Jilly Cooper, *Polo* (1991)

The Cotswolds can boast some very grand addresses. HRH the Prince of Wales and the Princess Royal both live within five miles of Tetbury (at Highgrove House and Gatcombe Park). The region is littered with estates and manors (some of them gently satirized in Jilly Cooper's novels) and countless celebrity homes lurk at the ends of Cotswold drives. Most imposing of all, on the eastern edge of the Cotswolds is the seat of the Duke of Marlborough—the only British stately home to call itself a palace. In fact, Blenheim Palace is a relatively recent upstart. Three hundred years ago it replaced a Cotswold palace which had been visited by royalty for over a thousand years.

WOODSTOCK PALACE: KINGS AND QUEENS IN THE FOREST

The land that is now the Blenheim Estate was once a royal hunting park, with a history dating back to the tenth century. Probably founded by Ethelred the Unready, the park formed the south-east corner of Wychwood Forest, an ancient woodland covering most of the Oxfordshire Cotswolds. Saxon kings stayed in a wooden hunting lodge, but this was replaced by King Henry I with a much grander palace built from stone.

John William Waterhouse, *Fair Rosamund* (1917). Woodstock Palace can be glimpsed through
the window of Rosamund's bower

Henry used Woodstock Palace as a country retreat and place to entertain foreign princes and kings, and it was here that a special ceremony was held, in January 1114, for the marriage of his twelve-year-old daughter, Matilda, to Henry V, the 32-year-old Emperor of Germany. Guests at the royal palace could enjoy hunting, coursing and hawking, and were introduced to King Henry's menagerie of exotic animals, including a leopard, a lynx, a camel and a porcupine.

Henry I's passion for Woodstock was shared by his powerful grandson, Henry II, who is believed to have kept his favourite mistress there. Rosamund Clifford is said to have stayed in a "bower" close to the royal palace, but safely hidden away from Henry's jealous queen, the formidable Eleanor of Aquitaine. Rosamund's secret love nest in the forest had all the ingredients of a fairy tale, and a fantastic story grew up around it after her death. The legend of Fair Rosamund tells of a bower fashioned like a maze, with a tangle of passageways leading to its heart. Here, she and Henry conducted their affair until the wicked queen came up with a cunning plan to track her down. According to the story, Eleanor followed a thread attached to her husband's spur, which led her through the labyrinth to her beautiful rival, who she either poisoned or stabbed to death.

Fair Rosamund's tragic tale has been told by artists, novelists and poets. In the sixteenth century the Tudors delighted in the image of a wicked Plantagenet queen, and the legend was the subject of several popular poems. Thomas Delaney's *Ballad of Fair Rosamund* describes King Henry "at Woodstocke" constructing an elaborate bower for his lover's "defence against the furious queene":

> Most curiously that bower was built
> Of stone and timber strong
> An hundred and fifty doors
> Did to this bower belong.
> And they so cunninglye contriv'd,
> With turnings round about,
> That none but with a clue of thread
> Could enter in or out.

Later, the Pre-Raphaelites fell under Rosamund's spell. William de Morgan, Arthur Hughes and Sir John Waterhouse all painted Fair

Rosamund in her bower, emphasizing the fairy-tale elements of her story. William de Morgan's image shows the evil queen, framed by venomous creatures, advancing on her defenceless victim. Hughes' Rosamund stands in a garden, with Queen Eleanor hovering at the gate, and Waterhouse shows Fair Rosamund waiting for her lover in a tower. As she gazes longingly down at Henry's palace she is unaware that Eleanor is lurking behind a curtain, waiting to pounce. Waterhouse painted his Rosamund in the final months of his life and it is one of his most haunting images.

The real story of Rosamund is rather more mundane. Rosamund Clifford grew up in Clifford Castle on the River Wye, before moving to Godstow Nunnery, close to Oxford, to be educated by nuns. There she was spotted by the young King Henry who took her as his mistress for the next ten years. Rosamund probably lived close to the royal palace, but she was never in danger from Queen Eleanor, who was far too busy pursuing her own interests in France. By 1176, the affair was over and Rosamund returned to Godstow nunnery, where she died a few years later, but she is not entirely forgotten at Woodstock. A jumble of stones beside the lake at Blenheim Park is known today as Fair Rosamund's Well. It is reputed to mark the exact spot where the famous bower stood.

King Henry II's famous sons, Richard and John, both hunted at Woodstock. Two of Edward I's sons were born in the palace, and Edward III brought his court to the Cotswolds for the birth of his eldest son in 1330. (The son was given the title Edward of Woodstock but was later better known as the Black Prince.) In 1464 Elizabeth Woodville is believed to have been walking in Wychwood Forest when she met King Edward IV out hunting. Famously beautiful with "heavy-lidded eyes like those of a dragon", she captivated the king who married her secretly.

In the summer of 1554 Woodstock Palace became a royal prison when Princess Elizabeth was banished there by her half-sister, Queen Mary Tudor. Earlier in the year Mary had been threatened by a series of uprisings and she suspected that Elizabeth was involved. In March 1554 the twenty-year-old Elizabeth was imprisoned in the Tower of London, where she stayed for three months before being sent to Woodstock. The journey to the Cotswolds took four days, and the young princess was cheered all the way along her route.

At Woodstock Park Elizabeth was confined to the gatehouse, as the rest of the palace had fallen into ruins. She was allowed some exercise, closely watched by guards, but her health declined as she waited to discover her fate. After almost a year of house arrest, Elizabeth was finally released in April 1555. Later an inscription was found scratched on a windowpane in the gatehouse:

Much suspected by me,
nothing proved can be,
Quoth Elizabeth prisoner.

When she became queen, Elizabeth avoided the scene of her captivity, but hunting at Woodstock was resumed in the reign of James I, when the king took over the few habitable rooms left in the palace, leaving his court to sleep under canvas. Later Charles I was a regular visitor to Woodstock Park, even finding time to hunt during the Civil War. For a short while during the conflict the palace acted as royalist garrison before falling to Cromwell's troops in 1646. The Civil War marked the end of the palace's role as a royal residence, and in 1704 Queen Anne granted Woodstock Park to the 1st Duke of Marlborough (see below).

MINSTER LOVELL AND A DREADFUL DOOM

Ten miles west of Woodstock, the romantic ruins of Minster Lovell Hall stand in the water meadows beside the River Windrush. The Hall was built in the fifteenth century for Francis, Viscount Lovell, a close friend and favourite of King Richard III. Lovell fought with Richard in the Wars of the Roses, escaping from the enemy at the Battle of Stoke, after which he was never seen again. According to some rumours, he fled to his Cotswold home, where he stayed hidden until he starved to death—a tale that was apparently confirmed in 1708 when a skeleton was found in an underground room at the Hall.

The discovery of human remains evidently made a profound impression on the local people, because a second, much more colourful tale was soon in circulation. This was the story of young Lovell and his bride, who played a fatal game of hide-and-seek soon after their wedding feast at Christmas time. In 1884 the story was recorded as *The Ballad of the Mistletoe Bough*, a tragic tale in four verses, ending with the following mournful lines:

O sad was her fate! In sportive jest
She hid from her lord in the old oak chest
It closed with spring—and dreadful doom
The bride lay clasp'd in her living tomb.

Minster Lovell Hall was bought by Sir Thomas Coke in 1602. Perhaps the eerie stories linked to the Hall made it an uncomfortable place to live, but for some unexplained reason one of his ancestors decided to dismantle the house in the mid-eighteenth century. Today an expanse of ruins remains, including an entrance passage with a finely carved roof. Close to Minster Lovell Hall (which is now in the care of English Heritage) are a large medieval dovecote and a small parish church dedicated to St. Kenelm, the Cotswold boy martyr.

SUDELEY CASTLE AND THE TUDORS

While Woodstock Palace has disappeared without a trace, another Cotswold home with royal connections has been scrupulously preserved. Sudeley Castle sits in a wooded valley close to Winchcombe. It was built around 1460 by an admiral in the royal navy, but the castle did not stay long in his family. Seized by the crown during the Wars of the Roses, it became the property of the English royal family.

In 1532 King Henry VIII visited Sudeley with his second wife, Anne Boleyn, but the most dramatic years in the castle's history began immediately after Henry's death. In 1547 the young King Edward VI granted Sudeley Castle to his uncle, Thomas Seymour, and in the same year Thomas married Catherine Parr, widow of Henry VIII. The secret marriage took place only four months after Henry's death, and there is evidence that it was a love match, as the pair had been sweethearts before Catherine's royal marriage. For a year the Seymours divided their time between London and the Cotswolds, bringing a large entourage with them to Sudeley. But the good times were short lived. In September 1548 Catherine died, shortly after giving birth to a daughter. Six months later Thomas was arrested. Accused of 33 charges of treason against King Edward, he was executed in the Tower of London in 1549.

Catherine Parr was buried in the chapel at Sudeley, with Lady Jane Grey acting as chief mourner, but within a century her tomb had been lost. The castle was at the heart of several battles in the English Civil War

and by the end of the conflict it was left in ruins. Catherine's tomb was discovered in 1728 during some renovation work, and in the following century the queen was given a second burial in the chapel, where her remains are interred in a marble monument. Visitors to the chapel can admire her effigy and see the scratched inscription from her original tomb. Elsewhere in the castle are many royal portraits and mementoes, including a love letter written by Catherine to Thomas Seymour.

Following the destruction of the Civil War, Sudeley Castle was allowed to fall into ruins until the nineteenth century, when it changed hands twice, ending up with its current owners, the Dent-Brocklehursts. Under their supervision, major renovations were carried out, with the aim of creating the perfect English castle. Standing against a background of densely wooded hills, the castle is surrounded by extensive grounds that feature a Tudor knot garden and parterre. It has been called the most romantic castle in England and has recently been reinvented as the ultimate wedding venue. In 2007 super-model Liz Hurley's "Wedding at the Castle" was a society event of the year, with a vast marquee in the grounds and all guests requested to wear pink. In fact, Hurley's wedding would have struggled to compare with a party thrown by her royal namesake. In September 1592 Queen Elizabeth I stayed at Sudeley as part of a grand summer progress, and held a three-day festivity to commemorate the English victory over the Spanish Armada four years earlier. Sadly, no detailed records of the event survive, but the autumn feast held at Sudeley Castle was remembered as one of the longest royal parties in English history.

BLENHEIM PALACE: ENGLAND'S GRANDEST STATELY HOME

Blenheim Palace, in Simon Jenkins' words, "brooks no argument". More a monument to national pride than a family home, it was designed by Sir John Vanbrugh in the short-lived style of the English Baroque. To some the Blenheim effect is magnificent; others have responded differently. For A. A. Gill it is "the most miserably dour gaff in England". Jenkins sees it as "most un-English", comparing the palace to "an army lined up for battle."

The story of Blenheim began on a German battlefield when Commander John Churchill led the English to victory against the French. In 1704 the Battle of Blenheim put a decisive end to Louis XIV's conquest of Europe and earned the undying gratitude of Queen Anne. Churchill's

reward was a title (he became the 1st Duke of Marlborough), the gift of Woodstock Park and a massive grant of £240,000 to spend on his new home. It was an unusually generous gift, but the story of Blenheim's construction is not a happy one. By 1710 the grant had almost run out, leaving Vanbrugh's grandiose palace very far from complete. To make matters worse, Sarah Churchill, 1st Duchess of Marlborough, had quarrelled with her former friend Queen Anne, and her husband had also fallen from royal favour. For the next four years the Marlboroughs were forced into ignominious exile in France, only returning to England after the queen's death.

In 1716 work resumed at Blenheim, this time at the Marlboroughs' personal expense. It was not long, however, before Sarah had managed to fall out with Vanbrugh, who abandoned the building to a team of local masons. Sarah went on to complete the palace after her husband's death, describing it bitterly as the nation's "monument of ingratitude", and when Vanbrugh returned to view his achievement, he was turned away at the gate on the orders of the duchess. He had planned to preserve the ruins of the royal palace, but Sarah gave orders for it to be razed to the ground. Today the site of Woodstock Palace is marked by a small stone plinth surrounded by trees on a patch of raised ground close to Vanbrugh's bridge.

Work on Blenheim Palace came to an end in the 1730s, and the park was finally completed thirty years later when Capability Brown created his famous landscape (described in Chapter Thirteen). Designed to be viewed from a distance, the palace looks most magnificent when approached by the drive that runs beside the great lake. Inside, a sense of grandeur is maintained in a series of ornate state apartments offering stunning views over the park.

MARLBOROUGHS, VANDERBILTS AND CHURCHILLS

After all the dramas of its construction Blenheim enjoyed a quiet interlude but by the 1890s the estate was in serious financial trouble. Desperate for funds, Charles Spencer-Churchill, 9th Duke of Marlborough, turned to the New World for salvation, proposing marriage to Consuelo Vanderbilt, a fabulously wealthy American heiress. The wedding was held in New York in 1896 and hailed as the society event of the year, but Consuelo was weeping behind her bridal veil. Transported from the pleasures of New York, she was faced with a dilapidated country pile and a daunting programme of repairs.

One of the most striking portraits at Blenheim is a study by John Singer Sargent of *The Ninth Duke and Duchess of Marlborough*. Painted in 1905 when the couple had been married for nine years, it shows Charles and Consuelo with their two sons, John and Ivor (famously described by Consuelo as "the heir and the spare"). The family makes a handsome group, dominated by the elegant Consuelo (as a young girl she had been forced to wear a ramrod fixed to the back of her dress). But behind the glamour lay deep unhappiness. In 1906 the 9th Duchess of Marlborough shocked society by leaving her husband, finally divorcing him in 1921. Charles went on to marry Gladys Deacon, an eccentric American with artistic interests, but this marriage was also not a success. Gladys took to dining with a revolver by the side of her plate, while Charles became so desperate to be rid of his wife that he temporarily closed down the palace to drive her out. Even after she left, however, the spirit of Gladys remained at Blenheim. The carved stone sphinxes on the lower terrace are said to be modelled on her and an enormous painting of one of Gladys' eyes glares down from the ceiling of the great north portico.

Today, the 9th Duke is largely forgotten, but his cousin is world-famous. In the autumn of 1874 Lord Randolph Churchill and his wife were staying with the 8th duke, when the heavily pregnant Lady Randolph had a fall in the park. Twenty-four hours later she gave birth to a son named Winston. During his childhood years the young Winston paid frequent visits to Blenheim, where he played with his cousins and absorbed the story of his distinguished soldier ancestor. Today at Blenheim Palace you can stand in the room where Sir Winston Churchill was born and view a gallery celebrating his life. You can also take a short walk to Bladon churchyard, to see the great man's simple grave.

DYRHAM PARK AND *THE REMAINS OF THE DAY*

Seventy miles west of Blenheim, at the other end of the Cotswolds, another stately home sits in a splendid park. Reached by a long, sweeping drive, Dyrham Park is surrounded by 270 acres of parkland and a formal garden with lakes and ponds. Dyrham was chosen by Ismail Merchant and James Ivory as the setting for their film *The Remains of the Day*. The film (based on a novel by Kazuo Ishiguro) evokes a world of elegant but faded country life, and Dyrham provided the perfect backdrop for its story.

The history of Dyrham Park began in 1686 when William Blathwayt, a prominent civil servant, married the heiress of Dyrham and set about converting her modest family home into a grand mansion. The house became an obsession, which occupied him until his death thirty years later, long after his wife had died. Blathwayt's creation is strikingly cosmopolitan. The grand eastern façade was built in the latest elegant French fashion. The house was filled with paintings and porcelain from the Netherlands, and the staircases were carved from American timber.

Blaythwayt built Dyrham to impress, but the house was not quite what it seemed. The magnificent eagle crowning its roof suggested a noble pedigree that Blaythwayt could not claim, and the opulence of its furnishings was underpinned by skilful wheeling and dealing. Wherever Blaythwayt went in the service of the crown, there were bribes and backhanders in the form of gifts for his country mansion. Blathwayt always hoped that Queen Anne would grace him with a visit, but she never came, perhaps recoiling from his flamboyant taste. In the 1700s Dyrham Park must have shouted "new money". With the passing of three centuries it has mellowed into a gracious stately home.

Chastleton and Stanway: Houses with Memories

Not all the Cotswold country homes put on a grand public face. Chastleton House, in the northern Cotswolds, is a handsome Stuart manor house that has always been a private family home. Built between 1607 and 1612 by a wealthy merchant, Walter Jones, the house remained virtually unchanged for the next four hundred years. No great historic events ever took place at Chastleton, but the rules of croquet were devised in its garden, and a secret chamber over the porch has an intriguing link with the English Civil War. After the Battle of Worcester in 1651 the Royalist Arthur Jones escaped back home to Chastleton, with Cromwell's soldiers in hot pursuit. There his enterprising wife kept him hidden in the secret room while she laced the soldiers' beer with laudanum, allowing her husband to make a speedy escape.

In 1991 Chastleton House was taken over by the National Trust, who adopted a policy of "conserving as found". Its rooms are now scrupulously clean, but they still contain some domestic clutter. Visitors can wander through the great hall, parlours and bedrooms, and children are encouraged to search for Arthur's secret room. Most atmospheric of all is the Long Gallery with its Jacobean barrel ceiling decorated with plasterwork designs. The gallery runs the whole length of the house, and was used by the family for gentle promenading in rainy weather. Nicholas Cooper notes in his excellent guide to Chastleton: "The room is perhaps at its best in stormy conditions, when the rain beat against the casements and the floor creaks underfoot like the deck of a ship in heavy seas."

While Walter Jones was planning Chastleton House the Tracy family were busy building their family home in the village of Stanway. Stanway House lies at the foot of a steep escarpment four miles north-east of Winchcombe. It is approached through an ornate Jacobean gateway dating from around 1630, while the house itself was built in the 1590s in the style of a grand Elizabethan manor. Much of the charm of Stanway lies in its setting, with the manor house and gateway forming part of a group that includes the church, a medieval tithe barn and the formal water gardens. As H. J. Massingham wrote: "The repose and graciousness of old England are gathered into this small acreage, and the scene is yet more moving in winter when the bloom of the grey stone is seen set against the dark network of branches and the subdued greens of Stanway Hill."

Stanway House has remained in the hands of Tracy descendants since it was first built, passing first to the Earls of Wemyss and then to the Neidpaths, and has managed to keep the atmosphere of a family home. (According to Simon Jenkins, "Visitors who complain of the mess [at Stanway] are sent at once to the nearest National Trust property.") The Great Hall still feels stranded in the sixteenth century, with its large oak table set up for a game of shovelboard. Elsewhere in the house are fine examples of "Chinese Chippendale" furniture, pre-Raphaelite paintings and family portraits.

In the 1920s Stanway cast its spell over James Barrie, creator of *Peter Pan*. Barrie first came to stay in 1921 as the guest of his secretary, Lady Cynthia Asquith, daughter of the Earl of Wemyss. As Lady Asquith recalled in her biography of Barrie, he fell in love with the place immediately: "not only with the gabled sixteenth-century house, but with its atmosphere which—remote, cloistered, yet somehow welcoming—seemed, he said, at once to enfold him like a cloak." Barrie rented Stanway for several weeks that summer, returning every year until 1932 to play host to his numerous friends. The list of house guests from these years reads, in Lady Asquith's words, "like scores of items from 'Who's Who'", and includes Sir Arthur Conan Doyle, G. K. Chesterton, L. P. Hartley and H. G. Wells. Barrie's guests were expected to join in lively games of croquet and cricket, and to accompany him on sightseeing expeditions to the local villages. But life at Stanway was not all fun and games, as their host would suddenly plunge into a black mood, leaving his guests anxious and abandoned. Barrie's last summer at Stanway was especially dire and Lady Asquith recorded on the day he left, "I must, alas, admit that I'm glad the last day has come."

New Owners for Old Homes

At Chastleton and Stanway you are aware of centuries of history, but Upton House belongs to the 1920s when it was renovated by the 2nd Viscount Bearsted. Originally a hunting lodge dating from the reign of William and Mary, the house is part of a large country estate a few miles south of Edgehill. For the super-rich Viscount Bearsted, heir to the Shell oil empire, Upton provided both a country retreat and a place to display his growing art collection. In 1927 he supervised an extensive remodelling of the house in the Art Deco style. The result is a country home of no great architectural distinction, but which nevertheless provides an excellent showcase for the family porcelain, tapestries and paintings. Visitors to Upton can view English masterworks by Holbein, Hogarth, Stubbs and Reynolds as well as paintings by Old Masters such as El Greco, Rembrandt and Tintoretto. Also on display is a set of posters from the Shell collection, evoking an era when the English countryside began to open up to motorists.

Upton House offers a fascinating insight into the millionaire lifestyle of the 1930s, when friends motored down from London to enjoy a Cotswold country weekend. It was a way of life that largely vanished with the Second World War, but it has recently been revived with the arrival of a clutch of celebrities in the Cotswolds. The list of the mega-rich with second homes in the region reads like the contents page of *Hello* magazine. Liz Hurley, Kate Moss, Damien Hirst, Hugh Grant, Ruby Wax, Sam Mendes and Kate Winslet, Lawrence Llewelyn-Bowen and Jeremy Clarkson are just some of the famous names who have invested in a place in the Cotswolds.

Cotswold celebrities are now so thick on the ground that a special tour has been devised to view their homes—at least from the ends of their drives. But one Cotswold manor house stands out against the tide. Since 1969 Postlip Hall has been a housing co-operative shared by eight families who each play a part in the upkeep of their home. The fifteen-acre Postlip Estate lies in wooded country three miles west of Winchcombe, where a chapel and barn form a charming group beside the Jacobean manor house. For the past forty years the Postlip Community has lived co-operatively, farming their land and holding regular events to fund the estate. Once a year Postlip Manor is host to the Cotswold Beer Festival. Held in association with CAMRA (the Campaign for Real Ale), the festival attracts over three thousand visitors to Postlip and helps to keep the spirit of an ancient manor house alive.

Chapter Six

MILLS, STEAM AND MACHINERY

THE INDUSTRIAL AGE

"The whole of this region [the Cotswolds], though it seems now so Arcadian, is actually a depressed industrial area."

J. B. Priestley, *English Journey* (1934)

Castle Combe has been called the prettiest village in England. In fact—like many Cotswold places— it is a decayed industrial site. For three hundred years the village streets would have echoed to the clatter of weavers' shuttles and the thump of the fulling mills. The stink of burning sulphur would have filled the air, and the River Bybrook would have run red with dye. The village of Castle Combe is just one of hundreds of industrial sites in the Cotswolds, found especially in the south-west of the region. Behind the picture-book scene, there is a history of money-making, labour and suffering, as the Cotswolds experienced the age of industry.

HARD LABOUR AT CASTLE COMBE
Cloth-making at Castle Combe had its origins in the enterprise of a certain Sir John Fastolfe, a soldier in the service of the Duke of Clarence (and a possible model for Shakespeare's Sir John Falstaff). Fastolfe acquired the manor in 1409 and set about recruiting men for the French wars and clothing them in the red and white cloth made by his tenants. By 1454 a chronicler recorded seventy cloth-workers with their apprentices living at Castle Combe. Roughly fifty new homes had been built for the workers and strict closing times had been imposed on the local taverns (8 p.m. in winter and 9 p.m. in summer).

Cotswold cloth-workers were known for their love of liquor—and they certainly needed some respite from their labours. Hand-production of woollen cloth is immensely labour intensive, and even the youngest villagers would have played their part in the process. The work began with sorting, washing and drying the fleece before the woollen bundles could

Castle Combe: picturesque village or industrial ruin?

be "scribbled" and "carded" (loosened and stripped of impurities). Then the treated wool was taken to a stove house to be bleached by sulphur fires. Women and children had the jobs of combing, spinning and spooling the yarn, while the man of the house laboured at his loom, with a young apprentice to catch and throw his shuttle. Finished "pieces" were carried to fulling mills to be thickened and shrunk by repeated pounding from wooden hammers. Fulling was followed by "napping" (raising the "nap" of the cloth) and "shearing" (shaving off the excess nap). Finally, the pieces were soaked in stinking vats of vegetable dye before being laid on wooden racks to dry.

Some reminders of all this industry have survived at Castle Combe. The high-gabled cottages were specially constructed to hold the weavers' looms. Steps leading down to the Bybrook allowed easy access for washing the wool, and the handsome market cross provided a gathering place for merchants dealing in wool and cloth. A carving on the church tower displays the twin symbols of a weaving shuttle and shears, while monuments inside the church commemorate the lives of the local clothiers. One tablet to "Mr. WALTER FISHER, clothier, and MARY his wife, proudly relates how the couple

> left them six sons and four daughters,
> all decently educated and formed for the world
> by their industrious care and tenderness.

"A Truly Noble Manufacture"

By the time Sir John Fastolfe set up business in Castle Combe people had been making cloth in the Cotswolds for at least three hundred years. In 1185 Temple Guiting had the first known fulling mill in England, and early parish records are scattered with the names of fullers, weavers and dyers. By the end of the sixteenth century finished cloth had replaced wool as the region's main export, as Cotswold mills dispatched their precious bales of cloth, via the Merchant Adventurers of London, to markets in Europe, India and the New World.

For the enterprising men who ran the clothing business, there were fortunes to be made. The real Dick Whittington was a Gloucestershire clothier. The owner of several mills, he famously rose to be Lord Mayor of London (the "cat" that accompanied him on his legendary journey is believed to have been a trading ship). And the rise of Sir Baptist Hicks was just as meteoric. Starting out as the son of a Chipping Campden mercer, he rapidly became the richest man in England, Lord Mayor of London, and chief moneylender to the king. Hicks spent part of his fortune in his native town, where he paid for the handsome market hall, a set of almshouses and an extravagant home in the Italian style. Campden Manor was burnt to the ground in the English Civil War but its imposing ruins survive beside the church, looking oddly out of tune with the rest of the place. As R. P. Beckinsale wrote: "We wonder what the Campden masons thought as they shaped the stone for those spiral shafts and reared the magnificent house with a wide terrace and flanking pavilions." The edifice was crowned with a transparent dome in which a light burned after dark "to guide benighted travellers on the wolds" and to advertise the munificence of their local multi-millionaire.

More modest clothiers' homes survive in the southern Cotswolds. Here the mill-owners usually chose to live in a comfortable mill house, which doubled as a home and a place for fulling and storing cloth. Fine examples of mill houses survive in the Painswick valley, where Lovedays Mill, Cap Mill, Painswick Mill, Skinners Mill and Kings Mill all date from the seventeenth century. Also forming part of this group is the Kemps Lane roundhouse: a small circular building, used for drying wool.

By the 1700s the business of cloth-making dominated the Five Valleys surrounding the town of Stroud (Frome, Nailsworth, Toadsmoor, Slad and Painswick). Villages were filled with weavers' cottages while the local towns were busy centres for trade. Daniel Defoe rode this way on his *Tour thro' the Whole Island of Great Britain* (1724-27) and marvelled at the astonishing scale of the "truly noble manufacture":

> … those that see the quantity of wooll brought to the markets of Tetbury, and other towns, and the quantity sent from London, all into this one vale, would wonder how it was possible to be consumed, manufactured, and wrought up; so on the other hand, those that saw the numbers of people imploy'd, and the vast quantity of goods made in this part of England, would wonder where the whole nation should be able to supply them with wooll.

The goods that Defoe observed were partly undyed "white cloth" and part coloured broadcloth—a Cotswold speciality. Cotswold mills were famous for their dyes, including a range of subtle duns, browns and greens and some glorious scarlets and blues. The natural salts found in the local rivers produced especially brilliant and lasting colours, and Uley Blue and Stroudwater Scarlet were famous throughout England. Cloth from the Cotswold mills clothed the British army in scarlet and blue, and provided the gentlemen of the shires with blue tailcoats and hunting "pinks". Even the rejected cloth was put to good use, as wealthy clothiers founded charity "redcoat" and "bluecoat" schools, whose pupils became a walking endorsement of their benefactors' philanthropy.

One of the Cotswolds' most picturesque places is Arlington Row, the line of cottages straggling up the hillside at Bibury. But just like the cottages at Castle Combe these are in fact industrial dwellings, where large quantities of cloth were once produced. The commerical unit known as Arlington Row was converted from a sheep barn in the seventeenth century, when a local mill owner added high gabled rooms with large windows to illuminate his weavers' looms. The cottage weavers would have washed their finished "pieces" in the tiny stream that runs beside the Row, then crossed the bridge to Rack Isle to stretch them out to dry.

Arlington Row looks charming today, but life in a weaver's cottage was anything but pretty. Anyone who has read George Eliot's *Silas Marner* will remember the haunting figure of the weaver of Raveloe, pallid and undersized beside his peasant neighbours, spending "the livelong day" bent over his treadle loom, "his ear filled with its monotony, his eyes bent close down on the slow growth of sameness in the brownish web, his muscles moving with such even repetition that their pause seemed almost as much a constraint as the holding of his breath." Silas Marner was based on the weavers Eliot had known in Warwickshire—figures glimpsed through windows with a "bent, treadmill attitude" or trudging over the hills, carrying their load of finished cloth to the mill. Marner manages to grow rich through his toil, but most Cotswold weavers were not so fortunate, working all the daylight hours just to keep their families from starving. In the 1800s Joseph White remembered his boyhood as the son of a weaver at Randwick (near Stroud), woken at four every morning and working until nine or ten at night. In spite of his punishing hours as his father's apprentice, he still found time to study, attracting the notice of a wealthy patron. The weaver's son from Randwick ended his life as Professor of

Arabic at Oxford University, but he was left permanently crippled by his childhood labour.

The Coming of the Machines

The weavers of Arlington Row would have spent their working lives at home, simply crossing the fields to deliver their pieces to the nearby mill (which still survives at Bibury). But this way of life was soon to disappear. The invention of the Spinning Jenny in 1764 heralded a new age of machinery, and by the turn of the century mechanization of the cloth industry was well under way. In the opening decades of the nineteenth century Cotswold mill owners rivalled each other to devise the best machines for napping, fulling and shearing. (One of these shearing machines provided the inspiration for a famous invention when Edwin Budding of Stroud patented the first mechanical lawn mower in 1830.) In 1836 the power loom arrived, with its mechanically operated "flying shuttle" and the mill owners rushed to install the new machines.

All this progress was very bad news for the weavers, confronted with a choice of tending the new machines or seeing their families starve. Yet the shearers faced an even grimmer prospect. Men whose skills had once been in great demand suddenly found themselves ousted by the shearing machines. In 1802 a band of desperate men prepared to turn their shears on anyone who dared to take their work away, and the owner of Woodchester Mill received an ominous letter:

> Wee Hear in Formed that you got Shear in mee sheens and if you Don't Pull them Down in Forght Nights Time Wee will pull them Down for you Wee will you Damd infernold Dog. And Bee four Almighty God we will pull down all the Mills that heave Heany Shearing me Shens in We will cut out Hall your Damd Hearts as Do ee them and We will meoc the rest Heat them or else We will Searve them the Seam.

It is not recorded whether these threats were ever put into action, but Woodchester Mill prospered, staying in business for another eighty years.

With the invention of the machines came a new generation of mill buildings. In a frenetic period between 1800 and 1820 almost every cloth mill in the western Cotswolds was rebuilt and over a hundred new buildings were constructed. These vast new structures, usually rising to at least four storeys, still relied on fast-flowing water but also made use of steam power and were topped by chimneys belching smoke. Inside the mills, cavernous galleries were filled with noisy machinery: water wheels and fulling machines took up most of the basement; spinning, scribbling, carding and shearing machines were found on the lower floors; and loom shops occupied the upper storeys, illuminated by rows of high windows.

JOHN HALIFAX, GENTLEMAN: PERFECT PROGRESS AT DUNKIRK MILL?

One of the best examples of a later Cotswold mill stands in the Nailsworth valley. Dunkirk Mill was enlarged several times in the nineteenth century and has a working engine house that can sometimes still be seen in action. The prospect of the mill in its wooded valley made a profound impression on a Victorian novelist, when she stayed in the nearby village of Enderly. Dinah Maria Mulock, a.k.a. "Mrs. Craik", was a bestselling author of morally improving tales, and her Cotswold visit inspired her most popular work of all. *John Halifax, Gentleman* (published in 1856) tells the story of a noble orphan who rises to the position of gentleman, establishing a mill equipped with all the latest steam-driven machinery. Written especially for the Victorian middle classes, with their aspirations of progress through industry, it effectively captured the spirit of the age and was outsold only by *Uncle Tom's Cabin.*

Reading the story of John Halifax today, it is just possible to see the Cotswold mills through Victorian eyes. When Halifax first points out Enderby Mill to his friend, he is filled with a sense of philanthropic optimism:

> Do you like this, Phineas? I do very much. A dear, smiling, English valley, holding many a little nest of an English home. Fancy being patriarch over such a region, having the whole valley in one's hand, to do good to, or ill… [and] down in the valley—is the grand support of the neighborhood, a large cloth-mill!… Now, [with] just one or two of our modern improvements…

And, of course, the "improvements" do get made, as Halifax eventually takes charge the mill, hauling it single-handedly into the modern age. Mrs Craik's hero represents the ideal Victorian industrialist, as he brings the exciting inventions of the cities to his backward Cotswold valley.

> He was setting up that wonderful novelty—a steam-engine. He had already been to Manchester and elsewhere, and seen how the new power was applied by Arkwright, Hargreaves, and others; his own ingenuity and mechanical knowledge furnished the rest. He worked early and late—often with his own hands—aided by the men he brought with him from Manchester. For it was necessary to keep the secret—especially in our primitive valley—until the thing was complete. So the ignorant, simple mill-people, when they came for their easy Saturday's wages, only stood and gaped at the mass of iron, and the curiously-shaped brickwork, and wondered what on earth "the master" was about? But he was so thoroughly the "master," with all his kindness, that no one ventured either to question or interfere.

In the capable hands of the "master" all goes well, and the scene when the steam engines are first set in motion is one of the high points of the book, as the fearful villagers recoil in terror when the machinery cranks into life:

> Greater and lesser cog-wheels caught up the motive power, revolving slowly and majestically, and with steady, regular rotation, or whirling round so fast, you could hardly see that they stirred at all. Of a sudden, a soul had been put into that wonderful creature of man's making, that inert mass of wood and metal, mysteriously combined. The monster was alive!

> Naturally, the "monster" in this fable proves entirely benevolent. None of the workers lose their jobs and the whole valley benefits from the mill's astonishing productivity. However, the reality of life in the Cotswolds was very different…

"THEY SAY THE SUFFERING IS VERY GREAT INDEED"
As early as 1820 there were ominous signs that the enthusiasm (and greed) of the mill owners might have been misplaced. Many clothiers realized they had drastically overspent on ambitious building schemes and untried machinery. Competition was fierce from Yorkshire and France, and only the finest Cotswold cloth passed the strict standards of the Merchant Adventurers Hall, leaving many owners desperate for customers. There were also serious issues of overcrowding, as mills all along a valley competed for the same water supply. Faced with all these problems, only the larger mills survived, and hundreds of cloth-workers were laid off work. This was the situation that William Cobbett discovered when he visited in 1826:

> From Avening I came on through Nailsworth, Woodchester, and Rodbrough to this place. These villages lie on the sides of a narrow and deep valley, with a narrow stream of water running down the middle of it and this stream turns the wheels of a great many mills and sets of machinery for the making of wool cloth. The factories begin at Avening and are scattered all the way down the valley. There are steam-engines as well as water powers. The work and trade is so flat that in, I should think, much more than a hundred acres of ground, which I have seen today, covered with rails or racks for the drying of cloth, I do not think I have seen one single acre where the racks had cloth upon them. The workmen do not get half wages; great numbers of them are thrown on the parish... At present this valley suffers; and though cloth will always be wanted, there will yet be much suffering even here, while at Uly and other places they say the suffering is very great indeed.

Cobbett did not linger to investigate the suffering, although he did observe that, at least in the Stroud valley, nobody actually seemed to be starving. He also seemed unaware of the history of strikes in the area. In fact, the weavers of Stroud had resorted to violence just the previous year. In the words of the Rev. Francis Witts, parson of Upper Slaughter and local magistrate: "A certain degree of dissatisfaction has existed for some time about wages, which led to disorderly assemblages, actual violence and alarming tumult." In response to this "tumult", a company of the 10th Hussars was sent into the town "to assist the civil power in quelling a riotous uprising."

Six months later, Witts was recording judicial proceedings against another group of rioters:

> The business at hand at the Sessions was the trial of several weavers who, acting under the delusion so prevalent in all manufacturing districts, have been guilty of very serious riots and acts of disturbance at Wotton-under-Edge and its neighbourhood some weeks ago. They proceeded to great violence, assaulting the operatives who undertook work at a lower rate than was approved by them, proceeding to the to the demolition of workshops and factories, meeting in large companies and debating in their clubs measures to obtain higher wages and control over their masters.
>
> Of these misguided men several were of very decent appearance; one had been a serjeant and enjoyed a pension. They must be punished with severity since the indulgence shown to the Stroud rioters has failed in its effect. The worse cases now will receive two years incarceration in one of the Houses of Correction.

The circumstances that led decent men to resort to violence are revealed in a weaver's letter to a government inspector (quoted in Alan Sutton's *Cotswold Images*). George Risby had worked for the same employer for seven years, in which time he had seen piece rates fall from £2 to 1s 8d "on account of the multitude of hands and shortness of trade." His letter ends with a heartfelt appeal: "I am brought so weak that I am not able to work as I was two years ago. I and my children are very destitute of clothes… All that we, as Englishmen, want is plenty of labour, and that which sweetens labour. I have four miles a day to walk to my work."

Risby was one of thousands of Cotswold workers suffering from exhaustion and malnutrition. Another inspector's report makes desperate reading:

> The weavers are very much distressed: they are wretchedly off in bedding: [the] witness has seen many cases where the man and wife and as many as seven children have slept on the floor with only a torn quilt to cover them; sometimes he… has witnessed very distressing cases; children crying for food, and the parents having neither food nor money in

the house; he has frequently given them money out of his own pocket to provide them with a breakfast.

Between the years 1820 and 1844 a total of 78 Cotswold mills ceased production. When Sheppards of Uley folded in 1837 (after the owner had overextended himself by buying Gatcombe Park) a thousand workers lost their jobs. At least a hundred of them migrated to Australia or North America, while others faced the prospect of the workhouse —something dreaded more than starvation. In the words of one inspector:

> These men have a great dread of going to the Poor Houses, and live in constant hope that everyday will bring them some work; [the] witness has frequently told them they would be better in the house, and their answer has been "We would rather starve". [The] witness considers this wretched state stints the children in growth and... has often dropped in at meal times and found them eating potatoes with a bit of flick or suet.

CHANGING TRADES

After the lean years of the "Hungry Forties" the woollen industry made a brief recovery in the 1850s, but this revival proved to be short-lived. Meanwhile, the exodus from the Cotswolds continued as people left for the cities or the New World, and the mills were gradually abandoned or converted for other uses. By the 1900s mill buildings in the southern Cotswolds were turning out hosiery, hairpins, paper and walking sticks. Some were turned into engineering works, while others provided furniture-making workshops. Dursley and Stroud became the main industrial centres for the region, specializing in engineering and plastic products, although a few of the larger mills stayed in operation, mainly manufacturing specialist cloth such as baize for billiard tables. In 1939 R. P. Beckinsale counted just seven cloth mills in the south-west Cotswolds. In the year 2000 this number had shrunk to one.

BLANKETS AND BLISS IN OXFORDSHIRE

The story of industry in the Cotswolds is mainly located in the south-west. Without the advantages of swift-flowing rivers many woollen mills in the Oxfordshire Cotswolds had abandoned production by the seventeenth century. Nevertheless, some enterprises prospered. In Charlbury and Woodstock, glove making was the staple industry, and many Cotswold villagers worked at home as "glovers". Looking back on his Broadway childhood, Sid Knight remembered his mother's gloving frame, a sight "as familiar to me as the old clock on the mantelpiece", and recalled "the tens of thousands of hours" that his mother spent operating the treadle with her foot while she guided the needle around the leather seams.

On the south-east fringe of the Cotswolds, a thriving blanket-making business grew up around Witney. In 1677 the Oxfordshire historian Dr. Robert Plott wrote that Witney blankets "are esteemed above all others" and noted that the industry employed at least 3,000 workers "from eight years old to decrepit old age." In the following century the Witney Blanket Weavers' Company was granted a royal charter and built a handsome Blanket Hall in the High Street, where the blankets were weighed, inspected and given the Witney "mark". Trade was brisk throughout the eighteenth century, with the finest blankets produced for the domestic market and coarser weaves exported to North America, but major change arrived in the nineteenth century, as mechanization forced many smaller mills out of business. By the 1890s just a few manufacturers dominated the town. The most famous of these, Earlys of Witney, continued to operate a factory until 2002.

The towns of the northern wolds also had their industries. In the eighteenth century flax was grown around Moreton-in-Marsh, and over forty weavers were kept busy producing fine linen cloth, a business that continued until the twentieth century. There were silk mills at Blockley, Chipping Campden and Broadway, but as demand for ribbons declined in the 1880s the mills began to close. News of the closures at Blockley drew William Morris to the area with a scheme to set up a pottery in an abandoned mill. Morris' plans never materialized—something he later regretted bitterly—but one nearby mill was revived. In 1902 the Old Silk Mill at Chipping Campden had a new lease of life as the headquarters of C. R. Ashbee's Guild of Handicrafts.

In the north-east corner of the Cotswolds, Bliss Valley Tweed Mill, near Chipping Norton, is the region's most unusual industrial site. When the family mill burned down in 1872, its owner, William Bliss, chose to create a building that was closer to a stately home than a factory. Bliss Valley Mill was designed by Lancashire architect George Woodhouse in the style of a French château, and sits in its own parkland. The factory clock,

Bliss Valley Tweed Mill: a factory designed to look like a stately home

which could be seen by workers all over the valley, is set in a handsome domed roof, and even the factory chimney was modelled on a classical Tuscan column.

Bliss Valley Mill provided a splendid home for William and his family but it was also built with his workers in mind. Bliss was a model employer whose philanthropy had been recognized with a special medal by Napoleon III, and he planned to create a gracious place for his employees to work. The workrooms were light and airy, and the mill was furnished with a reading room, a chapel, and a set of workers' cottages. In the following decade the mill workers of Chipping Norton enjoyed some of the best facilities in England, but the factory's construction had consumed the family's wealth. William's son was forced to auction off parts of the mill and the twentieth century saw a slow decline in business, with a union strike in 1913 splitting the town in two. The end finally came in 1988, when the remains of the company moved to Cornwall, and in the 1990s the buildings were converted into luxury housing. Today the factory buildings house 46 apartments and cottages, while the old Wool House has been transformed into a leisure centre, with indoor swimming pool, sauna, squash court and gym.

CARVING UP THE LANDSCAPE: ROADS AND CANALS

The growth of industry in the eighteenth century was accompanied by a gradual improvement in Cotswold roads. The region's "rough uneven ways" had been notorious ever since Shakespeare's day, but by the 1700s local turnpike trusts had been formed, with the aim of improving some of the busiest routes. Major coaching roads ran between the cities of Oxford, Gloucester, Worcester and Bristol, and the towns of Tetbury, Burford, Broadway and Stowe became important stops for changing the horses. As well as providing stabling for horses, the Cotswold coaching towns rivalled each other in their provision of hospitable inns for travellers. The Lygon Arms at Broadway and the Snooty Fox at Tetbury both date back to coaching days.

While the roads of the central Cotswolds were relatively easy to upgrade, progress in the Five Valleys was desperately slow. In the 1700s a coach could take all day to make the journey from Chalford to Stroud and the roads up the western escarpment were notorious. It was hard enough for a light carriage to climb through winding lanes out of "the bottoms", but moving the heavy products of the mills was a transport nightmare.

The obvious solution for the region was a canal. If the Cotswold mill towns could be linked to the Thames and Severn rivers, all their products could be carried away by barge. The first important step was taken in the 1770s with the construction of the Stroudwater Navigation, connecting the River Severn at Framilode to Wallbridge, a suburb of Stroud. The eight-mile stretch of water was welcomed by the mill owners who used the canal to import coal and other heavy materials from the west, but the problem still remained of how to transport their products west to London. A far more radical project was the proposed Thames & Severn Canal, linking the two rivers by a channel that ran near Cirencester. This was the same scheme that Alexander Pope had suggested to Lord Bathurst of Cirencester Park back in the 1720s, describing in grandiose terms how "the Thames and Severn… are to be led into each others' embrace thro' secret caverns of not above twelve or fifteen miles, till they rise and openly celebrate their marriage in the midst of an immense amphitheatre, which is to be the admiration of posterity a hundred years hence…"

Lord Bathurst had wisely rejected Pope's proposal, but now a team of engineers began to make more practical plans. In 1783 work began on the Thames & Severn Canal, a waterway covering a distance of almost thirty miles from Wallbridge to Lechlade, with an extra side-branch leading to Cirencester. It was a formidable undertaking, requiring 44 locks and an underground tunnel through the limestone at Sapperton, but the potential rewards were immense. It was hoped that the finished canal would not only carry the products of the Cotswolds but would also serve as a vital route for transporting goods between the Midlands and London.

By far the most challenging part of the canal project was the construction of the Sapperton tunnel. Extending underground for two and a half miles, it was the longest tunnel ever built in England, and was hailed as an engineering marvel. Visitors flocked to admire the work, and in the summer of 1787 the Honourable John Byng ventured into the tunnel with his candle:

Nothing cou'd be more gloomy than this being dragg'd into the bowels of the earth, rumbling and jumbling through mud, and over stones, with a small lighted candle in my hand… When the last peep of daylight vanish'd, I was enveloped in thick smoke arising from the gunpowder of the miners, at whom, after passing by many labourers who work by small candles, I did at last arrive; they… are in eternal danger and frequently perish by falls of earth… The return of warmth and happy daylight I hail'd with pleasure, having journey'd a mile of darkness.

In November 1789, the first canal barge made the triumphant journey all the way from Stroud to Lechlade, but celebrations were to be short-lived. Just three months later the Oxford to Rugby Canal was opened, providing a far more convenient route from the Midlands to the Thames. Meanwhile, the Thames & Severn engineers struggled to maintain water levels. Leakage was especially severe where the canal ran over porous limestone, and the next century saw repeated efforts to improve the efficiency of locks and pumps. All these problems, coupled with competition from the railways, meant that the Thames & Severn never became a viable commercial concern. The last working barge passed through the canal in 1911, and in 1933 the waterway was abandoned. Eight years later working transport ceased on the Stroudwater Navigation and it was officially closed in 1954.

Today the Cotswold Canal Trust works to restore the two Cotswold waterways. Extensive stretches of towpath have been cleared for walkers, and portions of the Stroudwater Navigation are open for pleasure craft. Other reminders of the canals are the circular length-men's cottages at Chalford, Cerney Wick, Marston Meysey and Coates. The Tunnel House Inn at Coates was built in the 1780s to house the workers who built the Sapperton tunnel, and stands just thirty yards away from its handsome entrance portal. When R. P. Beckinsale visited this spot in the 1930s he described the abandoned tunnel entrance as "a more impressive sight than ever [with a] long line of murky darkness stretching away underhill" and recalled the days when bargemen "used to lie on ther backs and push the barge along with their legs."

GREAT RAILWAY ADVENTURES: ISAMBARD KINGDOM BRUNEL
Following the failure of the Thames & Severn Canal, the Cotswold mill owners faced the same transport problems as before, but now with a greatly increased volume of goods. There was an urgent need for an efficient method of transport between the capital and the West Country— and in the 1830s a new solution was found. In 1833, a group of Bristol merchants formed the Great Western Railway Company, appointing the 27-

year-old Isambard Kingdom Brunel as their chief engineer. With characteristic energy, Brunel took less than a month to plan the route of a railway
from London to Bristol, running north of the Marlborough Downs via
Reading and Bath. For most of its length Brunel's projected track ran
across fairly level ground, but as it approached the city of Bath it plunged
through Cotswold limestone to emerge close to the village of Box. Brunel
faced many objections to his plans, but the strongest protests were raised
against the railway tunnel at Box, which was denounced as "monstrous
and extraordinary, dangerous and impractical". At nearly two miles long,
the tunnel was longer than any railway engineer had dared to build before
(although half a mile shorter than the canal tunnel at Sapperton) and
Brunel's detractors asserted that passengers would be deafened as well as
suffocated.

All these objections were brushed aside by Brunel as he pushed ahead
with work on his tunnel. Construction involved the labour of 300 horses
and 4,000 men and the use of approximately one ton of gunpowder a day.
The work was slow and dangerous, and over the course of five years around
a hundred men lost their lives, but the final result was acknowledged as a
triumph. Box tunnel was finished in 1841, and the line from London to
Bristol was opened the same year. For some time afterwards, however,
many passengers refused to travel though the tunnel, preferring to travel
by road and rejoin their train at the other end.

While the work was progressing on the London to Bristol line, Brunel
was also occupied in the construction of a branch line from Swindon to
Cheltenham. Once again the route involved digging through limestone,
and the Sapperton railway tunnels—one short and one long—proved especially challenging to the engineers. A different set of problems emerged
at Kemble, where the line ran through the land of Robert Gordon, an ob-
durate Scot who loathed the railway and did his best to prevent its
progress. Work was delayed for two years before Gordon finally agreed to
a massive settlement of £7,500. Even then, the building of Kemble station
had to be postponed until after his death, and at the point where the route
passed his home the railway was hidden from sight under a special covered
way.

In 1844 Brunel surveyed the route for another Cotswold railway. This
time he was working for the newly formed Oxford, Worcester and Wolver-
hampton Railway (OWWR) and the projected route ran through the

Evenlode valley (the present-day Cotswold Line). Early on in the process Brunel had encountered some fierce opposition at Chipping Campden, where a local landowner, Sir John Fox, summoned the constables to keep the young engineer off his land. This, however, was a minor contretemps compared with a later drama on the site of the Mickleton tunnel, three miles north of Chipping Campden.

The Battle of Mickleton Tunnel is one of the most notorious incidents in railway history, and is notable for being the last pitched battle fought between private armies on English soil. It had all begun when the OWWR contractor, a Mr. Robert Mudge-Marchant, had refused to continue work, claiming he was owed money by the company. Brunel was sent in to sort out the problem and a scuffle developed between Brunel's and Marchant's men, so incensing Brunel that he decided to take drastic action. On the evening of 17 July 1851, Isambard set off for Mickleton with several hundred navvies. His plan was to force Marchant to use these men to take over the work. Meanwhile, Marchant had raised the barricades, and as he argued with Brunel, the rival workmen began to fight. After the local magistrate had read the Riot Act, Brunel retreated, but he returned the next morning and brawling broke out again. By now Brunel was determined to assert his authority, and he spent the next two days summoning reinforcements from the local towns. In the early hours of 19 July Brunel drove in his carriage to the tunnel with a crowd of excited men following behind and waited for his extra "troops" to arrive. Over the next few hours, a total of 3,000 men crowded into the field. Outburst of violence took place throughout the day, but although some bones were broken no serious injuries were sustained. Finally, at 6 p.m., Marchant recognized that his position was hopeless and agreed to Brunel's promise of an arbitrated settlement.

Brunel had triumphed by very dubious means. As Adrian Vaughan points out in his excellent biography (aptly subtitled "Engineering Knight Errant"), the great engineer had "carried out an illegal show of brute force. He had incited 300 men into a riotous assembly. If the law had been enforced impartially he would have been arrested, tried and, if found guilty, transported to as penal colony in Australia. But Isambard was too illustrious a gentleman for that fate."

Today the major railways through the Cotswolds still follow the routes that Brunel established: skirting the southern borders from Swindon to

Bath; crossing westwards from Swindon to Gloucester; and heading north from Oxford to Moreton-in-Marsh. Reminders of the Great Engineer can be seen in the station houses at Cirencester and Stroud (both designed by Brunel), the goods shed at Stroud and the classical entrance portal to the Box tunnel. The tunnel at Box has gained a certain mystique, with some enthusiasts claiming that it was deliberately aligned so that the rising sun shone directly through it on the morning of 9 April, Brunel's birthday.

Train-Spotting in the Cotswolds: The Reverend Awdry

In 1917 the Awdry family moved to the village of Box, settling into a house that stood "within sight and sound of the Great Western Railway's main line near Middle Hill." It was the perfect destination for young Wilbert, then aged five. As he later wrote: "I used to lie in bed at night, listening to the engines struggling up the hill to Box tunnel, and imagining that they were talking to themselves." Wilbert spent his childhood in Box village, and he often accompanied his "Railwayman Parson" father on his rounds, visiting his parishioners in their plate-layers huts, signal boxes and stations, and listening in to their stories of the GWR.

Wilbert grew up to be a railway-mad vicar, just like his father, and when he had a son of his own he began to tell him stories about trains. The stories became the Railway Series, featuring such characters as Thomas the Tank Engine and Gordon the Green Engine, and were soon a runaway success. Between 1945 and 1972 the Rev. Awdry wrote and illustrated 26 railway books, and played an active part in campaigns to preserve steam railways. Awdry's working years were spent away from the Cotswolds, but in 1966 he retired to Stroud, where he spent the last thirty years of his life. Setting off from the station on one of his frequent lecture trips, Awdry would have passed the stone goods shed, designed by Brunel in 1845, bearing its painted advertisement for the Great Western Railway (as it still does today). The Stroud Preservation Trust has plans to convert this famous railway monument into a museum for heritage and the arts.

Today's rail enthusiasts should head for Winchcombe, where one of Britain's largest collections of railway equipment is packed into a tiny house and half an acre of garden. Items on display at the Winchcombe Railway Museum and Garden include some original ticket booths and signal levers, as well as scores of railway signs, posters and maps. Just four miles up the road at Toddington, the Gloucestershire-Warwickshire Railway (bearing the famous initials "GWR") runs steam and diesel trains on a stretch of track between Toddington and the Cheltenham Race course. Plans are underway to extend the track all the way east to Broad-way. In the meantime, passengers can enjoy a twenty-mile round trip as they relive the age of steam in the Cotswolds.

Chapter Seven

"HEAVEN ON EARTH"

WILLIAM MORRIS AT KELMSCOTT MANOR AND

BROADWAY TOWER

"Kelmscott Manor [was] the object of Morris' deep affection. Perhaps no other Englishman, apart from the owners of truly ancestral homes, has ever felt such passionate attachment to a building… Morris now began to feel that every road led back to Kelmscott. The gable, grey stone building [became] his ideal imagined place of domesticity, gregarious-ness, happiness, fulfilment."

Fiona MacCarthy, *William Morris: A Life for Our Time* (1995)

"I have been looking around for a house… and whither do you guess my eye is turned now? Kelmscott… a heaven on earth; an old stone Eliza-bethan house… and such a garden!"

William Morris, Letter to Charles Faulkner, May 1871

In the spring of 1871 William Morris made a short but historic journey. In the company of Charles Fairfax Murray, a fellow artist and friend, he caught the morning train from Paddington to Faringdon. From there the two men travelled by horse and trap to Lechlade, where they enjoyed a leisurely lunch before driving through country lanes to the isolated hamlet of Kelmscott. By the banks of the River Thames they viewed a handsome Elizabethan farmhouse built in the typical Cotswold style—and Morris fell in love. On the following day, he wrote to a friend describing Kelm-scott Manor as "a heaven on earth", and within a week he had agreed a lease on the house and its surrounding farmland. Morris never abandoned his busy London routine but for the rest of his life he escaped to Kelmscott whenever he could. For him and his followers the "old grey house by the river" was to become a symbol of an ideal way of life, and the perfect em-bodiment of the principles of the Arts and Crafts movement. But in 1871

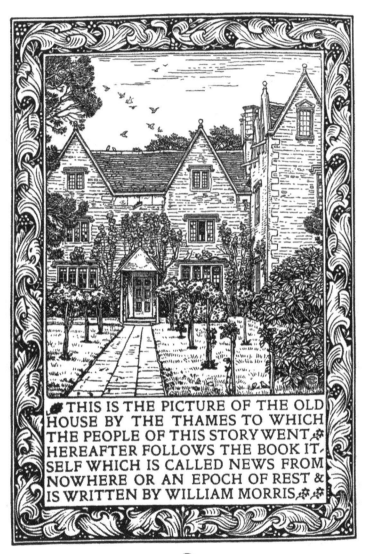

THIS IS THE PICTURE OF THE OLD
HOUSE BY THE THAMES TO WHICH
THE PEOPLE OF THIS STORY WENT
HEREAFTER FOLLOWS THE BOOK IT
SELF WHICH IS CALLED NEWS FROM
NOWHERE OR AN EPOCH OF REST &
IS WRITTEN BY WILLIAM MORRIS

Morris had some more personal reasons for seeing a country hideaway…

WILLIAM AND JANEY

The year he discovered Kelmscott Manor William Morris was 37 years old. A successful poet, designer and manufacturer, he was also a family man with a famously beautiful wife and two lively daughters, aged nine and ten. A decade earlier he had founded the firm of Morris, Marshall and Faulkner and Co., dedicated to the production of beautiful objects by traditional methods, and mainly thanks to his efforts it had grown steadily. Morris was endlessly inventive in his designs and under his leadership "the Firm" (as it was generally known) produced a stream of wallpapers, tapestries, furniture, stained glass and metalwork. But the Firm was not simply a commercial operation. It also embodied Morris' rejection of the soulless industrial age and his belief that people should have the right to work at a noble craft, creating objects of beauty and usefulness.

The Firm was based in Queen's Square, Bloomsbury, and ever since 1865 the Morris family had been living "above the shop". An earlier experiment in semi-rural living (in the Red House, near Bromley in Kent) had not been a success, and once back in London William immersed himself in the work of the Firm, supervising orders and production, producing designs and experimenting with new techniques. Much of the rest of his time was spent composing *The Earthly Paradise*, a lengthy verse epic, and reciting passages to longsuffering friends. Meanwhile, all was not well between him and his wife. Since the move to London Janey had become increasingly withdrawn and had begun to suffer from the mysterious ailments that would trouble her for the rest of her life. While William's life became increasingly frenzied, Janey took to the sofa, where she reclined languidly, beautiful and aloof.

The story of the marriage of William Morris and Jane Burden reads like one of Morris' romances. He was 23 years old when they met—inexperienced in love but filled with romantic literary notions. She was just seventeen, the uneducated daughter of an Oxford stable-hand. With her clouds of auburn hair, deep grey eyes and finely chiselled mouth, Janey was acknowledged by all Morris' circle to be a perfect "stunner"—the term the group applied to a certain type of beautiful young woman. But while his friends were content simply to admire Janey's beauty, Morris was determined to marry her.

Even in the earliest stages of the romance there were ominous signs. Morris' friend and fellow-artist, Dante Gabriel Rossetti, had been the first to spot Janey in Oxford, and from the start he claimed her as one of his models. Rossetti was six years older than Morris and a leading member of the Pre-Raphaelite brotherhood. A poet and painter of genius, he had a reputation for seducing beautiful women despite his long-term relationship with his muse and model, Lizzie Siddal. After her marriage to William, Janey continued to feature in Rossetti's paintings, and by the 1860s their relationship had acquired a dangerous intensity. When Lizzie died of consumption in 1862 Rossetti became dependent on Janey, visiting her almost daily and sending her passionate messages and poems.

By 1871 it was public knowledge that Janey and Rossetti were conducting a love affair. Life in the Morris family home had grown increasingly strained, with Janey and the girls suffering from a series of illnesses. Faced with a painful and difficult situation—Rossetti was his friend as well as a valued member of the Firm—Morris decided on an unusual course of action. He would find a place in the country where the lovers could be alone, away from the public gaze. As Fiona MacCarthy observes, "It was for its time—and even in ours—a socially unusual solution and Morris's generosity verged on the sublime."

"A LITTLE HOUSE OUT OF LONDON"

In early May 1871 Morris wrote to a friend in Rome expressing his concern about his daughters' health and resolving to look for "a little house out of London", and within just ten days he had achieved his aim—although the rambling Kelmscott Manor could hardly be described as a little house. But Morris did not take on the house on his own. Extending the generous offer to share the lease with Rossetti, he made his second journey to Kelmscott in the company of Janey and her lover. Rossetti christened the place an "Earthly Paradise" and instantly agreed to Morris' plan.

Once the joint lease on the manor was signed, Morris busied himself with decorating plans. His aim was to keep the house as bare as possible, papering the bedrooms with his famous wallpapers but leaving the living rooms plain and white. Morris was determined not to disturb the ancient spirit of the place, so some of the simple old furniture remained in place, while a set of tapestries stayed on the walls of the upper living room, their faded yellows and blues toning pleasantly with the surrounding plaster and wood.

By the end of June, Rossetti, Janey and the children were installed at Kelmscott. Morris came down for a day to plan more renovations, but by then he had other things on his mind. For several months he had been planning an expedition to Iceland—home of the sagas that inspired much of his poetry—and with his family settled in their country home he resolved to travel north as soon as he could.

The day before he left England, Morris wrote to Janey. Most of his letter was concerned with practical instructions, but he also expressed regret for the idyll he was leaving behind: "How beautiful the place looked last Monday: I grudged going away so; but I am very happy to think of you all happy there, and the children and you getting well." The letter ended poignantly, "Live well and happy." Later Morris admitted to a friend, "I know clearer now perhaps than then what a blessing and help [the] journey was to me; [and] what horrors it saved me from."

A SERPENT IN PARADISE

From July to September 1871 Janey and her daughters, Jenny and May, shared the "Earthly Paradise" of Kelmscott with Rossetti. They had a nurse for the girls, two servants from London and a local couple to lend a hand, but for most of the time the four of them had the manor to themselves. Rossetti took over the Tapestry Room, filling it with his painting equipment, while the next-door room became his bedroom. Janey was often in demand as his model, and the couple took long, romantic walks together by the river.

For Jenny and May it was a time of freedom. Rossetti had arrived with a stack of novels by Sir Walter Scott and he described how the girls devoured the romantic tales, sometimes reading an entire book in a day. In her memoirs May wrote about wild adventures, as she and Jenny indulged in their favourite sport of "roof riding" (which involved climbing out of the manor's windows and running across the ancient slates), but she also hinted at the troubled atmosphere in the house.

In the summer of 1871 Rossetti was 43 years old. Corpulent, balding and self-obsessed, he was in many ways an unprepossessing lover, but he could be immensely charming when he chose. In his cheerful moods he was a lively companion for Jenny and May, indulging in wild games of hide-and-seek in the attics and gardens. Yet the Morris girls regarded their mother's admirer with some alarm. He was already addicted to chloral, a liquid form of opium that would blight his later life, and had established a pattern of waking late and working through the night.

From the start Rossetti had mixed reactions to Kelmscott. To an elderly female acquaintance he wrote in ecstatic terms about "this loveliest haunt of domestic peace". Confiding in a close artist friend, he described the village as "the doziest clump of old grey beehives to look at you could find anywhere." As the weeks at Kelmscott stretched into months, he became morose, tramping doggedly around the fields and complaining of nightmares, induced by the bloodthirsty scenes in the tapestries on his studio walls. One of his best-known paintings from this time is *Water Willow*, a portrait of Janey that perfectly captures the melancholy magic of Kelmscott. In it she stands dreamily among the willow trees, while behind her are outlined the manor, the church and the boathouse, all freely rearranged by Rossetti.

By mid-September 1871 Morris was back in England, arriving at Kelmscott on a stocky Icelandic pony, much to the delight of Jenny and May. The returning hero stayed on for the next five days, telling his traveller's tales and taking long fishing trips on the river. But by then the summer was over and within a few weeks Kelmscott Manor had been shut up for the winter.

Back in London, Janey and Rossetti returned to their separate homes, although their affair continued more blatantly than ever. Away from the calming influence of Kelmscott Manor, Rossetti's moods became violent and unpredictable, with episodes of raving and delusions. In January he began a steep descent into depression, and by June his friends were so alarmed they took him off to Scotland to recover. There, Rossetti grew calmer but in September he wrote to Morris begging to be at Kelmscott once again, where he could be with "the one necessary person". It was a desperate appeal and once more Morris responded selflessly. Within a few days Rossetti was back in the manor, sending out a contented report: "here all is happiness again, and I feel completely myself."

Rossetti might have been happy to be back at Kelmscott, but life was not so easy for everyone around him. During the months that he had been away, his routine had grown even more erratic. Now he slept for most of the day, ate a huge dinner at ten and stayed awake for most of the night, dosing himself with chloral mixed with alcohol. Friends arrived at Kelmscott to help, but Janey was left to cope with the worst of his paranoia. Later she wrote of this period: "That Gabriel was mad was but too true, no one knows better than myself."

By late autumn it was clear that Rossetti intended to stay at Kelmscott indefinitely, and Morris allowed himself an uncharacteristic lapse into despair. In November he wrote to a friend, confessing that "this Autumn has been a specially dismal one for me… Rossetti has set himself down in Kelmscott as if he never meant to go away; and not only does that keep me away from that harbour of refuge, (because it is really a farce our meeting when we can help it) but also he has all sorts of ways so unsympathetic with the sweet simple old place, that I feel his presence there as a kind of slur on it."

For the next eighteen months Rossetti made Kelmscott his home. Janey and her daughters were often in residence. Several noisy dogs and a pet barn owl were given the run of the house, and a procession of friends and relations came to stay, including Rossetti's sister, the poet Christina. Sometimes racy girls arrived to pose for Rossetti (May remembered one who modelled in the nude) and some of the livelier guests indulged in boisterous games with May and Jenny.

As he recovered his strength Rossetti took up painting and drawing again, making many studies of Janey and her daughters. One of his favourite subjects was Janey as Prosperine, which he painted a total of eight times. Prosperine was a beautiful Greek goddess who was unhappily married to Pluto, God of the Underworld. Condemned to a life of mournful imprisonment, she was only rarely released into the sunlit world of love and happiness. Rossetti's Prosperine portraits rank among his masterpieces, but many people saw his choice of subject as a supremely tactless commentary on Janey's relationship with William and Rossetti.

Perhaps it was the Prosperine paintings that finally tipped Morris over the edge. In April 1874 he wrote an angry letter to Rossetti requesting that their joint lease should come to an end. In future, Morris suggested, Rossetti should pay the lease in full as the sole tenant of the house. It was the gesture of a hurt and angry man—and an enormous gamble. For a few months it looked as though Morris would lose Kelmscott Manor, but after a failed attempt to take on the lease alone Rossetti abandoned his claims to the house. A new lease was drawn up, with Morris sharing the costs with F. S. Ellis, a publisher and angler, and in July 1874 Rossetti left Kelmscott for good.

THE "OLD GREY HOUSE BY THE RIVER"

With Rossetti exiled from Kelmscott, Morris was at last free to enjoy his country home. His visits to the manor continued to be brief—he rarely stayed for more than four days at a stretch—but from the moment he arrived he plunged wholeheartedly into country life. Morris' letters from Kelmscott describe long rambles over the meadows, lazy afternoons in his garden and numerous fishing expeditions on the river. He also managed to explore the surrounding neighbourhood, driving by pony and trap to local churches and villages.

Morris wrote passionately about his country home, drawing a vivid picture of a "lowish three-storied manor house", with walls of weathered stone "buttered over" with a thin plaster. He revelled in the haphazard charm of his "beautiful and strangely naif house", but he reserved his greatest praise for the roof, "covered with the beautiful stone slates of the district, the most lovely covering which a roof can have." In particular, Morris admired the traditional Cotswold method of "sizing down" the roof slates, from the largest at the top to the smallest at the bottom, giving "the same sort of pleasure in their orderly beauty as a fish's scales or a bird's feathers." In the construction of Kelmscott Manor he recognized the virtues of careful craftsmanship and fitness of materials that were to become the guiding principles of the Arts and Crafts Movement.

One of the great attractions of Kelmscott for Morris was its rootedness in time and place. He loved the fact that the same families had lived in the village for countless generations and he saw the manor as having "grown up out of the soil and the lives of them that lived on it." Above all, Morris was always acutely aware of the beauty of his home. Even in 1872, when Rossetti was still a negative presence in the house, he could write ecstatically: "I am writing among the gables and rook-haunted trees, with a sense of a place being almost too beautiful to live in…"

Kelmscott Manor and its surroundings provided a rich source of inspiration for Morris. His frequent walks and fishing trips gave him the chance to absorb the colours and forms of plants, trees and birds, which he later converted into designs. (Morris very rarely drew from life, relying instead on his remarkable visual memory.) From 1875 to 1885 he produced

Morris in his meadow: carving by Ernest Gimson on a cottage in Kelmscott village

over sixty different patterns for fabrics, wallpapers, tapestries and carpets, many clearly inspired by Kelmscott. The flowers of his country garden—roses, carnations, marigolds, daffodils and tulips—make frequent appearances in William Morris designs. Two fabric patterns, Evenlode and Windrush, were named after local rivers and his famous Strawberry Thief design recalls the annual struggle to protect the manor's strawberry beds from greedy thrushes. In her memoirs May described a particular Kelmscott walk that provided the starting point for her father's Willow Bough designs.

Kelmscott Manor and village also found their way into Morris' writings. In his poem "The Half of Life Gone" Morris evokes the timeless way of life that he observed in the countryside around his home:

There is work in the mead as of old; they are eager at winning the hay,
While every sun sets bright and begets a fairer day.
The forks shine white in the sun round the yellow red-wheeled wain,
Where the mountain of hay grows fast; and now from out of the lane

> Comes the ox-team drawing another, comes the bailiff and the beer,
> And thump, thump, goes the father's nag o'er the narrow bridge of the
>   weir.

The sense of a harmonious, rural way of life informs Morris' most famous literary work. *News from Nowhere* was written in 1890, and presents a utopian vision set in the unimaginably distant year of 2012. For the famous frontispiece to the book, Morris chose an engraving of Kelmscott Manor and gardens, and this idyllic scene sets the tone for the rest of the vision in which the city of London has reverted to peaceful rural order. In Morris' brave new world London has become an idealized version of the Cotswold countryside, with thick woods covering Kensington and Putney and blackbirds singing in Piccadilly. On either side of the Thames are neat cottages, with communal gardens running down to the river, and everyone works joyfully for the common good. The vision culminates with a boat trip down the river to Kelmscott, where the contented villagers are seen gathering in their harvest and making merry—a picture based on Morris' first-hand observations of rural life.

The joyful scene in *News for Nowhere* when the travellers arrive at "the old house by the Thames" had its origins in a real adventure. In August 1878 Morris hired a steamboat equipped with a set of oars, and set off from London with Janey and May and three bachelor friends. The trip from London to Kelmscott took six days and was carefully stage-managed by Morris. At Oxford Janey disembarked and travelled on to the manor, to prepare the house for their arrival. Morris later described the magical scene as they approached the house at night, with lamps lit in all its windows to welcome them.

For Morris the writer of medieval romances, Kelmscott was the ultimate fairy-tale house. He saw his country home as the ideal destination of a knightly quest, and was eager for his friends to share his vision. In pursuit of his dream, he even created a topiary dragon as the magical guardian of his home, naming it Fafnir and inviting friends to witness the annual ceremony of clipping the dragon.

LATER YEARS AT KELMSCOTT

Kelmscott was the scene of many lively gatherings of friends, but it was also the place where Morris could escape to be with his family. Once Rossetti had left, an annual pattern developed with Janey, Jenny and May spending most of the spring and summer at Kelmscott, and William visiting whenever he could. Morris loved to spend time with his daughters and was devastated when Jenny suffered a series of epileptic fits, at the age of fifteen. After these episodes Jenny's health deteriorated fast and for the rest of her life she needed constant nursing care. Morris was greatly distressed by his elder daughter's illness, and he saw his visits to Kelmscott as a precious chance to spend some peaceful time with her.

By the time of Jenny's first attack, in 1876, Janey's affair with Rossetti was over, and she and William had developed an affectionate, accepting relationship. Shared concern for Jenny brought them closer, but Janey still sought comfort from other friends. During the 1880s she conducted a half-hearted affair with the poet Wilfred Blunt, who paid several visits to Kelmscott Manor. Blunt later described Janey's practice of leaving a pansy on his bedroom floor whenever she wished to be visited at night. On some of these occasions Morris was there too, sleeping alone in his splendid four-poster bed, but he apparently chose to ignore any nocturnal wanderings in the old house.

In 1892 Morris spent his first Christmas at Kelmscott Manor. Janey was away in Italy on a health cure, leaving William, Jenny and May to gather in the freezing house, along with May's husband, Henry Sparling, and her friend and admirer, George Bernard Shaw. It was an awkward occasion in many ways. May's marriage was crumbling, and the house was so cold that a thick layer of ice formed on the water jugs in the bedrooms. Yet, despite the chill, the two great socialists—Morris and Shaw—managed to keep themselves warm with some heated debates.

In his later years Morris' commitment to the socialist cause occupied most of his time and energy, although he still escaped to Kelmscott whenever he could. But as he reached his sixties, a lifetime packed with activity began to take its toll. At Kelmscott his marathon country walks were reduced to strolls and his fishing trips no longer started at dawn. In August 1896 he wrote to Jenny expressing "great distress that I cannot get down to Kelmscott, but I am not well, and the doctors will not let me." Six weeks later he was dead, at the age of 62. Morris died in London but he had made careful plans to be buried at Kelmscott, and on a wet and windy October day his coffin took a final journey to his country home. The route was the familiar one, taken hundreds of times by Morris in his lifetime, first by train from Paddington, and then by horse and cart through the country lanes to Kelmscott, but this time the coffin was carried on a painted farm cart decorated with branches of willow, vine and alder. At Kelmscott the church was decked out for harvest festival and Morris' grave was filled with the flowers from his designs. Gathered in the churchyard were family and friends, poets, artists and socialists, mingling with the workers from the Morris firms and the local villagers. Everyone agreed it was a fitting farewell for an extraordinary man.

After Morris' death the family continued to visit Kelmscott Manor. Janey bought the house the year before her death, and May made it her permanent home in 1923. Long divorced by the time she settled at Kelmscott, May was joined by the redoubtable Mary Lobb, a former Land Girl who had arrived to work at Kelmscott during the First World War. Large, loud and hearty, and prone to violent swearing, Miss Lobb always dressed in a knickerbocker suit—in striking contrast to the aesthetic-looking May.

During May's last years at Kelmscott Manor she and Miss Lobb retreated into the downstairs rooms, while the rest of the house became a shrine to her father. A new generation arrived to pay homage to Morris, including Evelyn Waugh, John Betjeman and Osbert Lancaster. Betjeman and his wife were frequent visitors to Kelmscott, and he wrote a moving account of the "uneven and rambling little house", with its glorious views across the meadows, describing it as a place that was "haunting and haunted", and "loved as only an old house can be loved."

May Morris died in 1938, leaving Kelmscott Manor to Oxford University, who in turn entrusted it to the Society of Antiquaries. Today the house is inhabited by full-time curators, and its rhythm of life has almost returned to the way it was in Morris' time. On certain spring and summer weekends (and on Wednesdays) the house comes alive with visitors, before it reverts to its sleepy, backwater existence.

KELMSCOTT TODAY

The most romantic way to arrive at Kelmscott is by the river path, but even if you come by road, you can still approach the house through its gardens. Walking up the path towards the old grey house, you may feel, as Morris certainly did, that you have entered an enchanted place.

Inside, Kelmscott Manor is low-ceilinged, small-roomed and domestic, a modest family farmhouse rather than the grand manor that its title suggests. All the downstairs rooms are light and airy, filled with fine examples of Morris' designs, but it is upstairs that a more personal story takes shape. In the Tapestry Room, a tangle of metal paint tubes provide a reminder that this was once the space where Rossetti set up his easels, while next door is the bedroom where Morris slept, once he had gained full possession of the manor. In this small, square room with its sturdy four-poster and its window opening onto the water meadows, Morris would have woken happy to be back in the place he loved best. He even wrote a (not very distinguished) poem, "For the Bed at Kelmscott", which May embroidered beautifully on a hanging round his bed:

> The wind's on the wold
> And the night is a-cold,
> And Thames runs chill
> Twixt mead and hill,
> But kind and dear
> Is the old house here,
> And my heart is warm
> Midst winter's harm.

Just along the corridor from William's cosy cabin, Janey's room is formal, leafy and cool. Entirely decorated with willow bough designs, it contains the famous Rossetti portrait of Janey amongst the Kelmscott willows. All the upper rooms are filled with beautiful fabrics, but for many visitors the best parts of the house are the "quaint garrets among the great timbers of the roof" where Morris liked to remember that tillers and herdsmen had once slept. In these spartan attic rooms, Morris' advice to "have nothing in your homes that you do not know to be useful or believe to be beautiful," is taken to its logical conclusion. Each of the twin bedrooms is furnished with just two beds, two washstands and a towel rail. The furniture is in the no-nonsense, rustic style of the original products of the Firm, and each bed has a cover with a different Morris design. Against the plain wooden floors and whitewashed walls Morris' colours and patterns sing out strongly, bringing nature into the house, just as he had intended his designs to do.

Views from Broadway Tower

Morris' affection for the Cotswolds reached beyond the immediate neighbourhood of his house and village. He considered Bibury, on the River Coln, to be the most beautiful village in England, with nearby Minster Lovell a close-runner up, and he was passionate about the area's tithe barns, cottages and churches. In his writings on the English countryside Morris often praised the honest workmanship of his local stonemasons, who knew instinctively how to create a sound and beautiful structure using materials that came straight out of the land.

Morris was a champion of the virtues of domestic, small-scale English countryside, and in 1877 he wrote an appreciation that reads like a description of the southern Cotswolds:

> The land is a little land... little rivers, little plains, swelling, speedily changing uplands, all beset with handsome orderly trees... all is little: yet not foolish or blank, but serious rather, and abundant of meaning for such as choose to seek it.

Yet despite his pleasure in the quiet valleys of the Windrush, Evenlode and Coln, Morris was also attracted by a very different Cotswold place. This was the turreted folly perched on Broadway beacon, on the north-east edge of the Cotswold escarpment.

Broadway Tower looks like a Saxon castle, but it was actually built in 1800 by the Earl of Coventry. The story goes that the Earl built it as a present for his homesick wife so that she could see her native Worcestershire. Inside the tower, three octagonal rooms house a small museum dedicated to William Morris, but the building's main glory is its astonishing view. Standing on the roof on a clear day, it is possible to see ten English counties.

In 1876 Morris' friend "Crom" Price took out a summer lease on Broadway Tower. Morris paid several visits to stay with Crom and gloried in the wildness of the place, writing to a friend, "I am at Crom Price's Tower among the winds and the clouds." Jenny and May also loved the sense of freedom there, and May later described Broadway Tower as "the most inconvenient and the most delightful place ever seen." In her memoirs she recalled that her father and his friends liked to take bracing baths on the roof "when the wind didn't blow the soap away."

Morris' journey to Broadway usually took him through Burford, and on one of these trips he made a distressing discovery. Stopping off to admire the town's parish church, he was alarmed to find a group of workmen scraping away at the medieval plaster, in the name of Victorian "modernization". Morris was profoundly upset by what he had seen, and as he continued his journey he resolved to take some action. In the following days at Broadway Tower he began to plan an ambitious campaign to safeguard the ancient buildings of England.

By the following year Morris had founded the Society for the Protection of Ancient Buildings, and for the rest of his life he was tireless in promoting its cause. The SPAB had an immediate impact, gaining the popular nickname of "Anti-Scrape" and rescuing countless buildings for posterity. Thanks to William Morris, famous national monuments like Peterborough Cathedral, and humble buildings like Kelmscott parish church have kept their medieval features almost intact. By the time of his death in 1896, Morris had unleashed an unstoppable movement to preserve his country's architectural character. Without his vision and energy the view from Broadway Tower could have looked very different from the way it does today.

Chapter Eight
SEEKING THE SIMPLE LIFE
ARTS AND CRAFTS IN SAPPERTON AND
CHIPPING CAMPDEN

"There was then [in the late nineteenth century] a feeling current—that men were out of tune with their surroundings. Industrialization had destroyed all creativity. Division of labour took away responsibility. Capitalism, the tyrannical "cash nexus", had a terrible effect on the British workman's soul. These were theories strongly voiced by both Carlyle and Ruskin. As a young man still at Oxford, William Morris read Ruskin... and realized that this was the new road on which the world should travel. His monumental energies from then on were directed to the betterment of life through revival of the handicrafts. From Morris's convictions, from his lectures and his writings and the many crafts he practised sprang the whole Arts and Crafts movement."
Fiona MacCarthy, *The Simple Life: C. R. Ashbee in the Cotswolds* (1981)

"Campden town
Is quiet after London-riot;
Campden street
Is kindly to the feet;
Campden wold
So bonny to behold
Is merry with the blowing wind & glad with growing wheat."
John Masefield, contribution to the *Campden Guild Songbook*

William Morris remained a country weekender all his life. Despite his passion for rural crafts, all his workshops were based in London and its suburbs, and he resigned himself to life in the capital, punctuated by brief escapes to Kelmscott Manor. In London, Morris named his Thames-side home Kelmscott House in a deliberate homage to his rural "heaven on

Chipping Campden: "We both wanted a better world… while the beauty of life—expressed in that Gloucestershire village was almost all in all to us" (C. R. Ashbee to F. L. Griggs)

earth". Comforted by the thought that the river beneath his window had begun its journey in the Cotswolds, Morris settled down at night to dream of Kelmscott. But for some of his followers dreaming was not enough. They believed it was time to leave the town behind, and head for the countryside in search of a better life.

BACK TO THE LAND: IN SEARCH OF A RURAL ALTERNATIVE
By the 1890s Morris and his friends had attracted a new generation of followers, and the Arts and Crafts movement had been born. Most of the new young members had trained, like Morris, as architect-designers, applying their talents to a range of crafts. Part of their inspiration was drawn from the past, as they copied traditional styles and methods of working, but their work was also a deliberate rejection of the industrial age. By designing beautiful objects to be made by hand, Arts and Crafts designers were taking a practical stand against the tide of shoddy goods that flowed from the factories. By providing work for skilled craftspeople they were voicing their protest against the demeaning labour of factory workers. A decision to join the Arts and Crafts movement was more than just a choice of a new style of art. It was a statement of belief in a simpler and better way of life.

Closely linked to the ideal of a simple life was a desire to leave behind the evils of the towns, and head for the countryside. The concept of a return to the land began as a response to the rapid industrialization of Britain at the start of the nineteenth century. As early as 1829 Thomas Carlyle had claimed that city life destroyed a man's spirit and dispersed his energies. Twenty years on, John Ruskin urged all sensitive men to escape from the cities and factories, and forge rural communities where they could engage in useful crafts and trades. For the truly committed members of the Arts and Crafts movement there was only one logical course of action—they had to take their crafts into the countryside.

GIMSON AND THE BARNSLEYS: THE START OF A DREAM
Two of William Morris' most fervent followers were Ernest Gimson and Sidney Barnsley. Both young men came from prosperous provincial families and both had arrived in London in the 1880s to study with Morris, drawn by the ideals of the Arts and Crafts movement. During the course of their training the men had become close friends, united by their hatred

of city life and a shared distaste for the commercial aspects of their profession, but at first they could see no obvious way to make their escape from London.

Like their mentor William Morris, Gimson and Barnsley were attracted to traditional crafts, and in 1890 they joined forces with three like-minded architects to set up a furniture-making company. Kenton and Company was based in Kenton Road, in the Bloomsbury district of London, and employed a team of skilled cabinetmakers to make the pieces the architects designed. For the other partners, the company provided an interesting sideline, but for Gimson and Barnsley it pointed the way to a new way of life. Both men developed a passion for hand-made furniture and set about gaining some practical skills. When the company folded after eighteen months, they realized they were no longer tied to London, and began to imagine a different way of living. Somewhere, they believed, they could find a place where they could live close to nature, learning from local craftsmen and adapting traditional skills to fit their modern designs.

At first, the move to the country seemed like an impossible dream. Although both men were cushioned by small private incomes, they had no experience of country life and were both intensely shy. Recognizing these drawbacks, they decided to invite a third partner to join them. Sidney's older brother, Ernest, was an old friend of Gimson from his years of training as an architect. At the age of thirty (almost two years older than Gimson and Sidney Barnsley) he was already running his own architect's practice and was married with two young daughters. Easy-going, practical and gregarious, Ernest was the ideal person to organize the business side of a country workshop. Ignoring his wife's objections, he joined in the plans with great enthusiasm and was soon leading the search for a place in the country.

The three friends' search took them all over England, but in the end they settled on the hamlet of Ewen as a starting place for their adventure. Ewen was three miles south-west of Cirencester in deeply wooded country, and they all felt certain they had found the right spot. In the remote valleys of the southern Cotswolds the traditions of English village life still continued as they had done for hundreds of years, and the villagers still practised their ancient country crafts.

From their earliest days in the Cotswolds Gimson and the Barnsleys felt at home. All three men proved to be natural countrymen, with a deep love of nature, and all enjoyed long rambles, setting off to explore (in the words of one of their friends) "a mystery land of difficult hills and deeply wooded valleys". It was on one of these walks that Sidney discovered the group's first real home.

PINBURY PARK: A WORKSHOP IN THE WOODS

In later years the story of the discovery of Pinbury Park took on a fairytale aspect, with Sidney stumbling through the trees to discover a sleeping beauty of a house lost in its hidden valley. Pinbury was a stone-built Elizabethan farmhouse, with many fine features that had crumbled and decayed. It turned out to belong to Lord Bathurst of Cirencester Park, who agreed that the men could live there rent-free in return for renovating his property. Within a few weeks a small craft community had been established at Pinbury, with Ernest Barnsley and his family living in the house, while Sidney Barnsley and Gimson converted the outbuildings into simple homes. As the most experienced architect of the three, Ernest Barnsley undertook most of the structural work, while Gimson moulded some exquisite plaster ceilings. One of the house's large, airy rooms was turned into a workshop where all three friends produced simple furniture, adapting techniques that they had learned from the local carpenters and wheelwrights.

For the next eight years Gimson and the Barnsleys lived and worked at Pinbury Park, restoring the house and making furniture. During this period they developed a distinctive style, using mainly local woods (oak, ash, elm and walnut) and creating contemporary designs that incorporated features from country carpentry, such as long metal hinges and visible joints. For all three designers fine craftsmanship was at the heart of their work, but while Ernest Barnsley and Gimson employed local craftsmen to work on their designs Sidney Barnsley worked alone, creating his own highly original pieces. One of Sidney's most remarkable creations from this time was a massive bow-fronted dresser carved from a solid piece of oak and inspired by William Morris' pronouncement that furniture "should be made of timber rather than walking sticks."

Life at Pinbury Park had a strongly utopian element. All three men were determined to live a simple life, although they struggled to survive until Gimson invited his cousin Lucy to stay. Lucy Morley had grown up on a farm and in spite of the handicap of being deaf she managed life at

Pinbury very efficiently. Under Lucy's guidance the small community soon became virtually self-sufficient, growing its own fruit and vegetables, baking bread, making cider and keeping hens and goats. Lucy's quiet, practical ways won the heart of Sidney Barnsley, and in 1895 the couple were married. Five years later Gimson married Emily Thompson, a vicar's daughter who shared his love of traditional English music. Gimson and Emily were childless but Sidney and Lucy had a son and a daughter, who were both born at Pinbury Park.

Pinbury Park: from left to right: Sidney Barnsley, Lucy Morley, Ernest Gimson, Alice Barnsley and Ernest Barnsley and their two daughters

The Pinbury years were intensely productive for Gimson and the Barnsleys, but they also made time for entertaining friends, as a stream of visitors arrived from London drawn by the simple appeal of the workshop in the woods. Some of these artistic friends were sorely tempted to settle in the Cotswolds. The architect and designer, Philip Webb, toyed with the idea of joining the Pinbury community, which he described as "a sort of vision of the NEW Jerusalem". Webb decided against the move, but Alfred Powell arrived to stay for just a few weeks, and never left the area. Powell later settled with his wife Louise in the village of Tunley, where they worked as ceramic decorators and played an important part in the Arts and Crafts community.

After eight years at Pinbury, the three men felt it was time to move on. By 1901 Lord Bathurst was keen to take over his house again and the three designers needed more workshop space. Acting once again as a generous patron, Bathurst arranged for Gimson and the Barnsley brothers to move to the village of Sapperton, a mile down the road. A generous plot of land in the valley below the church was set aside for the three men to build their own homes. At the same time, Bathurst offered Daneway House, to the south of the village, as the new site for their showrooms and workshops.

SETTLING IN AT SAPPERTON

At Sapperton, Gimson and the Barnsleys set to work designing their family homes, each creating a building that expressed his own character. Ernest Barnsley's Upper Dorvel House was by far the largest, consisting of an original cottage with two added wings and a dramatic, tower-like structure. Further up the valley, Sidney Barnsley's Beechanger was a characteristically modest design. Using local stone for the walls and roofing, he created a simple two-storey cottage in the traditional Cotswold style, with a workshop in the garden. Of the three houses Gimson's was the most experimental. The Leasowes was built in a compact L-plan. With its thick stone walls and flowing thatched roof it seemed to grow organically out of the landscape.

Once the three men had settled in Sapperton, Sidney Barnsley established a solitary routine of working at home on his furniture. Meanwhile the two Ernests took charge of the work at Daneway House, carefully restoring the fabric of the building as well as overseeing the furniture-making workshops. By this time all three designers had gained a national reputation, and a string of customers arrived to view their work, beautifully displayed in the whitewashed rooms of Daneway House. For the first three years at Sapperton Ernest Barnsley and Gimson ran the Daneway workshops together, but in 1905 some kind of rift developed between them. The cause of the estrangement is not now known, but it was apparently started by their wives and meant that the two men could only meet outside their homes. After 1905, Gimson took on the job of running the workshop single-handed, while Barnsley concentrated most of his efforts on architectural work.

ERNEST GIMSON: MASTER DESIGNER

In his Sapperton workshop Ernest Gimson worked on a variety of designs as well as practising as an architect. (His architectural work in the Cotswolds includes a design for Kelmscott village hall and a pair of cottages dedicated to Morris.) Gimson's furniture ranged from elaborate pieces for wealthy clients to cottage-style dressers, chests and chairs. He continued to model plaster friezes and designed a range of ornamental metalwork such as hinges, doorknockers and firedogs. Much of Gimson's work drew inspiration from the natural world: a plasterwork frieze could show spring honeysuckle or autumn hips and haws, and a pair of firedogs might feature hungry squirrels munching on acorns—all of them carefully observed on his daily walks in the local woods.

Ernest Gimson felt a deep sense of connection with his local community. Throughout his time in the Cotswolds he worked closely with local craftsmen and encouraged the young boys of the village to learn new skills. Richard Harrison, the toothless Sapperton wheelwright, was a lifelong friend and working companion, and Gimson also began a fruitful co-operation with the blacksmith's son, setting up a smithy to create a range of ironwork. With the encouragement of his wife Emily, who was a keen musician, he played a central part in the life of the village, putting on plays and helping to organize folk singing and dancing. In the words of the artist Fred Griggs, Gimson "taught Sapperton to enjoy itself."

In the final years of his life Gimson began to make plans for a utopian "craft-village". Ever since his twenties he had dreamed of establishing a self-sufficient community in which young craftsmen could live and work together. He had even purchased a plot of land close to Sapperton, ready to put his plans into action, but his utopia never became a reality. In 1919 Gimson died at the age of 55 after a long struggle with cancer. His tragi-

cally early death robbed Britain of one of its most inspiring architect-designers. As G. M. Trevelyan wrote: "There is no knowing how great his influence on the Modern Movement might have been."

After Gimson's death Daneway House was never the same again, and the following year the workshops were abandoned. Gimson's talented foreman, Peter Waals, moved with most of the men to a deserted mill in nearby Chalford, where he went on to develop his popular "Cotswold furniture". In Sapperton, the two Barnsley brothers continued to work on a range of projects. Sidney Barnsley designed and made his characteristic furniture, and was also in demand for his striking architectural designs, such as the library at Bedales School. In his later years, Ernest Barnsley became one of the leading architects in the Arts and Crafts movement, designing comfortable country homes but also working on cottages, schools and village halls—many of them in the Cotswolds. Ernest Barnsley's most ambitious project was Rodmarton Manor (described in Chapter Nine), an undertaking begun in 1909 and still not completed at the time of his death, at the age of 62. Ernest died in 1926, in the same year as his younger brother Sidney.

The peaceful village of Sapperton has hardly changed in the last hundred years. Its cottages have been lovingly preserved and the Bell Inn is a model of restrained good taste, but the most picturesque part of the village is the dip in the valley that encloses the church. Flanking the path leading down to the church are three plain slabs of limestone, marking the graves of Ernest Gimson and Ernest and Sidney Barnsley, and further down the valley are the houses they built. Standing in the field below the churchyard it is possible to enjoy the view the three men knew, and to share their sense of "a mystery land" of hills and wooded valleys.

Ashbee's Vision: The Start of the Guild of Handicrafts

While Ernest Gimson and Sidney Barnsley were setting up their London furniture firm, another young idealist was founding his own craft group in the East End. Charles Robert Ashbee, or CRA as he liked to be called, came from a middle-class London family and had studied at Cambridge, where he was influenced by the ideas of Edward Carpenter, a passionate believer in "crafts for the working man". After leaving Cambridge, Ashbee moved to Whitechapel (one of the poorest districts of London) and began to train as an architect, whilst involving himself in the socialist movement.

In 1888, at the age of 25, Ashbee founded his Guild of Handicrafts. The guild produced a range of fine craft items, such as jewellery, metalwork and furniture, but Ashbee's ambitions ran deeper than this. As Fiona MacCarthy explains in her excellent account of Ashbee's Cotswold years, the guild represented "his yen for simple useful things produced by honest toil; his hope that the British working man could build a new society; most of all, his burning faith in the reforming zeal of comradeship." With all these aims in mind, Ashbee chose his guildsmen (as he liked to call them) less for their practical skills than for their willingness to become comrades in a great endeavour. As well as learning and practising a craft, the guildsmen were encouraged to develop their own creative ideas and enrolled in a crowded programme of activities and education. When they were not busy in the workshops the men listened to lectures on art and socialism, attended lively suppers, sang traditional folk songs and acted in plays—all directed by Ashbee. They also played cricket, dressed in their flamboyant guild "uniform" of scarlet scarves and jackets embroidered with white pinks, the emblem of the guild.

For fourteen years Ashbee ran the Guild of Handicrafts in Whitechapel, but he still dreamed of building a new society in the unspoilt English countryside. If only the guildsmen could somehow be transported away from the city, Ashbee believed, they would be free to live simpler, healthier lives, shaped by the beauties of nature. In 1892 he had written a romance for the guild, which expressed his vision of a move to the country. *From Whitechapel to Camelot* describes the quest of a band of brothers who set off from London to find the perfect place to build a new city of Camelot. The story was meant as an inspiring piece of fiction, but as the lease on the London workshop approached its end Ashbee resolved to turn romance into reality. In 1901 he set out on a personal quest to find his Camelot in the English countryside.

Ashbee was thorough in his search, but once he saw Chipping Campden he knew his quest was over. The town had some significant advantages: several of its strong, stone houses stood empty, providing excellent housing for the guildsmen. Rents in the area were very low and there was a disused silk mill that could provide the perfect workshop for the guild. But it was the spirit of the place that really appealed to Ashbee. With its golden-coloured buildings and its vast, sweeping views, Campden seemed the perfect stage on which to turn his dream into reality.

CREATING CAMELOT: THE GUILD AT CHIPPING CAMPDEN
Ashbee arrived in Chipping Campden in the spring of 1902 along with his young wife, Janet, and a small band of guildsmen. They were followed over the next few months by more than a hundred men, women and chil-

dren who had taken the courageous step of making a new life in the Cotswolds. Cockney voices could soon be heard all over the town and the Old Silk Mill on Sheep Street was filled with the sound of men at work.

In his first few months at Chipping Campden Ashbee gradually settled his craftsmen into the mill. The offices and showrooms were on the ground floor, while the first floor was devoted to silversmiths' work and jewellery making. Cabinet-makers and woodcarvers took over the top of the building and the noisy smithy was set up in a nearby outhouse. Meanwhile, Ashbee was also faced with the challenge of finding places for the guildsmen to live. While the married men and their families moved into empty cottages in the town, Ashbee rented Braithwaite House, on the High Street, to provide a home for unmarried workers and visitors to the guild. A little further down the street he and Janet set up home in an old stone house that he renamed Woolstaplers' Hall. Ashbee saw Braithwaite House as a kind of university hall of residence, where young men could eat together and exchange ideas, while his home with Janet was the place where guild members gathered for music and poetry readings.

Work at the Old Silk Mill followed a calm and orderly pattern, with the men arriving at 7 a.m., and stopping one hour later for a communal breakfast. There were regular breaks throughout the day, and the working day ended at 5.30 p.m., leaving plenty of time for social activities. Ashbee encouraged his men to take a creative approach to their work and consulted them on many aspects of design. A visiting writer, Charles Rowley, was immensely impressed, and produced a glowing description of a "workshop paradise", where "Every window looks out onto a lovely common garden. Every workbench has a posy on it." Rowley concluded that Ashbee had achieved some kind of socialist ideal at Campden: "Nothing could be more delightful than doing rationally good work in such surroundings."

Once the guildsmen had settled into their new life, work progressed well. Ashbee had secured some generous commissions, and the guild was producing exciting new designs in a style that combined country traditions with the influence of Art Nouveau. It seemed that the dramatic move had done the guild nothing but good, and it was soon attracting new recruits. Some of these new apprentices were local men and boys, but others came from as far away as Scotland and Devon, drawn by the growing fame of Ashbee's experiment. When the young Alec Miller arrived from Glasgow he was delighted both by the guild and its fairy-tale setting:

I walked up Campden's one long street entranced and happy: a mile long street with hardly a mean house, and many of great beauty and richness. It was, after Glasgow… as foreign as Cathay and as romantic as the architecture of fairy-tale illustrations. It all seemed unbelievable! Was I really in the twentieth century, or the sixteenth?… I simply walked on and on, in an ecstasy of pleasure, with no thought but just wonder.

Ashbee was happy with the work of his newly transplanted guild, but his vision did not end at the workbench. He aimed to transform the lives of his guildsmen—and to shake up Chipping Campden in the process. Within a few months of arriving in the Cotswolds he had set up a library stocked with literary classics and socialist works, and a small museum displaying examples of fine arts and crafts. He founded a sports club for the guildsmen and encouraged them to play hockey, football and cricket with the locals. Most importantly, in Ashbee's eyes, he urged his men to immerse themselves in the beauty of the countryside, leading parties of guildsmen on hikes and bicycle rides.

Despite his strictly egalitarian principles, Ashbee's style was always to lead from the front. Tall, elegant and debonair, with dark wavy hair and a foppish Van-Dyke beard, he was the epitome of a romantic figure, but many people found him alarmingly intense. There was also something disturbing about his delight in the healthy physiques of his young apprentices. (Fiona MacCarthy reveals that Ashbee's diaries recount several "spiritual" relationships with young men, although there is no evidence that they ever developed into anything physical.) Fortunately for Ashbee, his young wife Janet provided the perfect foil for his intensity. Fifteen years younger than Ashbee, his "comrade wife", as he liked to call her, was attractive, fresh-faced and direct, with a natural talent for getting on with people. At Campden she displayed remarkable maturity, keeping a watchful eye on the emotional welfare of the young guild members, who tended to see her as a kindly older sister. Janet also formed an immediate bond with the children of the town and soon became a familiar figure in Campden, dressed in a billowing skirt and fisherman's jumper, leading a ragged collection of children through the streets.

GOOD YEARS FOR THE GUILD

By January 1903 the Guild of Handicrafts was thoroughly at home in the Cotswolds. While a few of the locals still regarded the Londoners with suspicion, they had ceased to be openly hostile to them and some new friendships had developed. To mark the start of the year the guild put on a performance of Ben Johnson's *The New Inn*. Dozens of Ashbee's friends arrived for the play including the young poet John Masefield, who instantly fell in love with Campden. From then on the New Year's play became one of the high spots of the Campden calendar, with later productions featuring actors from the town.

Profits from the New Year's play went towards another of Ashbee's projects—the building of an outdoor bathing pool just to the south of the town. By August the pool was finished and in September 1903 Ashbee held the first Campden Aquatic Sports, a series of swimming races featuring contestants drawn from the guild and the town. Like the New Year play, the Aquatic Sports became an annual event. A surviving photograph shows a lively occasion with the contestants wearing short woollen costumes while the poolside is packed with crowds dressed in their summer best.

In 1904 Ashbee's programme of improving activities entered a new phase, as the Campden School of Arts and Crafts opened its doors to students of all ages. The school was based in Elm Tree House in the centre of the town, with a large barn at the back providing a convenient lecture hall. All the classes were free and the school offered training in the "three Hs" of Hand, Heart and Head. Take-up at the school was impressive, with over 200 students enrolling in the first year. Of this total there were ninety men, sixty-five women and fifty children drawn from a mixture of guild families and locals. Ashbee and the guildsmen gave instruction in a range of crafts, along with classes in drawing and design. Janet led practical sessions on cookery, laundry and gardening. Music featured strongly on the curriculum and there were also daily exercise sessions held in the yard. But perhaps the most remarkable feature of the school was its lecture programme. During the first six months there were fifteen lectures, often given by visiting speakers, covering art and design, local history and folklore, socialist ideas, music and literature. For those who were willing to join the school the Ashbees were offering a rich cultural diet.

With the establishment of the Campden School some people in the town began to recognize the important role that the Ashbees were playing in their community. Not only could their children be given a better-than-average education but there was also the chance of employment in the guild. Yet just as the Ashbees were gaining some genuine acceptance, the fortunes of the guild began to decline.

THE END OF THE DREAM

By the start of 1906 things were looking bad for Ashbee. Some of his best young apprentices had left Chipping Campden in search of new kinds of work, while several older members were suffering from ill health. During the previous year the workshops had been forced to work reduced hours, and for the first time in its eighteen-year history the guild had made a financial loss. The isolated position of the guild had always made marketing difficult, but now Ashbee was faced with serious competition. Items in the Arts and Crafts style were being sold by the Liberty store in London at much lower prices than the guild could offer. At the same time, some of Ashbee's wealthy clients had turned their attention to new obsessions such as the motorcar. Ashbee tried to rationalize, producing cheaper items in response to customer demand, but the workshops entered a slow and painful decline.

In early 1908 Ashbee reluctantly agreed that the guild should go into liquidation. It was a sad conclusion to his dream, but it was not the end of Arts and Crafts in Campden. Some of the guildsmen felt so settled in the Cotswolds that they decided to continue working there, with new backers supporting their work. Among the long-term survivors was Ashbee's master silversmith George Hart, one of the original London apprentices. Hart kept on working on the first floor of the Old Silk Mill for the rest of his life, passing on his skills to his sons, and the Hart workshop is still operating in the Silk Mill today.

Following the collapse of the guild the Ashbees stayed in the Cotswolds for eleven more years, and for most of that time they continued to run the School for Arts and Crafts. Ashbee was kept busy with design and architectural work, but in 1919 he decided to take on a different challenge, travelling to Jerusalem to advise on the reconstruction of the city. When they returned to England four years later the Ashbees turned their backs on the Cotswolds, moving into Janet's old family home in Kent. By this time Ashbee was sixty years old, and had lost his passion to change the world. Settling down to live a quiet country life, he devoted

much of his time to writing his memoirs.

In his old age Ashbee looked back fondly on his great experiment, and Campden came to symbolize all that was beautiful and noble in his life. As he wrote in a letter to Fred Griggs, the artist who shared his love of Chipping Campden: "We both wanted a better world and were both quite out of touch with the one provided us, while the beauty of life—expressed in that Gloucestershire village was almost all in all to us."

CHIPPING CAMPDEN TODAY

Chipping Campden is still a stunningly beautiful place. On a sunny day, walking down the town's gently curving High Street, with its glorious views of the hills beyond, is an exhilarating experience. Less commercialized than nearby Broadway, Campden has a good supply of "real" shops as well as several galleries and studios. Ashbee's handsome home, Woolstaplers' Hall, stands on the High Street, but his legacy can be seen most clearly in the Old Silk Mill on Sheep Street. Once the lively working heart of Ashbee's guild, the mill is still filled with workshops and studios. The ground floor provides a gallery space and café, and on the first floor you can visit the workshop of David Hart, master silversmith and grandson of one of the original guild members.

Stepping into the Hart workshop feels like being transported back to Ashbee's time. Here, in a low-ceilinged workroom, David Hart and his son and nephew still work at the original wooden benches. Forty-year-old invoices, designs and drawings hang from hooks in the ceiling. The benches are scarred and pitted by decades of work, and Ashbee's original order books are kept in a small side office. Today the workshop produces silver vases, goblets and candlesticks for clients all over the world, and many of its pieces are based on Ashbee's designs. The silver is still worked by hand, using Ashbee's original tools, and the workshop is filled with the sound of planishing hammers.

Chapter Nine
ARTY CRAFTY COTSWOLDS
THE NEXT GENERATION

"Ever since the eighties… in the lost valleys of the Cotswolds a handful
of devoted Artists and Craftsmen had been living the simple life according to the doctrines of William Morris, surrounded by hand-woven
linen, vegetable dyed, and plain unstained oak furniture by 'gode
workmen wel ywrought'."

Osbert Lancaster, *Home Sweet Home* (1939)

William Morris started something big in the Cotswolds. After the first
craft communities had been established (in Sapperton and Chipping
Campden) many others followed, as craftsmen and women moved to the
countryside, drawn by the prospect of the simple life. At the same time,
some talented local people began to join the Arts and Crafts movement,
setting up workshops of their own in towns and villages. By the 1930s,
there were craft communities all over the Cotswolds, providing an easy
target for city satirists. But what was the reality behind the caricature?

CAMPDEN CRAFTS

By the end of the First World War Ashbee's experiment in the Cotswolds
had finally run its course, and in 1919 he and Janet left Chipping
Campden for good. But the town the Ashbees left behind was a very different place from the one they had moved to seventeen years earlier. At
the Old Silk Mill, the traditions of Ashbee's Guild of Handicrafts continued in the work of talented carpenters, woodcarvers and silversmiths.
George Hart, the silversmith, won prizes for his trophies, and the carver,
Alec Miller, had developed his skills to become a sculptor. Also living in
the town were F. L. Griggs, the etcher and illustrator, and Paul Woodroffe,
the stained glass designer. Griggs had settled in Campden in 1903, and the
following year Woodroffe moved to Westington, at the southern end of the
town.

At the Hart Workshop, Chipping Campden, the craft traditions established by C. R. Ashbee
have continued uninterrupted for over a hundred years

Fred Griggs was 28 years old when he first arrived in Campden as a promising young artist. He had been commissioned to produce romantic illustrations for a series of popular guides, *Highways and Byways of England*, and in Chipping Campden he found the perfect subject for his talents. For the next 35 years he lived in Dover's House on the High Street, leading many campaigns to preserve the medieval beauty of the town. (He was responsible for making sure the telephone wires ran underground so the glorious sweep of the High Street would not be interrupted.) Like Ashbee, Griggs loved the local folk traditions and made strenuous efforts to preserve them, even introducing some new "traditions" of his own, such as an annual feast for bell-ringers held at the Lygon Arms.

Griggs' most famous works were his etchings of "Anglia Perdita", a series of fantasy scenes in the visionary tradition of Samuel Palmer and William Blake. These images present a vision of vanished England, featuring Gothic buildings in an idealized landscape, and the Cotswold scenes around his home fed perfectly into this myth. Griggs detested the ways of the modern world (it was said that his wife only dared to buy an electric iron after his death). Nevertheless he believed that his lost vision of England could sometimes be glimpsed in Campden—at certain times when the light was right and the church bells were pealing.

Paul Woodroffe was just one year older than Fred Griggs, but while Griggs was lively and gregarious, he was a confirmed bachelor with a penchant for cold baths. In Campden he led a solitary life, dividing his time between book illustration and stained glass design. Woodroffe's windows were created in a set of outhouses in his cottage garden, where he worked with a team of local assistants. During his Campden years he established an international reputation as a stained glass designer, producing work in the Art Nouveau style. His most famous commission was for the Lady Chapel of St. Patrick's Cathedral, New York, a project that lasted for fourteen years. Every stage of the process was executed in Woodroffe's garden workshop before the finished windows were shipped to the United States, bringing the art of the Cotswolds to Fifth Avenue.

FINE FURNITURE IN BROADWAY

Chipping Campden made a lasting impression on one young schoolboy. In 1904 the twelve-year-old Gordon Russell enrolled as a boarder at Campden Grammar School, where he was to stay for the next three years.

It was a formative time for the boy who would later become one of England's leading furniture makers, and his passion for handmade furniture must have been nurtured by his early contact with the Campden guildsmen. Russell was also inspired by the architecture of the town, spending many hours sketching the High Street from his dormitory window. In later life he described the powerful impact that Campden had on his imagination, with its "wonderful setting of splendid stone buildings forming a street hard to match in Europe."

Gordon Russell's family had come to the Cotswolds to pursue a dream. Originally from Derbyshire, his father, Sydney Russell, had spotted a rundown coaching house when he was travelling through the Cotswolds, and had immediately recognized the place's potential. Moving his wife and sons to Broadway, Sydney made the Lygon Arms into his life's work, lovingly restoring all its details and filling its rooms with fine antique furniture. (Today it is one of Britain's best-known country house hotels.) By the time Gordon left school he was deeply involved in his father's project, and at the age of fifteen he was put in charge of the repair workshops, supervising the work of carpenters, blacksmiths, stonemasons and silversmiths. Soon he was designing simple items, and in 1919 (after returning from fighting in France) he set up his own furniture-making workshop.

Most of Russell's early pieces were made by hand but he gradually introduced more machinery. He had seen the dilemma of designers like Ashbee, who were forced to sell their hand-made items to the very rich, and he resolved to produce more affordable works. A passionate believer in good design, he maintained it was possible to use skilled machine work to produce "decent, well designed furniture for ordinary people".

By the mid-1920s Russell's prize-winning furniture was selling all over the world, but with the arrival of Modernism in the 1930s he decided it was time for a change of direction. Handing over the role of chief designer to his brother Dick, Gordon became involved in promoting design in industry, eventually becoming director of the Design Council of Great Britain. Under Dick Russell's direction, the Gordon Russell Company began mass production, and in 1935 work was transferred from the Cotswolds to a London factory. The firm that had begun in a Cotswold workshop had entered the modern age.

In 2008 the Gordon Russell Museum opened in Broadway. Housed in one of Russell's original workshops, the exhibition displays the work of the firm over a period of sixty years, from its Arts and Crafts origins to the age of mass production. The museum's collections include over a thousand original designs for furniture, metalwork and glassware, as well as filmed interviews with designers and craftsmen.

PLAIN POTTERY IN WINCHCOMBE

Gordon Russell was a great supporter of country crafts, and in 1926 he organized a special event: an exhibition of traditional skills to be held in the Russell workshops. Most of the craftsmen were local, but Russell persuaded the potter, Bernard Leach, to travel up from Cornwall for the event. In May 1926 Leach duly set out on his unreliable motorbike to make the three-day journey to Broadway. The sidecar of his bike was weighed down with tools and a potter's wheel, and perched on the pillion was his young apprentice, Michael Cardew.

Cardew was 25 years old when he puttered into Broadway on the back of Leach's bike. Brought up in London and educated at Oxford University, he had developed a passion for traditional pottery as a child on holiday in Devon. In 1923 he became Bernard Leach's first apprentice, joining a famous studio that combined English craft traditions with the influence of Japanese ceramics. It was a wonderful training for a young apprentice, but Cardew realized that he did not want to be a studio potter like Leach. His real interest lay in traditional craft pottery, of the sort that had once flourished in villages all over England.

Cardew later wrote about the pleasures of his week in Broadway. He enjoyed working with the soft local clay and played his part in the lively discussions on the future of crafts. But the most significant event of the week was the visit he made with Sydney Russell (Gordon's father) to the village of Greet, just outside Winchcombe. Greet Pottery had closed down twelve years earlier and was lying empty, overrun by hens. Poking around in the abandoned workshops, Cardew felt inspired: "the whole pottery gave out a feeling of generosity and good old-fashioned country ways of working."

Before the end of the year Cardew had moved to the Cotswolds to take up the biggest challenge of his life. Since the 1800s the pottery at Greet had produced flowerpots, chimney pots and a range of "farmhouse ware", but production had ceased in 1915 following the death of the last master potter. Fortunately, one last link with the past had survived. Elijah

Comfort had worked as a thrower in the old pottery and, at the age of 63, he agreed to take up his job again. With the help of Comfort and Sidney Tustin, a fourteen-year-old apprentice, Cardew set to work to bring the pottery back to life.

In his autobiography, *Pioneer Potter*, Cardew gives a vivid account of the hardships he faced at Winchcombe Pottery, as he experimented with clays and glazes and battled with the ancient kiln. For the first two years he survived on almost no money, sleeping and eating inside the pottery, until he finally found the time to build himself a wooden hut in the grounds. Even after his marriage in 1933 he continued to live in the hut for three more years with his wife and two baby sons.

Cardew's ambition was to make household ware at a price that people could afford, but he also wanted his pots to have a strong aesthetic appeal. Using the local red-coloured clay and following strictly traditional methods, he gradually developed his trademark style: large round-bodied jars, pots and bowls glazed in warm yellows and browns and decorated with bold incised patterns. As he grew in confidence Cardew began to make bigger pots, struggling to create giant cider jars with round bodies and narrow necks; a process he described as "an excruciating kind of fun" and also "a sort of magic". In 1931 Cardew exhibited his work in a London exhibition and was praised as an outstanding craft potter. Almost single-handedly he had managed to revive the dying traditions of craft pottery in England.

After the early struggles to build up the pottery, the 1930s brought great success, but by then Cardew was growing restless. In 1936 he returned to Cornwall, leaving the 22-year-old Ray Finch in charge of the pottery. Finch was the perfect person to continue the work at Winchcombe. Trained in ceramics at the Central School in London, he shared Cardew's enthusiasm for country pottery, but was also keen to develop his own designs. Apart from a brief interruption during the Second World War Finch continued working as a master potter well into his nineties, gradually handing the work over to his son. Today, Mike Finch and his team still create dishes, jugs and plates in the Winchcombe style, but they never flaunt their famous reputation. Passing a scruffy brick building by the side of a lane, you would have no idea that this was one of Britain's best-known potteries.

WOMEN DESIGNERS IN THE COTSWOLDS

Most of the early Arts and Crafts pioneers were men, but in the 1900s some talented women made their mark in the movement. In 1901 Katharine Adams moved to the northern Cotswold village of Weston sub Edge. As an unmarried woman of 39 she still lived with her parents, but she had plenty of work to occupy her. When she was a child Katharine had lived close to Kelmscott Manor, and had been inspired by William Morris' hand-printed books, with their exquisite tooled leather bindings. This experience marked the start of a lifelong interest. By the time she moved to Weston she had a growing reputation as a bookbinder.

Adams produced a range of fine leather bindings, some of them decorated with incised gold patterns. One of her most famous books was William Morris' *Story of Sigurd the Volsung*, bound in scarlet leather with a golden oak tree on the front. Adams' career flourished while she was in Weston and she set up a workshop, employing two local women. She eventually married, aged 56, and moved to Oxford where she continued bookbinding, but her Cotswold years were her most productive, resulting in over 200 books. A Katharine Adams binding is now a rare collector's item, but you can see some fine examples of her craft in the Court Barn Museum in Chipping Campden.

One of the most colourful figures in the Arts and Crafts movement was the weaver Ethel Coomaraswamy (now better known as Ethel Mairet). Ethel was the sister of Fred Partridge, who had travelled from Devon to join Ashbee's Guild of Handicrafts, and as a girl she made several trips to visit her brother in Campden. In 1902 Ethel married Ananda Coomaraswamy, a wealthy poet and philosopher, and after a period of living in his native Ceylon the couple decided to settle in the hamlet of Broad Campden, one mile south of Chipping Campden. With the help of C. R. Ashbee they converted a derelict Norman chapel into a dramatic home for their collection of Indian art. (The Ashbees later took over the chapel, living there from 1911 to 1917.) The Coomaraswamys added an exotic element to Campden society, holding candlelit soirées to discuss eastern poetry and philosophy. Ethel also astonished the locals by the way she dressed: a tiny birdlike woman, she wore sack-like dresses during the day and changed in the evenings into colourful flowing robes and dramatic Indian jewellery.

Ethel had been fascinated by the traditional crafts of hand dyeing and weaving that she had seen in Ceylon, and back in the heart of English sheep-rearing country she decided to set up a loom of her own. Soon she was immersed in the design and creation of original textiles, and had also begun the experiments with dyeing that would occupy her for the rest of her life. In 1913 Ethel left Broad Campden with her second husband, Philippe Mairet, settling at Ditchling in Sussex. It was during her time at Ditchling that Ethel created her best-known work, but her career as a dyer and weaver had started in the Cotswolds.

Soon after she moved to Sussex Ethel Mairet formed a close friendship with the textile designer Phyllis Barron. The two women shared a fascination with natural dyes, sometimes exhibiting their work together, but Barron's real working partnership started in the early 1920s when she met Dorothy Larcher. Within ten years Barron and Larcher prints had become so popular that the partners had outgrown their London studios. They were attracted by the Cotswolds, where they had several artistic friends, and they found the ideal place in Painswick. In March 1930 Barron and Larcher moved to Hambutts House, a handsome Georgian home with a large stable block, which they converted into workshops. With the help of three local women they were soon producing large quantities of hand-dyed and printed cloth to be made into outfits and soft-furnishings.

Barron and Larcher textiles drew their inspiration from French and Indian designs, but their two-colour patterns also had a very modern feel. The cloth was dyed in giant sunken vats, and laid out on long tables to be stamped with pattern blocks. Like William Morris, Phyllis Barron enjoyed

experimenting with traditional recipes for dyes, using a range of minerals and plants, but her greatest love was indigo. This deep blue dye required large quantities of uric acid, which Barron obtained by throwing "piddle parties"—riotous occasions held in Hambutts House in which the guests were entertained in return for plentiful jugs of urine.

Business was brisk in Painswick for Barron and Larcher, and their workshop was kept very busy, supplying cathedrals and palaces, shops and private customers. At the start of the Second World War, however, the partners decided it was time to retire, moving to a smaller house in the town. Visitors to their home in these later years described the experience of entering an interior that seemed to be made up entirely of Barron and Larcher textiles, in a range of soothing tones of indigo, rust and faded black.

"ARTY CRAFTY" LIFESTYLES
Arts and Crafts in the Cotswolds had their comic aspects. In Chipping Campden some of the arty incomers adopted what they took to be a "rustic" style of dress, with knickerbockers and flannel shirts for men, and smocks and billowing skirts for women—much to the astonishment of the town's residents. Some members of the movement liked to gather for evenings of traditional song and dance, even staging mummers' plays— productions that were sometimes performed to a bemused local audience.

For many adherents of the movement, the Middle Ages represented the high point of English culture, and they gladly sacrificed personal comfort in order to recreate an authentic medieval atmosphere in their homes. The Ashbees' home at Woolstaplers' Hall was strikingly different from the average Edwardian house, with its bare wooden floors, whitewashed walls and uncompromisingly plain oak furniture. But not all followers of the movement could live up to these ideals. In a letter to Ashbee just before his marriage, guildsman Will Hart apologized for Dora, his future wife, who was "the sort of girl whose idea of living is preferably in a modern house with modern conveniences." It is not known how Ashbee responded, but Dora would certainly have had the support of Henry James. After visiting the American actress Mary Anderson in her Arts and Crafts-style home in Broadway, the famous novelist wrote her a pitying letter: "You, if I may say so, have made yourselves martyrs to the picturesque. You will freeze, you will suffer from damp. I pity you, my dears."

Another visitor to Mary Anderson's home was E. F. Benson, creator of the comic *Mapp and Lucia* novels, and the flamboyant actress was probably the model for his Lucia. In his first book, *Queen Lucia* (published in 1920), Benson's heroine holds court in the fictional Cotswold village of Riseholme, based reputedly on Broadway. Lucia lives in a charmingly converted Arts and Crafts home with a living room so spartan and comfortless that "you had to be in a frantically Elizabethan frame of mind to be at ease there." In this picturesque setting she plays the virginals, while her architect husband declaims his (terrible) poetry to the long-suffering residents of the town.

In 1920s Broadway Mary Anderson stood out as a notable oddity amongst the stolid townsfolk. Yet within ten years the town had been gripped by a mania for Arts and Crafts. When John Moore visited in 1937 he found himself surrounded by sellers of hand-made furniture, scarves and raffia, and even contemplated wearing a notice to announce his hatred for all things home-made: "The place is a haven and headquarters for all manner of arty-and-crafty people, it is the refuge of every conceivable kind of crank... And the racket is quite a profitable one... it's your money they want in Broadway." The movement that had begun with the high ideals of William Morris had somehow—at least in Broadway—slipped into a pantomime, with money-making at its heart.

DESIGNING COTSWOLD HOMES
Queen Lucia's house in Riseholme is in many ways a typical Arts and Crafts Cotswold home. Cleverly converted from three small cottages, it presents a charmingly old-fashioned face to the world, but it is also fitted with all the latest gadgets cunningly disguised as antique features. This combination of old and new elements can be seen in many Arts and Crafts houses, and works especially well in the Cotswolds, where traditional materials are so widely used.

Some outstanding architects worked in the Cotswolds in the opening years of the twentieth century. Gimson and the Barnsleys, C. R. Ashbee, Detmar Blow and Guy Dawber all designed Cotswold buildings, ranging from large country homes to village halls and cottages. Ernest Barnsley made an especially significant contribution to the architecture of the Cotswolds, both in his small-scale buildings, and in his long-term project at Rodmarton Manor (see below). By the time of his death in 1926, the Arts and Crafts style was beginning to go out of fashion, but his work was continued by his son-in-law, Norman Jewson.

Norman Jewson was the last of the great architect-designers in the Cotswolds. Like many other figures in the Arts and Crafts movement he had trained in London but had grown tired of city life. Jewson described his arrival in the Cotswolds in his romantic memoir, *By Chance I Did Rove* (1950). Catching a train to Cirencester in 1907, he hired a donkey and cart to explore the countryside. The donkey was not a success, proving very obstinate on the hills, but the young architect did manage to ramble through the Cotswolds for several weeks, before finally ending up in Sapperton. There he presented himself to Ernest Gimson and was invited to become an "improver". It was the start of an idyllic period in Jewson's life, in which each day began with a three-mile walk from the village of Oakridge Lynch over the fields to Sapperton. In his memoir, Jewson recalled his daily walk down Tunley Lane, "a great place of wild flowers":

> Periwinkle and deep crimson Bloody Cranesbill grew there, as well as a
> pink flowered wood sorrel, so at Gimson's suggestion I picked and
> brought with me a different wild flower each day and made a drawing
> of it. This was part of his training of me in design...

Under Gimson's direction, Jewson was introduced to a range of traditional crafts, learning to work with plaster, stone, wood and metal. He was a fast learner, and soon became an invaluable member of the Sapperton group, working closely with Gimson, and helping Ernest Barnsley in his architectural work. In 1911 he married Ernest Barnsley's daughter Mary, moving into a cottage in the village, where he lived for the next thirty years. Jewson worked on new designs and renovations, aiming in all his work to create buildings with "good manners" that were "able to take their natural place in their surroundings without offence." His legacy survives in many parts of the Cotswolds, but perhaps his greatest achievement was the resuscitation of the Tudor manor house at Owlpen.

OWLPEN MANOR: "RESUSCITATED DREAM-PLACE"

Norman Jewson had first discovered Owlpen Manor before the First World War while he was cycling in the woods near Uley. Later he described his astonishment as he stumbled across the abandoned house in its exquisite garden. Jewson immediately recognized that Owlpen was a house of the highest quality, but it was in a terrible state. The roof had partly fallen in, the great stone bay window had come loose from the walls, and massive ivy roots were snaking across the floors. He was desperate to save the house, but in the end he had to wait until 1925 before it came on the market and he could raise the funds to achieve his dream.

Once he had purchased the manor Jewson embarked on a meticulous programme of restoration. His aim was not to rebuild, but to return the

house to the way it had been at the end of the nineteenth century, simply adding a few decorative details. Eighteen months later, Jewson's work was completed, but the project had proved so expensive that he was forced to put his dream house back on the market again. Owlpen Manor was bought by Barbara Bray, who turned out to be an ideal guardian, paying grateful tribute to Norman Jewson as "the magician of this resuscitated dream-place." Owlpen is now the home of the Mander family, who open it to the public on regular days in the summer.

Visitors to Owlpen Manor today can spot Jewson's delicate touch in his moulded plasterwork (look out for the panels featuring an owl). The house is filled with items from the Arts and Crafts period, and in the Great Hall there is a famous etching by Fred Griggs of Campden. As a close friend of Jewson, Griggs was involved in every stage of the restoration work, and his dream-like picture of Owlpen Manor perfectly captures the mysterious spirit of the place. The etching shows the house dwarfed by an avenue of giant yews (which have since been cut down). Running along its base is a handwritten dedication:

> To my friend NORMAN JEWSON, who, with one only purpose, & at his own cost & loss, possessed himself of the demesne of OWLPEN when, for the first time in seven hundred years, it passed into alien hands, & with great care & skill saved this ancient house from ruin.

ARTS AND CRAFTS ON DISPLAY: TWO MUSEUMS AND
RODMARTON MANOR

Anyone wanting to see Cotswold Arts and Crafts should visit two great
local collections. The Cheltenham Art Gallery and Museum has a spacious, white-walled gallery devoted to Arts and Crafts, with special emphasis on work from the Cotswolds. There are tables and chairs by Gimson
and the Barnsleys, furniture and textiles by William Morris, Winchcombe
pots and Barron and Larcher textiles. One of the most fascinating exhibits
is the piano that Ashbee gave to his wife, decorated with his hand-painted
scenes of Camelot and inscribed with one of his poems. At Court Barn
Museum in Chipping Campden the focus is on work from the northern
Cotswolds, with designs by Ashbee, etchings by Griggs and glass by
Woodroffe, as well as fine examples of Katharine Adams' bookbinding and
Michael Cardew's pots. Both museum displays follow Arts and Crafts principles of good design, and at Cheltenham you can experience some of the
movement's original impact as you move from the oppressively heavy Victorian Room into the light and colour of the Arts and Crafts Gallery.

For the total Arts and Crafts experience the place to visit is Rodmarton Manor. The house is the masterpiece of Ernest Barnsley, who designed
the pleasantly varied façade in the traditional Cotswold style. Its exterior
also features details by Norman Jewson. (Look out for his mouldings on
the drains, featuring owls, monkeys and cockerels.) Inside, the house is
filled with Arts and Crafts furniture. Many of the pieces are by Sidney
Barnsley, including a solid dresser built into a recess, and there are chests
and chairs designed by Ernest Gimson and Ernest Barnsley. Dominating
the entrance hall are two giant painted chests, decorated by Alfred and
Louise Powell, and the couple's ceramics are displayed throughout the
house.

Rodmarton Manor is not just the product of famous names. The
house is filled with the work of the local carpenters, blacksmiths and
needlewomen who were involved at every stage of the building. True to the
spirit of the Arts and Crafts movement, Ernest Barnsley saw the enterprise
as a chance to preserve traditional skills and educate local people, holding
craft demonstrations in the half-finished house. When Ashbee visited Rodmarton in 1914 work on the manor was still under way, and workers of
all kinds were busy inside and out. Delighted by what he saw, Ashbee reported:

"I've seen no modern work equal to it…The English Arts and Crafts Movement at its best is here—so are the vanishing traditions of the Cotswolds."

COTSWOLD CRAFTS TODAY

The influence of the Arts and Crafts movement can still be seen in the Cotswolds. The town of Chipping Campden is a major craft centre, with Ashbee's Old Silk Mill still providing a space for studios and workshops. In the Five Valleys around Stroud many of the old weaving mills have been turned into studio and foundries, housing sculptors and potters, furniture makers, weavers and stained-glass designers. There are regional craft centres in Cheltenham, Cirencester and Painswick, and a craft community on Bredon Hill. In the village of Whittington, near Cheltenham, John Randle has been running the famous Whittington Press since 1972, continuing the traditions of typesetting revived by Morris and Ashbee.

Pottery is especially strong in the Cotswolds. Apart from the famous Winchcombe Pottery, the region has two outstanding craft potters. John Jelfs, at Cotswold Pottery in Bourton-on-the-Water, concentrates on form, decorating his pots with glazes made from local wood ash and clay. At the Old Forge in Chedworth, David Garland makes colourful plates and jugs decorated with bold abstract designs. Garland sees himself as an inheritor of the English Arts and Crafts movement and keeps a photo of Michael Cardew by his wheel.

Chapter Ten

A COTSWOLD LIFE

LAURIE LEE IN THE SLAD VALLEY

"I was set down from the carrier's cart at the age of three; and there with
a sense of bewilderment and terror my life in the village began."
Laurie Lee, Cider with Rosie (1959)

From the famous opening sentence of *Cider with Rosie* we are immersed
with Laurie in his lush Cotswold valley. Laurie Lee grew up in the village
of Slad in the years following the First World War, but he waited until he
was in his thirties before he started to write about his childhood. By that
time he had established his literary reputation as a poet, and in *Cider with
Rosie* (published in the United States as *Edge of Day*) he uses his poet's skill
to recreate the sounds, smells and sights of his country childhood. The
result—part memoir and part fiction—captures a fleeting time in the life
of the English countryside, just before the ancient ways disappeared. It
also describes a very particular place in the Cotswolds.

LEES IN THE VALLEY
At the heart of *Cider with Rosie* is Laurie's family home, standing on a
steep slope by the side of the road from Stroud, with its long garden
stretching down the valley to a small lake. The house still stands by the
roadside in Slad today but it is no longer the crumbling wreck that Laurie
recalls, "with rooks in the chimneys, frogs in the walls, mushrooms on the
ceiling." Nowadays the garden looks much tidier too. In Laurie's time it
was a tangle of currant and rose bushes, strawberry plants and apple
trees—a terrifying jungle waiting to be explored.

Twenty years after he left the Slad valley Laurie could still picture his
childhood home, shaped like a letter T with its "hand-carved windows,
golden surfaces [and] moss flaked tiles." Living in the cross-stroke of the
T were two ancient crones, locked in cheerful enmity, while the down-
stroke was home to the Lees: eight children and their mother, crammed

Laurie Lee's childhood home: "a cottage that stood in a half-acre of garden on a steep bank above a lake… [with] rooks in the chimneys, frogs in the cellar, mushrooms on the ceiling, and all for three and sixpence a week"

into a warren of interconnected rooms. An attic with bulging ceilings provided a bedroom for the girls, while the boys slept on the first floor, three to a room. There was a scullery with a pump and a sink, usually filled with washing or vegetables. And at the heart of the house was the kitchen, dominated by a temperamental stove, where the family spent noisy evenings together.

Reading *Cider with Rosie*, one can feel the closeness of Laurie's family life, filled with pranks and squabbles, squeals and false alarms. But there are tragedies too. Before Laurie was two, his four-year-old sister Frances died "suddenly, silently, without complaint" and his mother never entirely recovered from her loss. All Laurie's siblings are vividly drawn, but the undisputed heroine of the book is his mother, Annie. In Laurie's affectionate portrait Annie Lee is brave, fanciful and disorganized, as she wages a losing battle to run her home and family. Hints of his mother's history emerge through Laurie's book: Annie had married a widower when she was 31, cheerfully taking over the care of his four children before having four more babies of her own. But her selflessness was not rewarded. After joining the army in 1914 Reg Lee never came home again, while Annie was left to bring up the family alone, always clinging to the belief that he would return one day. The character who emerges from *Cider with Rosie* is a passionate, generous countrywoman who loved flowers and sunsets, babies and fine china, and who passed on to Laurie her imaginative response to the world.

SCENES FROM SLAD

Cider with Rosie tells the story of Laurie Lee's childhood, but it also provides a record of rural life in the early twentieth century. Alongside his family portraits Laurie draws a picture of the village of Slad: "a scattering of some twenty or thirty houses" buried in a valley, with all the villagers' needs supplied by "a church, a chapel, a vicarage, a manse, a wooden [meeting] hut, a pub and a school."

One of the funniest chapters in *Cider with Rosie* is "Schooldays", which relates young Laurie's experiences at the two-room village school. "Outings and Festivals" describes a village charabanc outing and the annual parish tea, and "Winter and Summer" contrasts the wintry activities of skating and carol singing with lazy summer picnics and slapdash cricket games. Scattered through the book are local legends and stories, linked to special places in the landscape. There are memories of fêtes and haymaking, and portraits of village characters with names like Cabbage-stump-Charlie and Willy-the-fish. But the darker side of village life is not forgotten. A chapter called "Public Death, Private Murder" contains an account of a casual murder on a dark county lane and records the toll of winter deaths from poverty and "self-slaughter". The chapter ends with the poignant fate of Joseph and Hannah Brown, a couple who lived together contentedly for fifty years before being forcibly parted and taken off to the workhouse, where they both died within the week.

The closing chapters of *Cider with Rosie* chart the final years of Laurie's childhood and the end of an ancient way of life. While Laurie is discovering the joys of cider with Rosie, gleaming motorcars begin to appear on the old white roads, frightening pedestrians and horses. Within a few short years, Laurie observes, "the village would break, dissolve and scatter, and become no more than a place for pensioners." In the meantime he records how the traditional ways gradually slipped away, as most of the horses died, people stopped keeping pigs in their back yards and the old flutes and cornets were replaced with modern "wirelesses". By the end of the book Laurie is looking towards the future, but in *Cider with Rosie* he has left an unforgettable record of a vanished way of life.

AFTER ROSIE

The story of *Cider with Rosie* ends soon after Laurie reaches the age of fourteen, with a sense of his world opening out. In fact, the real-life Laurie lived at home until he was nineteen, although as he grew older he spent less time in Slad. Laurie's first move away from the village came when he was twelve years old and began attending the Central School in Stroud (a fact that is omitted from *Cider with Rosie*). His next three years were spent at school in Stroud before he started work as an office boy for a firm of chartered accountants in the town. Neither school nor office work held much appeal for Laurie, but there were other pleasures in his life. When not getting to know the local girls, he spent most of his time reading, writing poetry and playing his violin. Music, in particular, provided him with an escape from the narrow confines of village life. By the time he left school Laurie had formed a musical trio with a couple of friends and they were soon in great demand for local dances. Later he joined the Painswick Orpheans, a group that specialized in jazz and swing, and his evenings and weekends began to fill up with gigs, outings to the cinema and adventures with girls.

By the time Laurie was sixteen, he was travelling to Gloucester and Birmingham to visit friends. He had also found an interesting destination closer to home. This was the Whiteway Colony, a group of free-thinking liberals living in a community four miles away from Slad. The colony had been founded in 1898 and was run according to strict utopian principles, with everybody holding their land in common (an experiment described in Chapter Three). The early years at Whiteway had been extremely hard, but by the 1930s a frugal but creative way of life had evolved, with colonists growing their own fruit and vegetables, making bread, sandals and pots, and sometimes even weaving their own clothes. The colonists lived in a maze of self-build houses and caravans, and free-thinkers of all kinds were welcomed. In the 1930s Whiteway provided a home for communists, pacifists and refugees, including several supporters of the Spanish Republicans.

For a young man like Laurie, the Whiteway Colony was a fascinating place. It had a lively cultural life, based around the wooden community hall, and the place was humming with ideas. For four years in the early 1930s Laurie was a regular visitor at Whiteway, watching performances of folk dance and ballet, attending gramophone recitals and sometimes performing jazz on a Saturday night. Laurie often stayed on after these events, joining in the debates on the international issues of the day, and this experience must have played a part in his later involvement in the Spanish Civil War. By the spring of 1934 the colony also held a romantic attraction for Laurie in the shape of Cleo, the sixteen-year-old daughter of a communist agitator. Tantalizingly little is known about her, but she probably played an important part in awakening his political consciousness.

When Laurie met Cleo he was nineteen years old and desperate to see more of the world. This urgent need for escape is voiced in the opening chapter of his second book of memoirs, *As I Walked out One Midsummer Morning* (1969):

> I was propelled, of course, by the traditional forces that had sent many generations along this road, by the small tight valley closing in around one, stifling the breath with its mossy mouth, the cottage walls narrow-

ing like the arms of an iron maiden, the local girls whispering, "Marry me, and settle down."

With pressures like these in his life, it was only a matter of time before Laurie left, and in June 1934 he made up his mind. On a bright Sunday morning he headed down the road, carrying "a rolled-up tent, a violin in a blanket, a change of clothes, a tin of treacle biscuits and some cheese." It was the start of many years of adventures, told in *As I Walked Out* and *A Moment of War* (1991). But it was not the end of his life in Slad.

RETURN TO SLAD
Laurie Lee never completely left the Cotswolds behind. For the rest of his life he could still relive his childhood experiences in the Slad valley, and at the age of 31 he began to write them down. It was fifteen years before he completed *Cider with Rosie*, but when it was finally published in 1959 the book was an instant success. From that time on Laurie Lee was identified in the eyes of the public with his Cotswold home. Meanwhile, the profits from *Cider with Rosie* helped to finance his return to his Slad.

The return to Slad was a gradual process, and Laurie never abandoned his London home, but the first move came in the summer of 1959, just a few months before *Cider with Rosie* was published. It had been a tiring year, and Laurie felt in need of complete change of scene. While his wife Kathy was away in Greece, he decided to accept a friend's offer of a furnished house in Slad for the summer. The house was Woodside Bungalow, in a corner of Slad called the Vatch, which in Laurie's childhood still had a working mill. Laurie's first summer in Slad for over twenty years turned out to be brilliantly sunny, just like the summers he remembered. Many of his old schoolmates were still in the area, greeting him in the village shops and pubs, and most of the country sounds and sights were unchanged. Laurie rode to Stroud by bicycle, played cricket at Sheepscombe and dined at Steanbridge House, the mansion that had once belonged to the village squire. When Kathy returned to England in the autumn, Laurie brought her down to Woodside Bungalow and took her on long walks through the countryside of his childhood.

By the following year Laurie was making regular visits to Slad, usually with Kathy, and much of the summer of 1960 was spent at Woodside Bungalow. Laurie played music with his old friends at Painswick and drank in the local pubs. The runaway success of *Cider with Rosie* had turned him into a local celebrity, and he was in constant demand for opening village fêtes and umpiring cricket matches.

In 1961 Kathy began to look for a permanent home in Slad. She found Rose Cottage, a Cotswold stone house in the heart of the village, with a long, thin garden and a splendid view over the valley. By September the Lees had moved in and were setting about the task of taming the garden. Always ambivalent about his old village, Laurie seemed happy to be back so long as he could escape to London whenever he wanted. In the early mornings he pottered in his garden and most evenings he strolled the few yards across to the Woolpack. It was a special time for Laurie and Kathy, especially when they discovered that Kathy was pregnant after twelve years of trying to conceive. According to Kathy, the reason for this "miracle" was a minor operation. Laurie claimed her pregnancy was a piece of Cotswold magic.

A Child in the Valley

Jessy Lee was born in 1963, when her father was fifty years old. For Laurie, watching his daughter grow up in the Slad valley was a special pleasure. He took her on all his familiar walks, and held family picnics in the places he had known half a century before. Twenty years later he wrote in the *Sunday Times*, "I'd been away from this valley for twenty years, when suddenly she appeared and was born here... It was almost as though my return to Slad was not only to revisit my childhood, but also to find Jessy."

Of course, Jessy's childhood was nothing like her father's. During their daughter's early years the Lees had a nomadic life, migrating between Chelsea and Slad with frequent trips abroad, and later Jessy was sent to boarding school. Yet in spite of the interruptions she still felt that Slad was where she belonged. Like her father, she returned to live there many years later.

The Return of the Native?

With the publication of *Cider with Rosie*, Laurie Lee became a "national treasure". Usually he played up to the role of a genial countryman, giving interviews in the Woolpack with a pint of cider in his hand. Yet the real Laurie Lee was far more complex than his reassuring public persona suggested. As Valerie Grove reveals in her sensitive biography, Laurie was a man of secrets, who waged a constant struggle with illness and depression. Perhaps unsurprisingly for the man who wrote *Cider with Rosie*, alcohol and women played a significant role in his life, and although his love for Kathy was never in doubt there were other relationships (including another daughter) that Laurie chose to keep secret.

Laurie's attitude to his Cotswold roots was equally complicated. He had intense feelings for the place where he grew up, but a quiet country life was never enough for him, and once the winter rains set in he grew desperate to escape. As a younger man he had made frequent trips abroad in search of warmth and sunlight, and even in his sixties he established a way of life that often kept him away from the Cotswolds. With the support of the ever-tolerant Kathy he would usually spend weekdays in London, where he was a regular at the Chelsea Arts Club, returning only for weekends in Slad with his family.

In *Cider with Rosie* Laurie recounts the story of how he nearly died as a child, and a whole chapter of the book is devoted to his childhood ailments. The pattern of sudden fevers that began in early childhood lasted all his life and he also suffered from minor epilepsy. Yet in spite of his frequent bouts of illness, Laurie still managed to survive to the age of 82. In his sixties he began to lose his sight, and by the time he was eighty he was almost blind. By then he and Kathy had moved to Littlecourt, the house next door to Rose Cottage, where they had installed a large picture window to make the most of the view. In the last few years of his life Laurie spent most of his time at home in Slad, becoming a regular customer at the Woolpack.

On 13 May 1997 Laurie died at home with Kathy and Jessy by his side. He was buried in the churchyard in Slad, beside his mother Annie and infant sister Frances. On his gravestone is carved the simple epitaph he had chosen: "He lies in the valley he loved."

SLAD TODAY

The village of Slad can still be recognized from the descriptions in *Cider with Rosie*. Its stone cottages cling to the steep valley sides, and their roofs sparkle in the sun, just as Laurie observed, "like crystallized honey". Approaching the village from Stroud, visitors pass the church where Laurie once sang in the choir and the village school (converted into a house). On the right is the Woolpack Inn, filled with photographs of Laurie, and

Laurie Lee in the Slad valley: "I used to think the whole world was like my valley. But when I went out into the world to try my fortune I realised there was only one place like this"

neatly tucked behind it Rose Cottage and Littlecourt.

Twenty yards further along the road, a grassy bank drops down to a solid stone house, built in the shape of a T. This is Rosebank, Laurie's childhood home, known in his day as "Mother Lee's cottage". Today the house is much smarter than in Laurie's time, but apart from a new side porch its structure is unchanged. Beyond the house the garden drops steeply down to the lake where Laurie loved to skate, and beside the lake is a large cream-coloured mansion. This is Steanbridge House, where the village squire once lived, presiding over a way of life that has vanished forever.

Chapter Eleven

PICTURING THE SCENE

WRITERS, ARTISTS AND MUSICIANS IN THE

COTSWOLDS

"You hills of home, woodlands, white roads and inns
That star and line our darling land, still keep
Memory of us; for when first day begins
We think of you and dream in the first sleep
Of you and yours—
Trees, bare rock, flowers
Daring the blast on Crickley's distant steep."

Ivor Gurney, "Crickley Hill" (c.1917)

"Yes, I remember Adlestrop…"

Edward Thomas, "Adlestrop" (1914)

On 23 June 1914 the London to Worcester train stopped for a few minutes at a deserted country station. A passenger looked up, registered a name and took in a perfect rural scene. He noticed willow trees and rosebay willow herb growing by the tracks and haystacks drying in the sun. He saw "high cloudlets" in the sky and heard a blackbird sing, and in that moment his vision opened out, as "mistier" and "farther and farther" he became aware of "all the birds/Of Oxfordshire and Gloucestershire."

The passenger was the 36-year-old writer and poet Edward Thomas, and his Cotswold epiphany became the poem "Adlestrop". Less than three years later he was killed in action in the First World War, not long after his celebrated poem had been published. "Adlestrop" became an emblem for a vanished pastoral England before the horrors of the Great War. It has also become the best-known poem about the Cotswolds, a poetic snapshot of the spirit of a place.

WILLIAM SHAKESPEARE: "HIGH WILD HILLS" AND JUSTICE SHALLOW'S COUNTRY

Five centuries before Edward Thomas' train steamed through the Cotswolds, William Shakespeare was making frequent journeys across the wolds. His route from Stratford to London would have taken him through the northern Cotswolds, and his journeys to Gloucester (either from Stratford or London) involved a long, hard drive over the western hills. In Shakespeare's day travelling over the stony Cotswold uplands must have been a bleak, spine-jarring experience. In *Richard II* (Act II, scene iii) the Earl of Northumberland complains bitterly about his ride to Berkeley Castle:

These high wild hills and rough uneven ways
Draw out our miles, and make them wearisome.

A much more affectionate picture of the region emerges in *Henry IV, Part II*, (Act III, scene ii) when Sir John Falstaff arrives at the Gloucestershire farmhouse of his old friend and local magistrate, Justice Robert Shallow. Here, all is comfort and good cheer as the company gather round

Shallow's hospitable hearth. It is easy to imagine the homely atmosphere in the solid stone Cotswold farmhouse, with its low-beamed ceiling, mullioned windows and roaring fire.

Altogether Falstaff pays three visits to Shallow at home. When he first arrives he reviews a motley collection of locals as possible recruits for the king's army. The roll-call is unpromising: Mouldy, Shadow, Wart, Feeble and Bullcalf all step up for inspection—and all prove true to their names. Falstaff's second visit to Shallow takes place in Act V, scene i. This time he is overwhelmed by Shallow's offers of hospitality, confused with chaotic orders for the running of the farm. Finally, in Act V, scene iii, Falstaff admires Shallow's orchard before joining him and his friend Justice Silence in a drunken meal.

From his first speech Justice Shallow emerges as garrulous, self-satisfied and parochial. Yet despite his failings he is an endearing character. Amidst the drama of war and politics, Shallow's country farmhouse, surrounded by apple orchards, provides an oasis of rural contentment. Many critics have seen Shakespeare's portrayal of Justice Shallow and his companions as a nostalgic tribute to the traditional, rural way of life that Shakespeare knew as a boy growing up in Warwickshire.

Shakespeare was fond enough of Justice Shallow to use him in a second play. In *The Merry Wives of Windsor* Shallow is accompanied by his young cousin, Slender, who has fallen in love with Mistress Anne Page. As in *Henry IV, Part II*, Shallow is a pompous but well-meaning country gentleman. He also emerges as a lover of country sports when Slender enquires, "How does your fallow greyhound, sir? I heard say he was outrun on Cotsall." The line reveals Shallow's lack of success as a sportsman and can also be read as a clue to the whereabouts of his home. "Cotsall" probably refers to the famous "Cotswold Games", held near Chipping Campden, which locates Shallow's farmhouse in the northern Cotswolds. This part of Gloucestershire lay on Falstaff's route between London and the north. It was also the part of the Cotswolds that Shakespeare crossed on his frequent journeys from Stratford to London.

On Bredon Hill with Housman

About ten miles due east of Chipping Campden is Bredon Hill, a high limestone outcrop forming the far north-western edge of the Cotswold region. Rising to 981 feet, the hill is topped by a stumpy eighteenth-century tower known as Parson's Folly. In the 1830s the writer and traveller William Cobbett marvelled at the view from the summit of Bredon, describing it as "one of the very richest spots in England". It is also the subject of a famous poem by the scholar poet, Alfred Edward Housman (1859-1936).

"Bredon Hill" was published in 1896 in a collection of 63 short poems entitled *A Shropshire Lad*. The collection sold slowly at first, but following the outbreak of the First World War Housman's nostalgic depiction of rural life struck a chord with English readers and the book became a best-seller. As the title suggests, most of the poems are set in the Shropshire countryside around Ludlow, yet "Bredon Hill" belongs to an area at least thirty miles further south. Clearly, the dramatic Cotswold landmark had claimed a special place in Housman's personal landscape.

Like most of the poems in *A Shropshire Lad*, "Bredon Hill" tells a tragic story. A young man on the hillside surveys the view of "the coloured counties" stretched out below him and listens to the church bells peal "in steeples far and near." He remembers how he lay with his love "among the springing thyme" dreaming that the bells would peal for their marriage. But with the coming of winter the dream turned to nightmare, and the bells tolled instead for his sweetheart's funeral. The poem ends on a mournful note, with the young man answering the bells as they summon him to his own death: "I hear you, I will come."

The haunting rhythms of "Bredon Hill", with its theme of tolling bells, have appealed to several composers, but perhaps the most evocative musical setting of the poem was written by the Cotswold-born Ralph Vaughan Williams.

Ivor Gurney: Poetry and Music at Cranham and Crickley

Lying directly south of Bredon Hill is a series of wooded hills and cliffs that form the north-western Cotswold Edge. This was the dramatic countryside that inspired the poet and musician Ivor Gurney (1890-1937). Gurney grew up in Gloucester and sang in the cathedral choir, developing a precocious talent for composing. From an early age he was inspired by nature and by his late teens he had explored all the countryside around the city of Gloucester. Many of his walks took him to the steep, wooded valleys around Birdlip (the village where his mother had been born) and to the high ground at Cranham and Crickley Hill, where he spent many solitary days striding through the landscape, scribbling down ideas for tunes as he walked.

In 1911 Gurney won a scholarship to the Royal College of Music, where his genius was immediately recognized, but he was so homesick for Gloucestershire that he was unable to finish his degree. Three years later he joined the British army and was posted to France. In the horror of war Gurney's thoughts turned constantly to his native landscape, and he began to write floods of poetry, contrasting the blasted battlefields of northern France with the gentle, wooded landscape of Gloucestershire. The powerful poem "Crickley Hill" is typical of Gurney's double vision at this time, as he describes a walk with a fellow soldier in the lanes at Buire-au-Bois, which is magically transformed through their shared memories into a remembered hike on a Cotswold hill:

O sudden steep! O hill towering above!
Chasm from the road falling suddenly away!
Sure no men talked of you with more love
(O tears! Keen pride in you!)
Feeling the soft dew,
Walking in thought another Roman way.

You hills of home, woodlands, white roads and inns
That star and line our darling land, still keep
Memory of us; for when first day begins
We think of you and dream in the first sleep
Of you and yours—
Trees, bare rock, flowers
Daring the blast on Crickley's distant steep.

In August 1917 Gurney was gassed at Passchendaele and sent back to Britain, and the following year he was discharged from the army. In a highly emotional state he wrote and composed compulsively, revising poems and songs he had written on the Front, and adding many more. His first poetry collection, *Severn and Somme*, was published in the autumn of 1917 and *War's Embers* appeared two years later. In both collections stark descriptions of the horrors of war are juxtaposed with meditations on the Gloucestershire countryside. One of these countryside poems is the evocative "Cotswold Ways", which takes the reader on a past-haunted ramble around Birdlip and Crickley Hill. The poem opens intriguingly, "One comes across the strangest things in walks," and explores a set of chance encounters with fragments of Abbey barns, abandoned kilns and mounting-stones, carved Saxon faces and "Roman-looking hills."

By the early 1920s Gurney was acknowledged as a remarkably gifted composer and poet, but by this time his mental health was deteriorating. He began to lead a rootless existence, often walking alone all through the night, and surviving by a series of odd jobs, including singing in country inns. He took to eating erratically, often fasting for days, and composed and wrote in frenetic bursts, sometimes working for 22 hours at a stretch. It was a way of life that could not be sustained and in 1922 his family reluctantly committed him to an asylum. After a short spell in a Gloucester mental hospital Gurney was transferred to a larger establishment in Dartford, Kent, where he stayed for the rest of his life.

Gurney died from tuberculosis at the age of 47, still writing poetry right up until his death. The later poems are sometimes confused but always arresting, and many of them evoke the landscape of the Cotswolds. One of the most powerful of these later poems is "The High Hills", an imagined walk in the countryside round Crickley. In it, the poet struggles painfully as he tries to recapture the sense of walking on the high ground where beech "tangles wildly in the wind," and the poem is filled with a sense of sharp regret:

> The high hills have a bitterness
> Now they are not known

JAMES ELROY FLECKER ON PAINSWICK HILL

Cranham and Crickley will always be associated with Gurney, but there was another poet who walked these valleys and remembered them fondly from abroad. James Elroy Flecker grew up in Cheltenham, where his father was headmaster of Dean Close School. Until he was seventeen, when he was sent away to school, he attended his father's school in Cheltenham, and made frequent cycle trips into the local countryside. As an adult Flecker spent most of his life abroad, first in the Levant (the inspiration for his most famous poem, "The Golden Journey to Samarkand") and later in Greece, where he married a local girl. Dogged by illness and poverty all his life, he nevertheless managed to establish his literary reputation before dying from tuberculosis at the age of thirty. The poem "Oak and Olive", written in 1910, expresses Flecker's dilemma as an exile torn between England and Greece, and is infused with a sense of the shared cultural traditions of the lands of oak and olive. In the course of the poem Flecker describes his sentiments as he walks "in Athens town" but allows his thoughts to travel back to the scenes of his youth in Gloucestershire:

> Have I not chased the fluting Pan
> Through Cranham's sober trees?
> Have I not sat on Painswick Hill
> With a nymph upon my knees,
> And she as rosy as the dawn,
> And naked as the breeze?

The nymph on the poet's knee is, of course, entirely metaphorical, but the final stanzas of "Oak and Olive" offer a more rooted description of the Cotswold landscape. As Flecker lies "in Grecian fields, smothered in asphodel" his memories transport him, perversely, back to Gloucestershire:

> Then my heart turns where no sun burns
> To fields beneath low-clouded skies
> New widowed of their grain,
> And Autumn leaves like blood and gold
> That strew a Gloucester lane
>
> Oh well I know sweet Hellas now,
> And well I knew it then,
> When I with starry lads walked out—
> But ah, for home again!
> Was I not bred in Gloucestershire
> One of the Englishmen!

Hilaire Belloc: A Brief Voyage on the Evenlode

Nostalgia for a lost Cotswold landscape pervades a short poem by Hilaire Belloc (1970-1953), written in unusually winsome mood. Belloc first explored the Evenlode valley as a student at Oxford in the 1890s. Many years later he wrote "The Evenlode" as an elegy to a land of lost content:

> I will not try to reach again,
> I will not set my sail alone,
> To moor a boat bereft of men
> At Yarnton's tiny docks of stone.

With Belloc as a guide, the poem carries the reader on a dream journey "along the perfect Evenlode", under "open skies" and through "wandering mists". There are lyrical images of "hushed meadows" and the sound of waters "mingling in the brakes" before the poem ends with a vision of the Evenlode still wandering quietly through the "western wolds":

> A lovely river, all alone,
> She lingers in the hills and holds
> A hundred little towns of stone,
> Forgotten in the western wolds.

A Poet Laureate in Chipping Campden

The poet and novelist John Masefield (1878-1968) was not a Cotswold man, but he came to love the area. He had spent his childhood in Herefordshire and Worcester before leaving home at the age of thirteen to train as a sailor. After a short time at sea he resolved to be a writer and by his late twenties he had a growing reputation as a poet. In 1903 Masefield was living in London when he received an invitation from a friend in Chipping Campden. The friend was C. R. Ashbee, who had recently established his Guild of Handicrafts in the Cotswold town.

Masefield thought Chipping Campden was one of the most perfect places he had ever seen. He was also delighted by the Ashbees' simple way of life, sharing their enthusiasm for traditional plays and local folk songs. Between 1903 and 1905 Masefield made several visits to Campden, first on his own and later with his wife. After one of these visits he sent a thank-you poem to Janet Ashbee, in the manner of a traditional folk song, beginning with the lines:

When I from Campden town depart,
I leave my wits, I lose my art.

Later, Masefield wrote another poem in praise of Chipping Campden, intended for Janet's book of Cotswold ballads (a project that was never completed). The poem describes the town in ecstatic terms, finding "beauty everywhere/In that grey curving English street" and ends with a tribute to Ashbee's creation of a "city of the soul." Campden also provided the inspiration for Masefield's first play. In 1907 he wrote *The Campden Wonder*, based on a local legend of murder and intrigue. It was not a success, however, receiving only eight performances at the Court Theatre in London.

The Masefields' visits to Campden petered out after 1905, but this was not the end of their links with the Cotswolds. In 1932, two years after Masefield was made Poet Laureate, he decided it was time to look for a house in the country. For the previous thirteen years he had lived close to Oxford, but his wife Constance had been very ill and the couple were in need of somewhere quieter.

The place they discovered was Pinbury Park, an Elizabethan farmhouse in the Frome valley, five miles from Cirencester. The house was owned by Lord Bathurst and had been painstakingly restored by Ernest Gimson and the Barnsley brothers (described in Chapter Eight). Standing in its own wooded valley and surrounded by gardens, its setting was idyllic. Inside it had been stripped back to the original structure, with the addition of Gimson's exquisitely moulded plasterwork ceilings. In the early months of his tenancy Masefield wrote delightedly to a friend, "This is certainly a heavenly place." He was excited by the house's "old and romantic history" and thrilled by the appearance of dormice and wild ducks.

The Masefields stayed at Pinbury Park for the next six years and continued to enjoy the house and its surroundings. In November 1933 Masefield wrote: "the place is as lovely as ever, now that the leaves are off. The jasmine and the violets are out: the berries are scarlet on shrubs and trees, and the storm-cock loudly sings." In the peaceful Gloucestershire countryside Constance recovered her health, although they had to endure some bitterly cold winters and an occasional plague of rats. At the outbreak of war in 1939 the Masefields decided to move back closer to Oxford, but the Cotswold years had been a productive period. In 1937 Masefield published *The Country Scene in Poems*, a collection of verse inspired by rural life. The book contains poems on animals and farming, as well as celebrations of country events such as ploughing matches and county shows. While he was living at Pinbury Masefield also wrote his classic children's story, *The Box of Delights*, the tale of an enchanted box that grants its owners the power of time travel. Some of the adventures in *The Box of Delights* take place by a magical riverbank that may have been inspired by the Masefields' walks along the River Frome.

A SUPERTRAMP IN NAILSWORTH

The southern Cotswolds town of Nailsworth is famous for the steepness of its streets, and the outlying hamlet of Watledge is especially hilly. It was here that the self-taught poet, W. H. Davies (1871-1940) spent the last two years of his life, living contentedly with his young wife in a small stone cottage that they named "Glendower". In fact, Glendower was the fourth house he had occupied since arriving in Nailsworth ten years earlier. But this nomadic lifestyle was no novelty for Davies—the poet widely known as the "Supertramp".

William Henry Davies had an eventful life. Born into a poor family in South Wales, he was expelled from school at the age of fifteen, and soon embarked on a series of adventures that sent him across the Atlantic at least seven times. On one of his many journeys across North America his leg was injured when he fell from a train and had to be amputated just below the knee. No longer fit for manual labour, he made the decision that he should try to earn his living by writing poetry.

In 1899 Davies returned to Britain, where he continued to live a wandering life, writing poetry compulsively. Six years later, his talent was recognized when he sent a volume of self-published poems to some leading literary figures. Edward Thomas and George Bernard Shaw both admired Davies' simple style, with its combination of joyful appreciation of the natural world and squalid glimpses of urban life, and they encouraged him to write his memoirs. The resulting book bore the title (suggested by Shaw) of *Autobiography of a Supertramp*, and was a great popular success. For the first time in his life Davies gained some financial security.

"Glendower" in Watledge, W. H. Davies' last home:
"What is this life if, full of care,
We have no time to stand and stare?"

At the age of 52 Davies married Helen Payne, a young woman he had first met while she was working as a prostitute. (His frank account of their meeting and subsequent happy marriage was not published until 1980, after Helen's death.) The couple lived in Sussex for seven years before moving to Nailsworth in 1930, possibly to be closer to Davies' friend, the artist William Rothenstein. By the time he arrived in the Cotswolds Davies was nearly sixty and walking with his wooden stump was becoming hard. Nevertheless he still managed to explore the area, writing that: "in this little town… there are so many circular walks that I often find it difficult to decide which to take… But when the morning is quiet and sunny, I go anywhere, and lean on every stile or country gate I see."

During Davies' last years in Nailsworth he continued publishing poetry, including a volume of love poems, and also produced two prose works entitled *My Garden* and *My Birds*. One poem from this time, "Nailsworth Hill", presents a charming image of the moon "peeping" over the summit of the hill:

> She rests her chin on Nailsworth Hill,
> And, where she looks, the World is white.

In his last months at Glendower Davies was too weak to leave the house, but he still had a view of his cottage garden. Two lines from his most famous poem are inscribed on a plaque on the wall of his final home.

> What is this life if, full of care,
> We have no time to stand and stare?

T. S. ELIOT AT BURNT NORTON

One of the leading poets of the twentieth century had some intriguing Cotswold connections. The American-born Thomas Stearns Eliot (1885-1965) lived in England from the age of twenty-six, gaining a formidable poetic reputation for "The Waste Land", published in 1921. In the 1920s, Eliot found himself increasingly drawn to Anglicanism, and in 1927 he was baptised in Finstock Church (in the Oxfordshire Cotswolds) by a cler-ical friend who lived in Finstock Manor. In 1933 Eliot separated from his wife Vivienne, after almost twenty years of unhappy marriage (he would later commit her to a mental hospital). The following year he learned that his old friend Emily Hale would be spending the summer of 1934 in England with her uncle and aunt, Dr. and Mrs. Perkins. The Perkins took a six-month let on two cottages in Chipping Campden, repeating the arrangement in 1935 and 1937. During these three summers Eliot was a frequent visitor to Campden, staying at least five times in 1935.

It is not clear what Eliot's feelings for Emily were, but several people who knew him well claimed he was in love with her. They had first met when Eliot was a student at Harvard, and had performed in a play together. Subsequently, Emily had stayed on in Boston as a drama teacher and had never married. Unlike Vivienne, she was robust and cheerful, and Eliot clearly enjoyed exploring the local countryside with her. On one of their expeditions he discovered the manor house and garden of Burnt Norton in the woods above Aston-sub-Edge.

Burnt Norton is an unremarkable eighteenth-century manor house, built from local limestone in the traditional Cotswold style. Now used as a conference centre, it is surrounded by well-kept grounds, but in Eliot's time the gardens were neglected and their air of decay had a profound effect on him. Eliot may also have been intrigued by the strange history of Burnt Norton house, which gained its name from a dramatic incident in the eighteenth century, when a former owner burnt down the farmhouse on his estate after being abandoned by his mistress.

In 1935 T. S. Eliot wrote his long poem "Burnt Norton", which was first published in his *Collected Poems 1909-1935*. Later he composed three more companion poems ("East Coker", "The Dry Salvages" and "Little Gidding") and the four were published together as the *Four Quartets*. Eliot considered the *Four Quartets* to be his masterpiece. Filled with esoteric Christian and Hindu symbolism, the poems also carry some intensely personal meanings, and each of them has its starting point in a place of special significance for Eliot.

"Burnt Norton" opens with a meditation on the nature of time, and the lost nature of "What might have been", before moving into a remembered scene as:

Footfalls echo in the memory
Down the passage which we did not take
Towards the door we never opened
Into the rose garden.

Later in the poem there are images of "unseen music hidden in the shrubbery" and "an empty alley" leading "into the box circle/To look down into the drained pool"—all conjuring up a fleeting experience in a garden. The symbol of the rose garden has multiple meanings in the *Four Quartets*, but it is also rooted in a real moment in the garden at Burnt Norton. It is possible that in that moment Eliot saw the direction his life might have taken, if he had married Emily and made the step towards "the door we never opened."

U. A. Fanthorpe at Wotton-under-Edge

The small market town of Wotton-under-Edge is tucked under the edge of the high western Cotswold escarpment. Towering above it is Nibley Hill, with spectacular views across the Severn valley, and nearby is the steep-sided valley of Ozleworth Bottom. Simultaneously dramatic and ordinary, Wotton was home to one of England's most popular poets for thirty years.

Ursula Askham Fanthorpe, who died in 2009, has been described (by Carol Ann Duffy) as "an unofficial, deeply loved laureate". Her poems are reassuringly accessible, celebrating the English landscape, history and people, and many of them are rooted in the Cotswolds. In "Wotton Walks" she describes the ancient web of walks surrounding her home town, all of them leading back "To where Wotton pleats herself on her shelves/Above the vale, under the Edge." There is a similarly vivid sense of landscape in "Owlpen Manor", where the ancient manor house is pictured "like an old dog half asleep" lying in its "narrow, hand-carved valley". Other Cotswold poems take the reader to wilder places. In "Tyndale in Darkness" Fanthorpe pictures William Tyndale, the translator of the Bible whose monument crowns Nibley Knoll, standing on the high ground looking out "over moody Severn across the forest/To the strangeness of Wales." In her early poem "Earthed" she recognizes the menace of "serious Cotswold uplands, where/Limestone confines the verges like yellow teeth,/And trees look sideways."

Several Fanthorpe poems celebrate Cotswold characters and their language. In "Three Poems for Amy Cook", written in memory of her Wotton neighbour, she attempts to capture Amy's "wit and way with words" which is "Swift and surprising, like the road from Nibley." "Local Poet" presents a countryman with a voice that is "Double Gloucester" and

"Strong Language in South Gloucestershire" delights in the improbable names of the local villages and their ancient ancestry. In Fanthorpe's Christmas poem "The Invitation" her characters are the local Wotton foxes who speak in a seductive Gloucestershire burr, as they urge the infant Jesus to "Forget they beastly men" and "Come live wi wee under Westridge/Where the huntin folk be few." Like many of Fanthorpe's poems "The Invitation" is filled with affection for the ancient, gentle ways of the Cotswolds.

John Buchan's Adventures in Wychwood Forest

The Cotswolds have inspired story-tellers as well as poets. In 1919 the Scottish novelist, John Buchan (1875-1940) moved to Elsfield Manor, four miles north of Oxford. At that time the three-storey manor house was surrounded by fields and had fine views over towards the Cotswolds to the west. Elsfield became the Buchan family home, and John made it his base for frequent excursions into the Cotswolds, adopting the region's valleys as a southern substitute for the Scottish Highlands.

At the time of his move to Elsfield, Buchan had already made his name with the fast-paced thriller, *The Thirty-Nine Steps* (published in 1915). He was also an active politician, journalist and publisher, but he still found time for country life. Buchan explored the local countryside on horseback and on foot, tramping through forests and fishing in rivers—and put this romantic landscape into his novels.

During his first year in Oxfordshire Buchan wrote *Mr. Standfast*, the third in his series of Richard Hannay novels that had begun with *The Thirty-Nine Steps*. Like all the Hannay stories, it is packed with action, but this adventure ends with the hero marrying and settling down. In a deliberate mirroring of Buchan's own life Hannay moves into Fosse Manor, an ancient stone manor house in the Oxfordshire Cotswolds, where he enjoys the life of a gentleman farmer. Just like his creator, the Scottish-born Hannay feels at home in the Cotswolds, "anchored at last in the pleasantest kind of harbour."

Richard Hannay is not the only Buchan character to inhabit the Cotswolds. In 1923 Buchan published a historical novel that linked his twin passions for Scotland and the Cotswolds. Midwinter traces the adventures of a supporter of Bonnie Prince Charlie as he embarks on a dangerous mission to gain support for his cause in the English Midlands. In his verse dedication of the book Buchan expresses his "twin loyalties" to "Wychwood beneath the April skies" and "the deep heath by Fannich's lake", announcing his intention to write a tale that "haply tries to intertwine" the two. Midwinter was a huge commercial success, being hailed by critics at the time as "the greatest historical novel ever written." Eight years later Buchan drew once more on his knowledge of the Cotswolds to create another historical blockbuster. The Blanket of the Dark (published in 1931) is a fast-moving tale set in the reign of King Henry VIII. The action takes place in the towns and villages of the Windrush and Evenlode valleys, and some of its most exciting scenes are set in the depths of Wychwood Forest.

J. B. Priestley's Hitherton-on-the-Wole

When J. B. Priestley travelled through the Cotswolds in preparation for writing his *English Journey* (1934), he already knew the region well. Less than five years earlier he had created the fictional Cotswold village of Hitherton-on-the-Wole in his picaresque novel, *The Good Companions* (1929). At the start of this story, Miss Elizabeth Trant is found living in a village with a "grey cluster of roofs" and a "square church tower in the middle" situated somewhere equidistant between Chipping Campden, Cirencester, Burford and Cheltenham. It has been suggested that the model for Hitherton is Bourton-on-the-Water. In fact it could be any small village in the Cotswolds, of the sort that is usually passed unnoticed on the way to somewhere more important.

> Sometimes motorists, hurrying from lunch at Oxford to tea at Broadway or Chipping Campden, lose their way and find themselves at Hitherton, and the little books prepared for them tell them at once that Hitherton has 855 inhabitants, closes early on Wednesday… boasts a hotel, *The Shepherd's Hall* (3 bedrooms) and a garage J. Hurley & Son… But away they go the motorists… Thus when any strange and expensive looking motor car stops there, everyone at Hitherton, with the exception of Mrs Farley of *The Shepherd's Hall* and J. Hurley and Son, who are always hopeful, prepares at once to point the way to other and more important places.

Priestley's delightful parody of a guidebook entry is prefaced by a lyrical picture of the Cotswolds that could grace the introduction to any guide:

> Here are pleasant green mounds, heights of grass forever stirring to the tine of the south-west winds; clear valleys, each with a gleam of water; grey stone villages, their walls flushing to a delicate pink in the sunlight; parish churches that have rung in and rung out Tudor, Stuart and Hanoverian kings; manor houses that have waited for news from Naseby and Blenheim and Waterloo and Inkerman and Ypres… but have kept their stones unchanged… Here is a place [where] man has forsworn his mad industrial antics and settled himself modestly and snugly in the valleys and along the hillsides, has trotted out his sheep and put up a few tiny mills and been content.

The satire is gentle and affectionate. The Cotswolds of Priestley's *Good Companions* are beautiful, cosy—and deadly dull. Clearly, Elizabeth Trant has to get out of Hitherton as fast as she can, before she sinks forever into a life of spinsterhood in her pretty Cotswold cottage. By the end of the chapter she has made her escape, but not before the reader has been treated to a country auction at the Hall and has got to know a host of colourful local characters.

BARBARA PYM IN FINSTOCK

In 1974 the novelist Barbara Pym moved to the Cotswolds. She was 61 years old and, despite having published six novels before she was fifty, her literary career appeared to have petered out. Her seventh manuscript had been turned down by twenty publishers on the grounds that her gently comic stories of middle-class life were no longer fashionable, and her next book was also rejected. In 1971 she underwent surgery for breast cancer and three years later she suffered a minor stroke. For several years she had been spending weekends in the country with her sister Hilary, and now she decided it was time for a permanent move. After a long career at the African Institute, she left London for good, settling into Finstock, a small Oxfordshire village on the edge of Wychwood Forest.

In Finstock, Barbara joined Hilary in Barn Cottage, a converted wheelwright's shop in the oldest part of the village, and entered a social circle that revolved around church services, jumble sales and visits for tea and sherry. It was a way of life that she had captured brilliantly in her first novel, *Some Tame Gazelle*, published in 1950, and now she observed with interest how village life had changed in the intervening years. At the time of the move, Barbara was also busy completing another novel, *Quartet in Autumn* (a darkly comic exploration of the relationship between four office workers) and in 1976 she sent the manuscript to her old publisher, Jonathan Cape. Once again, the novel was rejected, but the following year her fortunes changed dramatically when Lord David Cecil and Philip Larkin contributed to an article in the *Times Literary Supplement*, nominating Barbara Pym as the most underrated writer of the century. Within a few months Macmillan had offered to publish *Quartet in Autumn* and later that year it was shortlisted for the Booker Prize. Buoyed up by this recognition, Barbara embarked on what was to be her final work: *A Few Green Leaves*, "the story of an imaginary village".

Barbara Pym is always sparing with details of setting, but her "damp West Oxfordshire village" bears a striking resemblance to Finstock. The unnamed village is set within an "almost idyllic setting of softly undulating landscape, mysterious woods and ancient stone buildings", and stands on the edge of a dank, ancient woodland. Apart from the church and its rectory and the manor house, Pym's village has a smattering of pretty cottages (mainly lived in by newcomers), a pub, a village hall and a doctor's surgery. Life in the village is presented through the eyes of Emma, a young anthropologist, who notes with clinical interest the disintegration of traditional rural patterns. In this fragmented community the church is no longer the hub of social life. People turn for help to the doctor rather than the vicar, and villagers eat ready-meals in front of the TV, leaving the newcomers to make jam for "village" events.

A Few Green Leaves was completed in 1979, just a few months before Barbara Pym's death from cancer. It has been described as the most elegiac of her novels, but it ends on a quietly hopeful note. In the final chapter, one of the novel's central characters reaches a decision to return to the village, and acknowledges "there's something rather lovely about the winter here."

JILLY (AND JOANNA) IN RUTSHIRE
Two of the UK's most popular female novelists have Cotswold connections. In 1982 Jilly Cooper moved to the village of Bisley (near Stroud) and has lived there ever since. Joanna Trollope was born in her grandfather's

rectory in Minchinhampton in 1943 and lived in Coln St. Aldwyns (near Cirencester) from 1984 to 2005.

Jilly Cooper began her writing career as a journalist before producing the first of her blockbuster novels in 1975. After her move to Bisley the novels continued to flow, but their setting changed to Rutshire, a fictional version of the Cotswolds. Between 1985 and 1999 Cooper wrote the six novels known as the *Rutshire Chronicles* (*Riders*, *Rivals*, *Polo*, *The Man Who Made Husbands Jealous*, *Appassionata*, and *Score!*). Since then she has published *Pandora* and *Wicked!*, set in Rutshire's neighbouring county of Larkshire, but still firmly rooted in the Cotswolds.

Cooper's novels are high-spirited romps, chronicling the adventures of the "county set"—all played out against the bucolic background of Rutshire (or Larkshire) villages and towns. Her larger-than-life characters have outrageous double-barrelled names, live in crumbling manor houses and keep dogs and horses. When they are not too busy bed-hopping, they ride, hunt and play polo and attend county balls in a delicious parody of upper-class country life in the Cotswolds. Cooper also delights in making local references in her novels, borrowing some of her characters' names, such as Ricky France-Lynch, Miss Miserden and Somerford Keynes, directly from Cotswold places. While Jilly Cooper is the queen of the rural "bonk-buster", her friend Joanna Trollope has been described as the mistress of the "Aga saga". Several of Trollope's early novels chronicle middle class life in country villages, town and farms. (*A Village Affair* and *The Rector's Wife* explore the challenges of village life, while the problems of farming families are examined in *Next of Kin*.) Trollope has stated that she made a deliberate choice not to site her novels in the countryside where she lived, but the influence of the Cotswolds on her writing is inescapable.

ARTISTS AND WRITERS IN BROADWAY

The Cotswolds have always attracted artists, but one special place became the focus of a lively artistic colony. In 1884 the American illustrator and painter Francis Davis Millet (1846-1912) "discovered" the picturesque village of Broadway, in the north-west corner of the Cotswolds. Once an important coaching stop, Broadway has a broad main street ending in a wide village green. Today it is a busy tourist centre, but in the 1880s its handsome buildings were attractively neglected and ivy-covered. Millet was delighted by this "quaint reflection of a long ago country village" and quickly made arrangements to move his family into Farnham House, overlooking the green. At the same time, he took over Abbot's Grange, a crumbling monastic ruin dating from the 1300s, which he converted into a wildly romantic studio. By the summer of 1885 Millet was welcoming his first visitors—mainly American expatriates like himself—and over the next few years Broadway became a regular summer artists' colony. Visitors to Broadway included the American painters Edwin Abbey, John Singer Sargent, Alfred Parsons and Edwin Blashfield, and the English illustrator Fred Barnard. Artists' models and writers also came to stay—among them the critic and essayist Edmund Gosse and the eminent novelists, Henry James and Robert Louis Stevenson.

Life in the Broadway colony centred round the atmospheric Abbot's Grange, where artists and writers worked and played companionably. Some work was achieved, but this was interspersed with tennis, dances, games and musical evenings. Edmund Gosse has provided an attractive picture of life at the Grange: "…in the morning, Henry James and I would write, while Abbey and Millet painted on the floor below, and Sargent and Parsons tilted their easels just outside. We were all within shouting distance, and not much serious work was done, for we were in towering spirits and everything was food for laughter." Surrounded by such exuberance, only Henry James maintained a sedate demeanour, but even he let out the occasional "genial chuckle". Sometimes the antics at Abbot's Grange spilled out into the village. On one occasion Fred Barnard, wearing fancy dress, chased a screaming American up and down the high street, while the locals looked on impassively. It seemed that nothing the artists did could disturb the villagers' calm. As Gosse reported, "Whatever we do or say or wear or sing they only say 'The Americans is out again.'"

Amidst the fun and games the artists sketched and painted local buildings and scenery. The Lygon Arms, where some of them stayed as guests, was a popular subject, and John Singer Sargent used the garden of Farnham House for his painting "Carnation, Lily, Lily Rose". The picture, which shows two girls in a garden at dusk, was painted over several months, since Sargent could only work on it when the light was a particular shade of purple. Each evening the whole colony would assemble to enjoy the spectacle of Sargent running forward over the lawn "with the action of a wagtail" to make a few rapid dabs on his canvas, before taking a final turn at tennis.

"Broadway and much of the land about it are in short the perfection of the old English rural tradition" (Henry James)

The idyllic summers at Abbot's Grange lasted until 1890, when Edwin Abbey moved to Fairford and the group dispersed. The Broadway colony did not leave a lasting artistic legacy, but it did provide great opportunities for fun. Henry James claimed that Millet had "reconstructed the golden age" in Broadway. When he was in the Cotswolds with his artist friends James enjoyed a rare sense of relaxation, prompting him to comment mischievously, "it is delicious to be at Broadway and not have to draw."

THE VIEW FROM FAR OAKRIDGE: ROTHENSTEIN, BEERBOHM AND DRINKWATER

Since the establishment of the Broadway colony, artists have painted thousands of Cotswold views, but a few painters stand out from the crowd. Sir William Rothenstein is particularly associated with the region. Living in the western Cotswolds for thirty years, he created some powerful images of stark, stone buildings against stormy skies.

In 1912 Rothenstein and his wife bought Iles Farm at Far Oakridge, near Stroud. It was a large property, consisting of a farmhouse, outhouses and barns set in 55 acres of land with glorious views over the Golden Valley. Rothenstein taught at the Royal College of Art, and served as official war artist in two world wars, but Iles Farm was his refuge where he could sketch and paint and entertain his friends. The farmhouse was carefully restored by his friend and neighbour Norman Jewson, and Rothenstein commissioned some special Cotswold pieces to furnish it. Ernest Gimson built an enormous cupboard, which was painted with Cotswold scenes by Alfred Powell (who lived in nearby Tunley), and Powell also created a ceramic punch bowl, decorated with scenes of Gloucestershire. Rothenstein loved the solid stone buildings of the Cotswolds, and he painted the local farms and barns in all kinds of weather. Writing about his passion for Cotswold stone, he once explained: "Stone buildings always move me—austere in grey weather, pale, livid even, against a stormy sky, they are warm and sparkling in the sunlight."

During their years at Iles Farm, the Rothensteins entertained a string of guests (including W. B. Yeats, John Galsworthy and Rabindranath Tagore) and established a lively circle of artistic friends. Some were Cotswold neighbours, like the poet W. H. Davies and the architect Norman Jewson. Others came to stay. The critic and caricaturist Sir Max

Beerbohm escaped to the Cotswolds for the duration of the First World War, renting Winston's Cottage in the village of Far Oakridge. Immensely sophisticated and urbane, Beerbohm refused to abandon his elegant city ways even in the depths of the country. Jewson described him emerging reluctantly into the local lanes "as if dressed for a garden party at Buckingham Palace." When Beerbohm left Winston's Cottage in 1918, a more enthusiastic tenant moved in. John Drinkwater was a successful playwright and a member of the group of young English poets known as the Georgians. For three years at Far Oakridge he plunged into Cotswold life, compiling a collection of humorous observations on the locals. Drinkwater's *Cotswold Characters* (1921) introduces a gallery of colourful villagers, including the "foreigner" Rufus Clay, who remained an outsider because he came from Painswick, seventeen miles away. His poem "The Cotswold Farmers" takes a more whimsical view of his surroundings, evoking the ghosts of labourers on the hills around his home:

> Sometimes the ghosts forgotten go
> Along the hill-top way,
> And with long scythes of silver snow
> Meadows of moonlit hay,
> Until the cocks of Cotswold crow
> The coming of the day
> ....
> They fold their phantom pens, and plough
> Furrows without a share,
> And one will milk a faery cow,
> And one will stare and stare,
> And whistle ghostly tunes that now
> Are not sung anywhere.

STANLEY SPENCER IN LEONARD STANLEY

Nine miles west of Far Oakridge is Leonard Stanley, a village on the Cotswold Edge that provided a refuge for the artist Stanley Spencer (1891-1959) in a stormy period of his life. In July 1939, with Britain on the brink of war, life was looking particularly grim for Spencer. He had divorced his first wife, Hilda, in 1937, marrying Patricia Preece later that year. Within two years, however, this marriage had also collapsed, and

Preece had claimed their house in Cookham, leaving Spencer homeless. In a desperately demoralized state, he set off on a holiday with two fellow artists, Daphne and George Charlton. The three of them rented rooms in the White Hart Inn, Leonard Stanley, close to the home of their mutual friend, Michael Rothenstein (whose parents lived at Far Oakridge). With the outbreak of war that autumn, the holiday turned into an extended stay, and Stanley did not leave the Cotswolds until the following spring, when he took up work as a war artist.

In his room above the bar, equipped with a piano and a cosy fireplace, Spencer at last had space to draw and paint again. George was absent for most of the week, busy with the transfer of the Slade School to Oxford, leaving Stanley and Daphne with plenty of time together. Daphne was motherly and tender to Stanley, cutting his fingernails and mending his shabby clothes, and they soon embarked on a passionate affair, recorded by Spencer in a series of (often erotic) drawings featuring "big Daphne" and "little Stanley". Soon after moving to the Cotswolds, Stanley began to record the loves of his life in a series of sketchbooks later known as the *Scrapbooks*. His drawings were annotated and squared-up ready for painting but only a few of them were turned into canvases. Of these, his image of Stanley and Daphne, lying on a tiger-skin rug in his room at the White Hart Inn, has become one of Spencer's best-known paintings.

Stanley Spencer also recorded several scenes in and around the village. In *Chestnuts*, Stanley, Daphne and a gardener are shown picking cabbages while the village children thread chestnuts for a game of conkers. In *Village Life, Gloucestershire* Daphne and Stanley look on as a small family group witnesses the coming of God. *The Woolshop* shows Stanley helping Daphne to choose knitting wool, with Stanley also stacking shelves in the shop, and was based on a visit to a shop in nearby Stonehouse. A few of Spencer's Cotswold sketches were incorporated into his later works. So a study of Daphne climbing Sandford Knoll was later used as a reference for the Assumption of the Virgin Mary and a church in Stonehouse surrounded by pavement featured in the large-scale work *The Resurrection and the Raising of Jairus' Daughter*.

Some of Spencer's Cotswold paintings are landscapes. *Leonard Stanley Farm Pond, Old Tannery Mills* and *Cottage Garden, Leonard Stanley* are carefully observed country scenes that can be compared to the Cotswold pictures of his contemporaries, including Gilbert Spencer, Stanley Badmin and James Bateman. All these works display a renewed interest in the English pastoral scene that was also expressed in the literature of the 1930s. For Spencer, however, the village of Leonard Stanley held a more personal significance. Infused by his passion for Daphne, it briefly replaced Cookham as his "sacred place".

Music from the Cotswolds: Vaughan Williams and Holst

Two great English composers have Cotswold roots. In 1872 Ralph Vaughan Williams was born in the village of Down Ampney, close to Cirencester, where his father was rector. Following his father's death when Ralph was three years old, the family moved away from the Cotswolds, but the composer maintained a lifelong affection for his birthplace. One of his most famous hymn tunes *Down Ampney* (the accompaniment to the hymn "Come down, O Love divine") celebrates the village where he was born.

In 1910 Vaughan Williams embarked on a project that combined his love of the Cotswolds with his enthusiasm for English folk song and legend. The two-act opera *Hugh the Drover* tells the story of a Cotswold horse-drover who gets into a fight over a beautiful girl and is held in the stocks before finally escaping with her to freedom. Set in the Cotswolds in 1812, it opens with a country fair and a display of Morris dancing. Work on the opera did not progress easily; over the next forty years Vaughan Williams made many revisions, finally publishing it with the new title of *A Cotswold Romance*. The opera has been recorded but only rarely performed, although it contains some memorable tunes, including a rollicking chorus by the Men of Cotsall and a romantic solo, "Hugh's Song of the Road".

Gustav Holst (1874-1934) was a friend and contemporary of Vaughan Williams and shared his passion for English folk music. Holst spent his childhood in Cheltenham (where there is an excellent Holst Museum) and after leaving school took up a temporary post in the Cotswolds. The nineteen-year old Holst became the village organist and choirmaster at Wyck Rissington, and soon took on an additional role, conducting the choral society at Bourton-on the-Water, one mile's walk away across the Dikler valley. When he was not making music Holst spent most of his leisure time hiking in the local hills. Imogen Holst has described how her father developed "a deep love of the Cotswold hills… [which] was always to remain one of the most precious things in his life."

After a year at Wyck Rissington, Holst moved to London to study music. He was to spend the rest of his life in the capital, but he never forgot his Cotswold origins and often returned to walk in the familiar countryside. He also dedicated his first major orchestral work to the region where he grew up. In 1900, at the age of 25, Holst completed his *Cotswold Symphony*. Pastoral and romantic in spirit, it expresses his affection for the Cotswold landscape. At the heart of the symphony is an elegy for William Morris, one of Holst's great heroes. In this gentle movement the composer aimed to convey Morris' vision of the English countryside: a "heaven on earth" that he had found in the Cotswolds.

Chapter Twelve

ECCENTRIC COTSWOLDS

COLLECTORS, DREAMERS AND DANGEROUS

GAMES

"He was… one of… a famous company, the eccentric English country
gentry, the odd and delightful fellows who have lived just as they pleased,
who have built Follies, held fantastic beliefs, and laid mad wagers."

J. B. Priestley, *English Journey* (1934)

In the autumn of 1933 J. B. Priestley's travels around the Cotswolds took
him to Snowshill Manor. He had already seen several Cotswold manors by
the time he arrived at the house, but from his first glimpse of its "Gothic
craziness" he knew that he had found something extraordinary. Climbing
up to the manor through a series of gardens, he sensed "that anything
might happen now, that we were trembling on the very edge of common
reality, that life might turn into a beautiful daft fairy tale under our very
noses." Snowshill Manor turned out to be every bit as strange as Priestley
had imagined. Today it is still preserved as a monument to one of the
Cotswolds' most eccentric characters.

SNOWSHILL MANOR: A HOUSE OF CURIOSITIES
Snowshill Manor occupies the heart of the hilltop village of Snowshill
(known to the locals as "Snozzle"), two miles south of Broadway. Surrounded by a series of "garden rooms" designed in the Arts and Crafts
manner, the house is a hotchpotch of different styles. Priestley observed
that the manor had "no sense, though an infinite antique charm". It was
probably this lopsided charm that first attracted Charles Paget Wade, who
bought Snowshill Manor in 1919 with the aim of turning it into a giant
cabinet of curiosities.

Wade was an architect, craftsman, antiquary and poet. The son of a
wealthy plantation owner in the West Indies, he was brought up as an only

Snowshill Manor: "The house itself had a Gothic craziness. There was no sense though infinite charm, in its assembled oddity of roofs, gables, windows, doorways" — J. B. Priestley

child in his grandmother's house: a place where, he later recalled, there was "seldom any laughter, and never any visitors or young folk". In these dismal surroundings Wade surrounded himself with objects. Later, he devoted his adult life to amassing treasures, mostly purchased in antique shops and country sales.

As a young man, Wade worked briefly as an architect before joining up to fight in the First World War. Once the war was over, he decided to look for a permanent home for his rapidly growing collection. Snowshill Manor—rundown, neglected and surrounded by thistles—proved to be the perfect place. Over the next thirty years Wade filled the house with more than 22,000 objects, including mechanical automata, clocks, children's toys, musical instruments, farm carts and implements, and a large number of bicycles. One of his special interests was samurai armour, and he was fascinated by anything connected with witchcraft and magic.

Once installed at Snowshill, Wade turned his property into a giant display case, labelling the rooms with appropriate names according to their contents, decoration or position in the house. "Dragon" was named after the roaring fire that Wade kept burning in the ancient medieval hall. "Seventh Heaven" was on the top floor, and "Meridian" was in the centre of the house. "Hundred Wheels" was filled with spinning wheels, carts and bicycles, while "Admiral" contained ships and globes. The "Green Room" housed Wade's collection of 26 suits of samurai armour, standing to attention like a ghostly army. The "Witch's Garret" was a secret attic room filled with objects linked to witchcraft, alchemy and the occult.

Nothing in Snowshill Manor was allowed to remind Wade of the twentieth century. The house was lit entirely by candles and oil lamps, and no modern kitchens or bathrooms were installed. To keep his museum intact Wade created a frugal home for himself in the old Priest's House in the manor's courtyard. At night he slept in a panelled box bed with a view of the stars. In the evenings he sat in a tall porter's chair by a crackling fire, studying his ancient tomes.

"Curiouser and Curiouser"

Despite his love of solitude, Wade could be welcoming, and some of his guests were treated to a tour they would never forget. Wade would usually greet them in fancy dress (he had a choice of over two hundred costumes), and trusted friends might even be invited to dress up themselves and enact a play in the Dragon Room. Visitors to Snowshill were usually charmed by Wade's fantastic tales, but they needed very strong nerves. Many years after he had toured the house as a child, one guest still remembered his feelings of terror as Wade burst out on him from one of the manor's many secret passages. Even more alarmingly, he remembered Wade sitting as still as a waxwork inside an inglenook fireplace, then suddenly leaping out from the flames with his long grey hair streaming behind him.

When Priestley visited Snowshill Manor, Wade was his personal guide, leading him on a fantastical tour through a warren of "ancient dim panelled rooms, in which there were collections of spinning wheels, sedan chairs, model wagons, weapons, old musical instruments... and blazing lacquer from Peking." The tour ended with a visit to Wade's workshops in the Priest's House: a set of "queer ramshackle rooms [containing] tools and implements of every kind, coats-of-arms, skulls, black letter folios, painted saints, colossal tomes of plain song, swords and daggers, wooden platters and I know not what else." Among all this confusion Wade was busy creating a miniature model of an old-fashioned seaport, complete with dwarf trees and even live goldfish swimming in its harbour. For Priestley, this was his host's final triumph:

> Most excursions of this kind, which begin with such promise, offering you some remote valley, some village or house drowned in time... have a bad trick of fizzling out; but not this one, which became curiouser and curiouser until at last... we landed at the seaport that was two feet high, in a harbour where the goldfish... came glittering like whales of red gold.

Priestley was just one of many well-known visitors to Snowshill. John Betjeman, Graham Greene and John Buchan all toured the house, but not everyone enjoyed the experience. Virginia Woolf went to Snowshill in 1935, and wrote a waspish letter to her sister, Vanessa Bell:

> We went 40 miles to see a necromancer [Charles Paget Wade]... who lives on a medieval farm which he has filled with old clothes, bicycles, mummies, alligators, Indian altars—not, I thought, very interesting, and I think rather a fraud, as he pretended to have no watch, and so I lost my train and only got back at 8.30.

At the age of 63 Wade amazed his friends by marrying a woman who had turned up at the manor one day, lost in a storm. Evidently his wife did not enjoy life at Snowshill Manor because she spent most of her time in Wade's plantation home in the West Indies. In the 1950s Wade left England to join her, making arrangements for the manor to be taken over by the National Trust. He still visited England to stay at Snowshill, and on one of these trips he died suddenly and was buried in the local churchyard.

Wade's collection is still in place at Snowshill Manor today. For some visitors the house has a sinister, claustrophobic feel. Others share the attitude of Virginia Woolf, quickly hurrying back to modern life. But for a few, like J. B. Priestley, the place is a giant box of delights, full of playful eccentricities.

SEZINCOTE HOUSE: A MOGUL FANTASY

Five miles west of Snowshill is one of England's most surprising sights: a turquoise-domed Indian palace sitting comfortably in its Cotswold valley. Sezincote House (pronounced See-zin-kt) is the only English country house to be built in the Mogul style. It was the dream home of Sir Charles Cockerell, who had spent his working life in India, where he had formed a passion for the dramatic, red stone palaces of the Mogul emperors.

In 1798 Charles Cockerell inherited a Gloucestershire estate and resolved to create his own Mogul palace in the Cotswolds. The obvious choice of architect was his brother, Samuel Pepys Cockerell, who had already designed a house for his friend Warren Hastings at nearby Daylesford. Undeterred by the fact that he had never visited India, Samuel relied on the advice and drawings of the artist Thomas Daniell to create his designs. The result is a surprisingly successful fusion of Muslim, Hindu and English Regency styles.

Sezincote House is built of Cotswold stone, stained orange-red to imitate Indian sandstone, and decorated with delicate geometric carvings. Its crowning glory is a flamboyant onion dome, inspired by Muslim mosques and palaces, while rising from the four corners of the roof are lantern-like "chatris". Curving out from the main house, an elegant, glass-walled orangerie ends in an octagonal pavilion whose many-arched windows are intended to resemble a set of peacock feathers. The house sits amongst picturesque grounds laid out by Humphry Repton, including a Persian paradise garden, giant statues of Brahmin bulls and a temple to

... Exotic Sezincote!
Stately and strange it stood, the Nabob's house
Indian without and coolest Greek within..."
John Betjeman, "Summoned by Bells"

the Hindu goddess Souriya.

The house and gardens at Sezincote are still a remarkable sight, but in the 1800s they must have seemed incredibly exotic. One early visitor was certainly impressed by his vision of India in the Cotswolds. After seeing Sezincote in 1812 the Prince Regent decided to build an Indian extravaganza of his own. The result was the Brighton Pavilion, which initiated a national craze for oriental designs. A century later, in the 1920s, Sezincote inspired the young John Betjeman, who stayed there as a guest of a university friend. Later, Betjeman recalled the excitement of arriving at Sezincote; driving through an avenue of oaks, and on towards

> The bridge, the waterfall, the Temple Pool
> And there they burst on us, the onion domes,
> Chajjahs and chattris made of amber stone:
> "Home of the Oaks", exotic Sezincote.
>
> *Summoned by Bells* (1960)

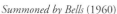

BATSFORD ARBORETUM: INSPIRATION FROM THE EAST

While Charles Cockerell found his inspiration in India, his near neighbour, Lord Redesdale, was influenced by his experiences in the Far East. Algernon Bertram Mitford, 1st Baron Redesdale, was known to his friends as Bertie (pronounced "Bartie"). In the 1860s he had worked as an ambassador in China and Japan before retiring to Gloucestershire, where he built himself a comfortable house near Moreton-in-Marsh. Batsford House was constructed in an unremarkable mock-Tudor style, but Redesdale's passion was his garden. Inspired by the concept of the Japanese "wild" garden, he aimed to create an oriental landscape in the Cotswolds with artfully grouped clumps of bamboos, trees and plants, combined with rockeries, streams and waterfalls, and even a hermit's cave. The Batsford Arboretum is open to the public and is especially famous for its rare bamboos, maples and cherry trees. The gardens have matured and changed since Bertie Redesdale's time, but the concept is still there: a landscape modelled on Japan and patiently transplanted to Gloucestershire.

MITFORDS IN THE COTSWOLDS

Bertie Redesdale died in 1916, leaving his house and title to his son, David Freeman Mitford. The following year the new Lord Redesdale moved into

Batsford House with his wife, Sydney, and their five children: Nancy (aged thirteen), Pam (ten), Tom (seven), Diana (six) and Unity (two). A few months after the move Sydney gave birth to Jessica (later known as Decca), and three years later Deborah was born. The Mitfords spent two years at Batsford House before moving to Asthall Manor, near Burford, in 1919. In 1927 they moved again to the newly built Swinbrook House, two miles east of Asthall.

Of the seven Mitford children, five gained fame or notoriety in adult life. Nancy was a comic novelist, whose pronouncements on "U" and "Non-U" etiquette for all social occasions made her the style guru of the 1950s. Deborah (usually known as Debo) married into the high aristocracy, inheriting the title of Duchess of Devonshire and becoming mistress of Chatsworth House. Diana caused a national scandal when she left her first husband for Oswald Mosley, the leader of the British Union of Fascists, while Decca took the opposite political route, joining the Communist Party and supporting the Republicans in Spain. Most notorious of all, Unity became a close friend of Adolf Hitler in the years leading up to the Second World War.

What was it in the Mitfords' country childhood that laid the ground for such dramatic adult lives? Fortunately, an excellent record survives in the writings of Nancy and Decca. For clever, ruthless Nancy, her childhood experiences provided perfect material for a comic novel. In *The Pursuit of Love*, the Mitford siblings are metamorphosed into the terrifying Radletts, a band of seven children cooped up in Alconleigh, a fortress-like country house based on the Mitfords' final home at Swinbrook. Nancy also made use of her parents in the novel, as David and Sydney Mitford become the terrifying Uncle Matthew and the vague Aunt Sadie, seen through the eyes of their fictional niece. Uncle Matthew is a particularly memorable creation, with his towering rages and irrational hatreds, his alarming habit of cracking his hunting whip and his passion for operatic arias played at top volume on his ancient gramophone.

When *The Pursuit of Love* was first published in 1945 its portrait of eccentric country life was viewed as the product of Nancy's fertile imagination. But most of its scenes and characters were shown to be true to life when Decca produced her memoir fifteen years later. *Hons and Rebels* tells the story of Decca's rebellion against her family background and includes a lively account of the terrors and tedium of her Cotswold childhood.

Later, the Mitford biographers added a wealth of detail to these accounts, providing a startling picture of a very unusual family life.

A Very Unusual Childhood

Nancy once described her three childhood homes as a gradual slide down the social scale, and her first Cotswold home was certainly the grandest. With its five separate staircases, dozens of rooms and exotic grounds, Batsford House must have provided a wonderful playground for the Mitford children, but it was ruinously expensive to run. After just two years at Batsford, the family moved to the more modest Asthall Manor, a rambling Jacobean manor house. Asthall was always intended as a temporary stopping place while the new family home was built. In fact the Mitfords stayed there for the next eight years, and it became their favourite family home.

Surrounded by beautiful gardens and with a spectacular view of the Windrush valley, Asthall Manor was immensely romantic. The nursery window looked out onto an ancient graveyard, and there was even a resident ghost whose footsteps could be heard at night pacing the terrace. Best of all, the children agreed, was the library, filled with Grandpa Redesdale's books and furnished with cosy armchairs. This glorious hideaway was separated from the rest of the house by a covered walkway, and became the children's special kingdom; the place where they indulged in their endless imaginative games, feuds and "teases".

Life for the Mitford children was firmly based at home. Despite the desperate entreaties of his older daughters, Lord Redesdale was adamant that none of his girls should run the risk of acquiring common habits by going to school. The girls were educated by a series of governesses, with varying degrees of success. The splendid Miss Mirams managed to give the older children an excellent early grounding, but (according to Decca) a later governess instructed her charges in the dubious art of shoplifting. In *Hons and Rebels* Decca claimed that Unity managed to frighten most of their governesses away. One unfortunate woman left in tears after an encounter with Unity's pet snake, Enid, wrapped around the lavatory chain.

Enid the snake was just one of the strange collection of pets kept by the Mitford children. In addition to the numerous family dogs, the house was full of pet rats, dormice and magpies. The girls were intensely involved with the chickens that Sydney kept for their eggs (Debo would often watch them for hours, studying their expressions intently), and Decca had a lamb, named Miranda, that accompanied her everywhere, sometimes even sharing her bed. The children's passion for animals led to constant warfare with Lord Redesdale's gamekeeper, who often found that his traps had been sabotaged. Nevertheless, they managed to enjoy the country sports of hunting and hare coursing. A favourite family sport was the "child hunt", in which Lord Redesdale chased through the countryside after a pair of his children with his bloodhounds in full pursuit. After a vigorous romp through fields and woods, the hunts usually ended with the human "hares" rewarding the slavering hounds with large chunks of meat. Apparently, the child hunts were greatly enjoyed by all, although they must have alarmed the Mitfords' country neighbours.

GAMES, QUARRELS AND HORROR AT SWINBROOK

Asthall Manor stands in the hamlet of Asthall, but it was the nearby village of Swinbrook that provided the focus for the Mitfords' social life. This was where Lord Redesdale had his shooting grounds, and where he eventually built the new family home. The girls made frequent expeditions to the village post office to post their letters and buy sweets, and church on Sundays was compulsory. Lord Redesdale held the patronage of Swinbrook church, a duty that he took very seriously. The choice of hymns was decided in advance by him (firmly avoiding any fancy foreign tunes) and sermons were never permitted to last longer than ten minutes. Just in case the vicar was tempted to digress, he would be confronted by the vision of Lord Redesdale consulting his stopwatch, and preparing to signal precisely two minutes before his time was up.

In 1927 the long-awaited house move took place, and the Mitfords finally took up residence in Swinbrook House. Every aspect of the new house had been carefully planned by Lord Redesdale, who boasted that his family would never need to leave home at all. Each of the seven children had their own bedroom, and there was a large schoolroom for their lessons. The house was surrounded by stables and garages, staff cottages and greenhouses, and even had its own squash and tennis courts. But Lord Redesdale's dream home was not a success. Its isolated position, standing on a high bluff north of the village, was very exposed, and its architecture was, in Decca's words, "frankly institutional". In *Hons and Rebels*, she famously describes the house as a mixture of a small barracks, a girls' board-

ing school, a private lunatic asylum and a country club, and acknowledges that it filled most of these roles for her family.

By the time of the move to Swinbrook House the four older children were no longer based at home, so Unity, Decca and Debo (aged thirteen, ten and seven) were left to entertain themselves. Deprived of their beloved library, the sisters took to gathering in a linen cupboard (the warmest place in a very draughty house) where they devised a set of fiendishly compli-cated games. Unity and Decca took the lead in all the games, inventing their own language known as "Boudledidge" and creating a secret society, known as the "Hons".

As the three youngest girls matured, the differences in their characters emerged. Debo developed into a natural countrywoman, perfectly happy with her country sports. Unity devoted much of her time to creating elab-orate historical collages such as "Hannibal Crossing the Alps", and Decca grew rebellious and discontented. In the volatile political climate of the early 1930s Unity and Decca formed opposing political allegiances: Unity nurtured a fascination for Hitler and the Nazis, while Decca followed the fortunes of the Russian communists. Soon the schoolroom at Swinbrook had been divided into two opposing camps, one side decorated with Unity's swastikas, the other covered in Decca's hammer and sickle designs.

In 1933 the schoolroom battle of loyalties took a serious turn when the nineteen-year-old Unity visited Germany with her sister Diana, and met Adolf Hitler. Unity was captivated by the Führer and returned the following year determined to catch his attention. Her campaign was successful and within a year she had become an honoured member of Hitler's circle. On her return to England Unity made no secret of her adventures, and there is even a story that she once startled the postmistress at Swinbrook by giving her a full Nazi salute. By 1936 Unity was spending most of her time in Germany, often in Hitler's company, and she was there when war broke out.

On the day that Britain declared war with Germany, Unity shot herself in the head in a public garden in Munich. She was dangerously ill but somehow survived and was eventually brought back to Britain in the full glare of a hostile British press. Her family were horrified by the changes in her. She had become childlike and irrational, and was incontinent and needed constant care. Sydney took on the task of nursing her grown-up daughter, taking her down to Swinbrook in the hope that the people who had known her daughter as a child would still be kind to her despite her terrible history. Back in her childhood village (although no longer in the grand Swinbrook House), Unity reverted to the behaviour and interests of her youth, living nine more years before she died in 1948.

Unity's suicide attempt triggered the break-up of the Mitford clan. After her return from Germany she and Decca never met again, and Decca spent the war years in America. As one of England's most high-profile fascist sympathizers, Diana was imprisoned for the duration of the Second World War, and Tom (the only boy in the family) was killed in action in Burma, six months before the end of the war. The family that had once enjoyed such exuberant games in the Cotswolds had been crushed and shattered.

Swinbrook Today

There are still many reminders of the Mitfords around Swinbrook. If you approach the village from Shipton-under-Wychwood, you will pass the gates to Swinbrook House, on the left-hand side of the road. The house stands on the brow of a hill, a tall rectangular building facing down the valley. Now softened by creepers, it has nevertheless kept its uncompromising air, but Swinbrook village is just as Decca described it: "a dozen grey cottages… huddled like Cotswold sheep, quiet and timeless." At the heart of the village is one of the loveliest parish churches in the Cotswolds. In the chancel a clear east window looks out on a perfect English scene and two sets of memorials commemorate the Fettiplaces, the original lords of the manor. The nave is filled with a set of varnished pews provided by Lord Redesdale and paid for, according to Decca, from his winnings on a racing bet. In the Mitfords' time the principal pew would have been entirely filled by the family, the girls all doing their best to make their brother "blither" (a family word for giggle). A more sombre reminder of the family dominates the back wall of the church, where two stone panels commemorate the lives of David and Sydney and their son, Thomas.

Beyond the church porch the graveyard is an attractive jumble of tombs, some of them surrounded by railings. This is where Decca recalls that the family pets were tethered while their owners attended church. In *Hons and Rebels* she describes (with some exaggeration) how the churchyard railings provided convenient cages for a sheep, several dogs, a goat and a dove "whose loud whelps, cooing and baaing blended nicely with the lusty voices of the village choir." Standing beside the path that leads from the churchyard out towards the fields are three simple stones to Nancy, Diana and Unity. Nancy's tomb is decorated by a mole, the animal on the Mitford coat-of-arms. Diana's simply states her name and dates. Unity's epitaph reads: "Say not the struggle naught availeth."

WOODCHESTER MANSION: THE HOUSE THAT WAS NEVER A HOME

In a list of England's weirdest houses Woodchester Mansion would have to come near the top. Hidden in its deep, wooded valley, the crumbling Gothic mansion was abandoned over a century ago when its Victorian builders suddenly downed tools, leaving their work half completed. Since then it has never been properly lived in and it is said to be one of the most haunted houses in the country.

Woodchester Mansion stands at the base of a steep-sided valley, two miles south of Stroud. On a sunny day it looks romantic and inviting, but for most of the year the house is in deep shadow. On the outer walls grotesque gargoyles leer down on visitors. Inside, corridors end in startling views of the valley beyond. Fireplaces hang suspended at a great height, and Victorian ladders remain propped up against exposed walls. The house is home to Britain's largest colony of rare horseshoe bats, which start to circle as soon as darkness falls. Only a handful of brave investigators have dared to stay the night in the empty mansion, where they have reported numerous sightings of ghosts, including a tall man in the chapel and a floating head in the bathroom.

The story of Woodchester Mansion began in the 1840s when William Leigh purchased a large Georgian manor house known as Spring Park. The house was named after the many springs in the area and stood in 400 acres of attractive grounds, although its position at the bottom of the valley was unhealthy and unwelcoming. Undeterred by these drawbacks, Leigh gave orders for Spring Park to be demolished, and began to plan a new house on the same spot.

Leigh was the son of a Liverpool trader and had inherited a small fortune from his father, but the driving force in his life was his Roman Catholic faith. The house he envisaged was to be a spiritual community inspired by the Gothic churches and monasteries he loved. Leigh consulted some of the leading architects of his day, but in the end the house was designed by an enthusiastic novice. Benjamin Bucknall was just twenty-one when he started work on his plans for Woodchester. Brilliantly inventive and passionate about Cotswold stone, he nevertheless lacked any practical experience. The result is a flawed masterpiece, reflecting the passions of two unusual Victorians.

Looking at Woodchester Mansion today, it is hard to imagine how it could ever have functioned as a family home. Constructed around a cloister-courtyard with a large chapel and a substantial brewery, bakery, and laundry, it is more of a monastic institution than a private house. Plumbing is almost non-existent (the whole surviving mansion has only one WC) and the kitchen is sited an inconvenient distance away from the dining room. The most exquisite part of the mansion is its chapel, with a delicate vaulted ceiling and rose window. Yet the chapel was planned to stand directly next door to the game larder, with its obnoxious odours of ripe hanging meat.

Despite the shortcomings in the Woodchester Mansion's layout, no expense was spared on its stonework. The house is constructed almost en-

tirely from Cotswold limestone, sometimes showing remarkable ingenuity. (A completed bathroom has bath, taps, pipes and water tanks all hewn from stone.) Inside and out the carved decorations are of the highest quality. One fireplace has an exquisite scene of the Garden of Eden, while ceiling bosses feature ferns and vines alongside mysterious faces of green men framed by leaves.

By 1852 work on the new mansion was under way, with a team of over a hundred workmen busy on the site. Meanwhile, William Leigh and his family settled into a large house on the estate. They were apparently in no hurry to move, and an intriguing rumour spread that the house was intended not as a family home, but as an English refuge for an unpopular Pope. Soon there were other rumours. It was said that workmen were falling to mysterious deaths. Ghosts were sighted and the locals whispered that the project was doomed. In 1868, after sixteen years of building, work on the house came to a sudden end and the workmen moved out, leaving behind a litter of tools that can still be seen in the house today.

Nobody knows why Woodchester Mansion was abandoned. Maybe William Leigh ran out of funds, or perhaps he simply lost faith in the project. (By 1868 all but one of his children had died.) Leigh's only surviving son did not share his father's taste for monastic living and kept away from the house. Later, Leigh's grandson stayed in the servants' quarters for a short time before the family eventually decided to sell up. During the Second World War Woodchester Mansion became a base for US and Canadian troops, and afterwards some of its rooms were used by a local school. In the 1950s the house was taken over by a local bat enthusiast, who maintained its roofs for twenty years. Finally, in the 1990s, a trust was established to carry out essential repairs whilst still keeping the house in its unfinished state. Today the mansion is used as a study centre for stonemasons and has been partially opened to the public. On certain days of the year visitors can follow a winding path into the valley to explore the mansion frozen in time.

TODDINGTON MANOR: DAMIEN HIRST'S TREASURE CAVE

While building work was progressing at Woodchester, another Gothic mansion was taking shape in the Cotswolds. Toddington Manor stands in over 120 acres of landscaped parkland close to the village of Toddington, four miles north of Winchcombe. The house was the pet project of Charles

Hanbury Tracy, who designed the house himself despite having no formal training in architecture. The result is a highly idiosyncratic building combining several different architectural personalities. From the east it resembles a stern medieval castle with towers and turrets. Viewed from the north, however, it seems more like a mixture of a Gothic church and an Oxbridge college. The house was in private ownership until the 1930s, and since then it has had a variety of roles, being used as an army barracks, a monastery and a school before lying empty for fifteen years.

In 2005 Toddington Manor was bought by the leading man of Brit Art, Damien Hirst. For most of the local residents this was good news (they had vigorously opposed a bid to convert the mansion into a hotel), but some of them must have felt a little alarmed. What could the man who loves to shock the art world be bringing to this quiet Cotswold village? Hirst has gradually revealed his plans for Toddington Manor. Over the next decade he will undertake a meticulous programme of restoration, with the help and advice of English Heritage. When finished, Hirst envisages that the mansion will provide the perfect showcase for his personal art collection, accumulated over the past twenty years. This collection, which he has named "Murderme", comprises over a thousand pieces, including works by Andy Warhol, Francis Bacon and Banksy, as well as many items reflecting Hirst's obsessions with sex and death. In an interview for *The Guardian* in 2006 he described his vision for Toddington as an "Aladdin's cave... stuffed with treasures... There won't be just art but totem poles, skulls of people who've been executed, macabre things."

Painswick Rococo Gardens: a miniature "landscape of delight"

Chapter Thirteen
SHAPING THE LANDSCAPE
GARDENS AND GARDENERS IN THE COTSWOLDS

"The transformation when you pass through the gate is immediate and stunning. On one side you are in a busy village, and on the other you are suddenly thrust into a rural Arcadia of the sort that seems incomplete without a couple of Gainsborough figures ambling by. Before me spread 2,000 acres of carefully composed landscape—stout chestnuts and graceful sycamores, billiard-table lawns, an ornamental lake bisected by an imposing bridge, and in the centre of it all the monumental baroque pile of Blenheim Palace. It was all very fine."

Bill Bryson, *Notes from a Small Island* (1993)

"How much I wish to be her guide thro that enchanted forest cannot be expressed: I look upon myself as the Magician appropriated to the place."
Alexander Pope, Letter describing the gardens at Cirencester Park (1722)

In the autumn of 1718 the poet Alexander Pope wrote a contented letter from Cirencester: "I am with Lord Bathurst in my bower, in whose groves we yesterday had a dry walk of three hours. It is the place of all others that I fancy…" The letter went on to outline how he spent his days: writing in the morning in his bower, hunting in the afternoon and drawing up plans for the estate in the evening. Together, Pope and Bathurst pondered elaborate schemes "to open avenues, cut glades, plant firs, contrive waterworks, all very fine and beautiful in our imagination." The result of their imaginings was Cirencester Park, a stretch of formal parkland extending west from the town. Combining regularity with romanticism, it was one of England's first experiments in the art of landscape gardening.

Cirencester Park: Alexander Pope's "Enchanted Forest"

Allen, 1st Earl Bathurst, inherited the family estate in 1704, at the age of twenty. Twelve years later he purchased the neighbouring Sapperton estate and plunged into the task of creating a park. Bathurst was a capable and energetic young man who enjoyed the company of poets and satirists, and chief among his friends was Alexander Pope (1688-1744). Apart from being a leading poet of the age Pope was an expert on the classical landscapes of ancient Rome and Greece and a passionate advocate of landscape gardening. With his encouragement, Bathurst rejected the formal rectangular gardens that had been the fashion in English country homes, and attempted to imitate the "amiable simplicity of unadorned nature". The result was a park whose paths still followed a strict pattern but which was softened by picturesque clumps of woodland.

While Lord Bathurst supervised the day-to-day work on his parkland, Alexander Pope paid frequent visits to Cirencester to check on the progress of the work. Pope would certainly have been involved in the construction of the classical temples scattered around the estate, including "the Sylvan bower" where he loved to write, hidden inside the copse known as Oakley Wood. In 1722 Pope wrote excitedly to the Honourable Robert Digby, offering to conduct his wife around the park: "How much I wish to be her guide thro that enchanted forest cannot be expressed: I look upon myself as the Magician appropriated to the place." The letter continues with Pope's ecstatic vision of the park's future glories, as he pictured it filled with glittering pavilions and colonnades. In reality, the park turned out to be far more low-key, although Bathurst did keep adding to the landscape for another fifty years. By the end of his life, he was able to see some of the results of his early plans. Sir Horace Walpole described the peer in his eighties enjoying "with philosophic calmness, the shade of those trees which he himself had planted half a century before."

Lord Bathurst could only imagine the vistas we enjoy today. From the viewpoint of Cirencester House (a rather plain, box-like structure shielded by a tall, semicircular hedge) the park resembles a large wood intersected by the straight Broad Avenue, with a set of rides radiating out towards the trees. Inside Pope's "enchanted forest" paths meander through the trees and ornamental buildings are artfully positioned. Some of the buildings are classical, while others are more eccentric. The castellated structure known as Alfred's Hall was the first "sham" castle in England and an object of considerable pride for Bathurst, who called it a "pretty little plain work in the Brobdingnag style." Bathurst was a friend of Jonathan Swift, the famous creator of Gulliver and the land of Brobdingnag, and Swift had lodged in an earlier version of Alfred's Hall. Bathurst later recalled an alarming incident; the day after Swift left the park the building collapsed, "conscious of the honour it had received by entertaining so illustrious a guest, it burst with pride."

EIGHTEENTH-CENTURY ELEGANCE: ROUSHAM, PAINSWICK AND STANWAY

Cirencester Park is a rare example of the short-lived "forest style" of landscaping that was soon to be eclipsed by more dramatic ways of shaping the land. By the 1730s a talented young architect called William Kent had introduced a new style to England. Kent was greatly impressed by the work of the architect Andrea Palladio, who had revived the classical style in Italy, and he adopted a similar approach, designing English houses and parklands in a classical, "Palladian" style.

William Kent's approach to the English landscape has often been compared to painting. Using perspective, light and shade, he created gardens that resembled the paintings of classical landscapes by such masters as Claude Lorraine and Nicolas Poussin. Kent's most famous creation is Stowe in Buckinghamshire, but he also shaped a spectacular landscape for Rousham House, just beyond the borders of the Oxfordshire Cotswolds. Here Kent introduced lakes and streams as well as temples, grottoes and statues. The result is a landscape of managed surprises, which was described by Sir Horace Walpole as "the most engaging of all Kent's works".

Kent's idealized landscapes proved immensely popular, and his elegant principles were soon being applied to gardens of all sizes. At Painswick in the western Cotswolds there is a rare example of a surviving small-scale garden in the picturesque style. Known today as Painswick Rococo Garden, it was created in the 1740s for Benjamin Hyett, the young owner of Painswick House, who transformed the hidden valley behind his home into a miniature pleasure park. Hyett's garden was constructed on a steep slope and incorporated winding paths through woods and an arrangement of miniature buildings. At the garden's entrance a statue of the boy god Pan establishes a mood of playful frivolity. The garden buildings include the Eagle House, the Pigeon House and the Red House, all built in a flamboyant Neo-Gothic style. Most spectacular of all is the Exedra, a semi-circular structure offering wonderful vistas through its arched windows. By the nineteenth century picturesque landscapes had fallen out of fashion, and the grounds of Painswick House were adapted for growing vegetables. However, in 1984 a campaign was launched to restore the gardens, with the help of an eighteenth-century painting showing them in their original state. Today the Painswick gardens have largely been reclaimed, and visitors can experience some of the pleasure and romance of an eighteenth-century landscape of delight.

Palladian gardens were famous for their elaborate water features, as seen at Rousham, where the gardens include cascades, fountains, and square pools. All these features were installed by Charles Bridgeman, and he was probably also responsible for the work at Stanway House. The manor house at Stanway (near Winchcombe) is set in steeply wooded parkland and its spectacular water garden was added in the 1720s. Over the last decade, a restoration programme has returned the eighteenth-century features to partial working order. Today, a formal canal runs along a terrace above the house, while a pyramid obelisk, eight ponds and a long cascade have all been reinstated. Adding to the effect is a modern single-jet fountain, claimed to be the tallest in Britain.

CAPABILITY BROWN AT BLENHEIM

While William Kent created elegant landscape scenes, Lancelot Brown worked with a broader brush. Brown rose to be head gardener at Stowe before embarking on a thirty-year career as a landscaper. A great enthusiast for his craft, he could always see an estate's "capability" for improvement, and soon earned the nickname of "Capability" Brown. Brown's approach to landscaping is sometimes known as the Serpentine style because it echoed the natural undulations of the English landscape, introducing sinuous lakes, sweeping drives and circular clumps of trees. He is famous today for his work at Chatsworth, Longleat and Bowood House, but perhaps his greatest achievement was the transformation of the grounds of Blenheim Palace.

When Capability Brown arrived at Blenheim in 1764 he took over a park that had already been partly tamed. In the 1700s Sir John Vanburgh had overseen the deforestation of the land (which had previously been a royal hunting park) and had imposed some grandiose features of his own. Surrounding the newly built palace was a broad parterre and a walled formal garden, while an enormous bridge spanned the streams of the marshy River Glyme. Vanburgh's bridge was a vast creation, rising to fifty feet and containing 33 rooms for parties and trysts. Its incongruous size had attracted much ridicule, prompting Alexander Pope to write:

the minnows , as under this vast arch they pass,
murmur how like whales we look, thanks to your Grace.

By the 1760s, such artifice was no longer in fashion. With the support of the fourth duke, Capability Brown set to work to "naturalize" the landscape, adding hills, planting copses and covering the parterres with extensive lawns. In a dramatic move, he dammed the River Glyme, creating a large lake in front of the palace. Ornamental cascades were built at the entrance and exit points of the river, and the lake was narrowed to pass under Vanburgh's bridge, flooding and submerging most of its rooms. The lake was seen as Brown's masterstroke, creating one of England's most picturesque views.

Other designers added more "improvements" over the following decades, including a set of pleasure gardens with formal flowerbeds, statues and follies. In particular, the 5th Duke of Marlborough (1766-1840) was a great garden enthusiast, importing plants and trees from all over the world and erecting a range of unusual buildings, such as a Swiss cottage, a Druid's temple and an Eskimo's hut. One of the more alarming features of the duke's gardens was a pivoted boulder, operated by a hidden spring and designed to roll out suddenly and surprise his visitors. Most of the follies at Blenheim were later dismantled, although the graceful Temple to Diana still remains—and was the site of Winston Churchill's proposal of marriage to Clementine Hozier in 1908. One generation earlier, Winston's mother Jennie described her first view of the Blenheim estate in a letter to her sister:

> As we passed through the entrance archway and the lovely scenery burst
> upon me, Randolph said with pardonable pride, 'This is the finest view
> in England.'

HUMPHRY REPTON (AND JANE AUSTEN) IN THE COTSWOLDS

Humphry Repton is generally regarded as the last of the great eighteenth-century landscapers. Less directly involved in the landscaping process than Kent or Brown, he acted as a consultant to the landowners of his day, recording detailed plans in his famous "red books". Over the course of his thirty-year career Repton undertook dozens of commissions, and he is associated with three very different Cotswold places. At Dyrham Park he acted as a "landscape improver", replacing the formal gardens with a park of gentle hills. At Sezincote he provided a suitable setting for an exotic Indian garden, and in the village of Adlestrop (near Stow-on-the-Wold) he remodelled the grounds of the manor house and rectory.

Sometime before 1806 Henry Leigh, squire of Adlestrop, commissioned Humphry Repton to work on his grounds. Leigh had rebuilt Adlestrop Park in the latest Gothic style and was keen to modernize his estate. At the same time he also commissioned Repton to design a new garden for his cousin at the rectory. The cousin was the Rev. Thomas Leigh, uncle to Jane Austen, an occasional visitor at the Cotswold rectory. When Jane stayed at Adlestrop in 1806 she was treated to a tour of the remodelled gardens at the rectory and the park. Her reaction to the changes is not known, but it can be guessed from a passage in her novel *Mansfield Park* (completed in 1811). In the novel her character Mr. Rushton gushingly describes an ancient country house whose grounds had been laid out "by an improver" with the result that "I never saw a place so altered in my life. I told Smith I did not know where I was… you see the house in the most surprising manner." In the discussion that follows Repton's name is mentioned several times as Austen highlights, with characteristic irony, some serious concerns about the "improvement" of country estates.

CHASTLETON HOUSE: A JACOBEAN WONDERLAND

The vogue for "improvement" that swept through England has left few examples of early gardens, but the remains of a Jacobean garden can still be seen at Chastleton House. Chastleton was built in the northern Cotswolds, in the 1610s and its grounds were probably laid out at the same time. Following the fashion of the time, they were divided into separate compartments or "courts". At the front of the house the "Fore Court" was mainly laid out as lawn, with a row of shrubs flanking the central path. On the eastern side of the house the large "Best Garden" was overlooked by the most important rooms, while the "Base Court" lay on the western side, close to the brew-house and the stable range. To the north of the house there was probably a bowling green, linked to a kitchen garden. Each of these garden courts was separate from its neighbours, and the Best Garden provided a private space for the master of the house and his guests.

Visitors have a splendid view of the Best Garden from the windows of the Great Parlour at Chastleton. No longer laid out with formal beds, it has retained its topiary ring: a large circle of bushes trimmed into different shapes. The bushes have been replanted at least twice and in the nineteenth century they were reshaped in some fantastical Alice in Wonderland forms, resembling a cake-stand, a cat, a teapot, a sheep, a chicken, a squirrel, a sailing ship, a peacock and a crown. Today their shapes have become intriguingly ill-defined.

Chastleton's other glories are its croquet lawns. In the 1850s the house was inherited by Walter Jones Whitmore, an eccentric young bachelor who devoted his time to inventing gadgets and playing croquet. At that time croquet had only just arrived from Ireland and had been taken up by a small band of enthusiasts, including the Rev. Dodgson (otherwise known as Lewis Carroll). Walter practised his croquet tirelessly at Chastleton, pondering different approaches and strategies, and in 1865 he wrote the definitive rules for the game, which were published by *The Field*. Two years later he organized the first ever croquet tournament in England, from which he emerged as the winner, and in the same year he published *Croquet Tactics with Coloured Diagrams*, billed as the work of "a Champion Player". Walter organized one more tournament before he died from cancer at the age of 41, but he is not forgotten at Chastleton. Today a perfect lawn is laid out for croquet in memory of the man who is known as the father of the modern game.

OWLPEN MANOR: GARDENS OF PARADISE

Owlpen Manor is one of the Cotswolds' most romantic places. Set in a steeply wooded valley seven miles west of Tetbury, the Tudor manor house is surrounded by seven terraces linked by gravel paths and steep stone steps. Most of the terraces date back to the sixteenth and seventeenth centuries and are laid out as formal parterres, with rectangles of lawn enclosed by low box hedges and flowerbeds. There is a circular walk around a Georgian millpond, a raised stilt hedge and a walled kitchen garden. Most dramatic of all is the Yew Parlour, dominating the western approach to the house. The parlour is made up of a group of closely-planted trees, trimmed to form a rectangular, roofless outdoor chamber. It was probably originally planted in the eighteenth century and has been known at various times as the "Green Drawing-Room", the "Ballroom" and the "Dancing Floor".

In 1848 Owlpen Manor was abandoned, as its owners moved to Owlpen House, a grand new mansion less than a mile away. Sitting amongst its terraces, just across the valley from their new home, the old manor house became a romantic destination for the family and their visitors, and its gardens gained a semi-mystical significance. To Owlpen's Victorian visitors the twelve yews of the Yew Parlour represented the Twelve Apostles, the seven terraces were the Seven Gardens of Paradise, and the narrow gate leading to the church was the Needle's Eye, the entrance to the ultimate Paradise Garden.

Life at the new mansion did not continue for long. By the 1840s Owlpen House was empty, and the original manor house was left to decay, although the gardens were carefully maintained. In 1914 Gertrude Jekyll visited Owlpen to make plans and notes on the gardens, and many others followed, especially after the house had been restored in 1926. Geoffrey

Jellicoe was moved by the Englishness of the Owlpen garden and its medieval sense of mystery, and admired the simplicity and scale of its plan, which he recorded carefully in a set of bird's-eye views. For Vita Sackville-West the gardens at Owlpen were "a dream", one of the places "one has seen and loved." Its "dark, secret rooms of yew... that made rooms in the garden with walls taller than any rooms in the house" were the inspiration for her famous yew parlours at Sissinghurst.

ARTS AND CRAFTS GARDENS IN THE COTSWOLDS

Ten miles east of Owlpen is Rodmarton Manor, one of the finest achievements of the Arts and Crafts movement. The house was designed by Ernest Barnsley who was also responsible for laying out the grounds. Barnsley was fascinated by the relationship between gardens and landscape, and he devised a set of gardens that became increasingly informal as their distance from the house grew. Today you can still see Barnsley's series of garden "rooms" at Rodmarton, enclosed by hedges and walls, while at the far end of the estate is his original Wild Garden, marking the transition from garden to farmland.

The gardens at Rodmarton Manor cover eight acres, but the same principles can be seen on a much smaller scale at Snowshill Manor, where the gardens slope down from the house in a set of terraced rooms, each enclosed by walls and gates. Incorporated in the garden design are a couple of barns, and all the woodwork is painted a distinctive turquoise-blue. The gardens at Snowshill were created by Baillie Scott in close collaboration with Charles Paget Wade, who bought Snowshill Manor in 1919. Inside the house, one enters a maze of rooms stuffed with Wade's possessions, and the gardens convey a similar impression: a set of linked outdoor rooms stocked with a profusion of plants and flowers. The blue of the garden woodwork was developed by Wade, who believed that no green paint could ever rival nature's greens.

MAJOR LAWRENCE JOHNSON AT HIDCOTE MANOR

Snowshill nestles in a cosy valley but as you travel north, the landscape changes. By the time you reach the village of Hidcote Bartrim, three miles north-east of Chipping Campden, you are in a region of high, bare ground and windswept fields. This was the unpromising canvas that Major Lawrence Johnson inherited when his mother bought Hidcote Manor in

1907. Over the next forty years, however, this self-taught genius created one of England's most influential gardens.

The gardens at Hidcote are famously divided into a complex structure of "corridors" and "rooms" formed by towering hedges. Hidcote's high hedges offer essential protection from the wind but also define the garden's character: a place of geometrical precision, softened by lavish plantings, and full of visual surprises and bold new views. Within his garden rooms Johnson focused on different ideas, sometimes concentrating on a particular colour or species (as in the White Garden, the Fuchsia Garden and the Red Borders), sometimes building a garden around a special feature (as in the Pillar Garden, Stilt Garden and Terrace Garden). Two of Hidcote's most dramatic features are the grassy Long Walk, leading to a gateway with spectacular views, and the Theatre Lawn, where plays are sometimes staged in an amphitheatre of yews. But the Hidcote gardens are not all formal. On the wilder outskirts of his estate Johnson established areas of woodland as well as a fern garden and a water garden.

Little is known about Lawrence Johnson the man. Born into a wealthy American family, he spent most of his adult life in England, attending Cambridge University before joining the army. After the First World War he retired from army life aged 47 and devoted the rest of his life to gardening and plant-collecting. In a never-ending quest for new species Johnson undertook botanical expeditions to the Alps, Kenya and South Africa, and swapped plants with collectors in Australia and Japan. (This enthusiasm for exotic species was shared by several other Cotswold plant collectors, most notably "Chinese" Wilson of Chipping Campden and Sir George Holford of Westonbirt.) Johnson never married and played the dutiful son until his mother's death, creating a special garden room for her at Hidcote known as Mrs. Winthrop's Garden. In 1948, after forty years of work in his Cotswold garden, he moved to France, leaving Hidcote Manor to the National Trust. Since then the gardens at Hidcote have provided inspiration for millions of gardeners. They are also the source of the famous "Hidcote lavender" with its distinctive deep violet flowers.

TWO WOMEN'S VISIONS: KIFTSGATE COURT AND BARNSLEY HOUSE

Less than a mile from Hidcote is another spectacular Cotswold garden. Kiftsgate Court is a handsome Georgian-fronted house standing on the

edge of the northern Cotswold escarpment. Today it is the centrepiece of an inspired garden begun in 1918 by a remarkable plantswoman, Heather Muir. With the help and advice of her friend and neighbour, Lawrence Johnson, Muir created a garden that shares some features with Hidcote (such as a series of colour-themed "rooms") but has a more relaxed and idiosyncratic character. Surrounding the house are a number of brilliantly colourful walks and terraces. The steep hillside to the south-west is planted with shrubs and trees and provides spectacular views of the Malvern Hills.

Since its creation ninety years ago, Kiftsgate has been in the care of three generations of women, passing from Heather Muir to her daughter Diany Binney, and then to her granddaughter, Anne Chambers. In the 1970s Diany commissioned a set of striking sculptures from Simon Verity, and Anne has converted a tennis court into a modern water garden. In 2003 the critic and gardener Robin Lane Fox reported from Kiftsgate: "the next generation's hand is no less firm and their eyes are no less discerning. The tapestry is richer and rarer than ever."

Rosemary Verey (who died in 2001) was one of Britain's best-known gardeners. The author of numerous garden books including *The English-woman's Garden* and *The Garden in Winter*, she is perhaps best known for her own garden in the Cotswolds. In 1951 she moved with her four children into her husband's family home, a seventeenth-century manor house in the village of Barnsley, but it was another ten years before she turned her attention to the garden. Over the next three decades the garden at Barnsley House evolved into an eclectic mixture of styles, combining historical designs with cottage garden planting and carefully planned vistas of the English countryside.

Despite its modest size— covering less than five acres—the garden at Barnsley House is full of variety. There is a laburnum and wisteria tunnel, a knot garden, a Gothic summerhouse and a neoclassical stone temple, imported stone by stone from nearby Fairford Park. Multiple layers of planting ensure that the garden stays colourful throughout the year, while fruit and vegetables form part of the total scheme, planted in ornamental potagers.

THE GARDENER PRINCE AT HIGHGROVE

Sometime in the early 1980s Rosemary Verey received a surprising telephone call. Convinced it was a hoax, she reprimanded the caller for making a joke so early in the morning. In fact the call was genuine: HRH Prince Charles was calling to ask her advice. It was the start of a long co-operation as her Cotswold neighbour took on the task of creating a remarkable garden.

Acting on advice from some of Britain's finest garden designers (including Rosemary Verey, Miriam Rothschild and Sir Roy Strong) the prince has created a set of themed spaces that encompass an Italian garden, an Islamic garden and a garden of the Southern Hemisphere. Some of the effects at Highgrove are extremely striking. At the back of the house a long path is flanked by a series of abstract topiary shapes. The black and white garden has white lupins and peonies mixed with black grasses, while the Victorian "stumpery" is a highly sculptural collection of old tree roots, which provides an ideal habitat for ferns and insects.

Not all the Highgrove estate is devoted to formal gardening. Since the 1980s the Prince of Wales has planted 10,000 trees and nine miles of hedgerows. His famous Wildflower Meadow covers four acres and includes over thirty varieties of endangered native plants. Over the last three decades gardening has clearly become a royal passion. A TV documentary celebrating Prince Charles' sixtieth birthday featured him happily at work in his garden at Highgrove. Ten years earlier, the poet U. A. Fanthorpe composed a birthday poem for her royal neighbour. Entitled "A Brief Résumé at Fifty", the poem surveys a very public life, but also celebrates the Prince as a private man, ending with a gentle benediction: "…may/Your Gloucestershire garden grow."

The Badminton Horse Trials: one of
the star attractions of the Cotswold
sporting year

Chapter Fourteen

THE COTSWOLDS AT PLAY

SPORTS, GAMES AND LEISURE PURSUITS

"It is not surprising that in those countries which abound in sunshine and fresh, health-giving air the inhabitants will invariably be found to be not only keen sportsmen, but also accomplished experts in all the games and pastimes for which England has long been famous… for this reason we have christened the district of which we write the 'Merrie Cotswolds'."

J. Arthur Gibbs, A Cotswold Village (1898)

To the young J. Arthur Gibbs, squire of Ablington Manor (near Cirencester), the "Merrie Cotswolds" offered the perfect playground: a place where the sun shone, the air was healthy and the natives engaged in wholesome sports and pastimes. Gibbs' *A Cotswold Village: Or Country Life and Pursuits in Gloucestershire* was published in 1898 and contains chapters on: "A gallop over the walls" (describing the joys of hunting); "A Cotswold Trout Stream" (on fly-fishing); "When the May-fly is Up" (more on fishing); "On the Wolds" (on shooting in the wolds); and "Cotswold Pastimes" (on traditional games and cricket). Early in his account Gibbs provides a list of the sporting events to be enjoyed throughout the year, starting in spring with trout-fishing in the Coln and Windrush, local hunt races at Moreton-in-Marsh and the larger race meetings at Whitsuntide, then moving on to summer when he enjoyed cricket matches and the Cirencester Horse Show. By September it was time for the shooting season to begin, with pheasant, quail and partridges to be bagged, and in the winter there was fox hunting with hounds. Surveying this endless round of pleasures, Gibbs concludes (somewhat complacently): "Time passes quickly for the sportsman who has the good fortune to dwell in the merry Cotswolds"—and the Cotswolds' image of a sporting playground is still very much alive today.

COTSWOLD GAMES.

Some Cotswold Games have an ancient pedigree. Robert Dover's first "Cotswold Olimpicks" were held near Chipping Campden in 1604

HUNTING COUNTRY

Hunting in the Cotswolds has an ancient pedigree. As early as the tenth century the Saxon kings of England were chasing stags and boar in Woodstock Park, the royal hunting ground in Wychwood Forest. Every English monarch from Ethelred the Unready to Charles II is said to have hunted at Woodstock, using a famous palace as their base. Nothing now remains of Woodstock Palace, but an elegant Tudor hunting lodge survives in the western Cotswolds, two miles east of Wotton-under-Edge. Around 1550, the lodge now known as Newark Park was built for Sir Nicholas Poyntz, a leading courtier of King Henry VIII. Poyntz lived ten miles away at Acton Court and the lodge was built with the purpose of entertaining his guests after a hard day's hunting. The lodge was compactly constructed on four floors, with kitchens in the basement and a set of reception rooms on the ground floor. A banqueting chamber occupied the first floor, and the top floor was reserved for sleeping quarters. Looking out from the lodge, Poyntz and his friends would have enjoyed spectacular views of his hunting grounds stretching over the valleys towards the River Severn.

Another major hunting ground in the western Cotswolds belonged to the Duke of Beaufort of Badminton Park. In the 1730s the 3rd duke was a keen participant in country sports, enjoying stag-hunting, hare coursing and hawking. Thirty years later, his grandson is credited with introducing fox hunting to Gloucestershire. By the early nineteenth century the Beaufort Hunt had become a lavish public event attracting hordes of eager spectators. On one memorable occasion, more than a thousand people were invited by the duke to join in a grand hunt breakfast on the lawns of Badminton House. The Beaufort Hunt is still active in south Gloucestershire, although the recent anti-hunting laws have somewhat altered the character of its meets.

EQUESTRIAN SPORTS

Hunting is just one of many "horsey" sports that can be enjoyed in the Cotswolds. There are major racecourses at Cheltenham and Bath. The wolds are home to some famous horse trials, and the local sporting calendars are full of point-to-points, polo games and gymkhanas.

Three significant events in the equestrian year are held in the western Cotswolds. In March the racetrack at Cheltenham hosts the Gold Cup, probably the most prestigious National Hunt horse race in Britain. The race is a steeplechase (a mixture of racing on the flat and jumping over hurdles) covering three miles with 22 fences. Steeplechasing at Cheltenham began in the 1800s, and the Gold Cup race acquired its famous name in the 1920s. The race is part of the four-day Cheltenham Festival, which also includes the Queen Mother Champion Chase. HRH the Queen Mother never missed the races at Cheltenham and was still attending her Champion Chase at the age of one hundred.

The Badminton Horse Trials, held in May, attract record-breaking numbers of spectators. Started in 1949 as a way of training British riders for international events, they have been called the world's most important horse trials. Today the four-day event includes dressage displays, cross-country races and jumping events, all held in the extensive grounds of Badminton Park.

Less than fifteen miles north-east of Badminton is Gatcombe Park, the home of the Princess Royal, an outstanding horsewoman who was a member of the British Olympic team in 1976. Since 1983 the princess has opened her grounds every August for the Gatcombe Park Festival of British Eventing. Like the Badminton Trials, the Gatcombe Festival features cross-country, show jumping and dressage events. The chance to see Zara Phillips in action on her home course makes this a star attraction for the horse-loving public.

While Zara Phillips draws the crowds at Gatcombe, other young members of the Royal Family appear on the polo field. Polo requires excellent horsemanship and nerve, and Princes William and Harry are both keen players, often seen playing at the Beaufort Polo Club. The Beaufort was founded in 1894 inside the walls of Cirencester Park and is the oldest polo ground in England. Its idyllic surroundings make it probably the prettiest as well.

The glamorous worlds of polo and horse-racing are mercilessly satirized in the novels of Jilly Cooper. For over twenty years Cooper has lived in the heart of Cotswold racing country, and is the proud owner of her own racehorse. Using her inside knowledge (and adding generous dollops of sex and scandal) she has produced two best-sellers: *Polo* and *Riders*. Some real-life memories of Cotswold sports are recalled by Xandra Bingley in *Bertie, May and Mrs Fish: Country Memories of Wartime* (2005). Bingley's account of her childhood on a farm near Cirencester includes some descriptions of hunting that are not for the faint-hearted, and a comic record of a family outing to the Cheltenham races.

Ancient Races

Today's horse racing events have some ancient antecedents in the Cotswolds. In 1621 a racecourse was established on the high ground between Bibury and Burford, and King Charles II became a regular at the races, sometimes in the company of his mistress Nell Gwyn. During Bibury Race Week the inns at Bibury and Burford were overtaken by members of high-society, intent on high-living. Their pleasure-loving monarch is believed to have stayed at the newly-built Bibury Court (now a country hotel).

Another royal regular at the Bibury races was the famously dissolute George IV, who usually stayed with Lord Sherborne, owner of the nearby Sherborne Estate. Sherborne came from a family of gamblers who owned a very unusual racing ground. In the 1630s John Dutton of Sherborne had paid for a deer course to be created inside his deer park, along with a small personal grandstand. The notoriously cruel pastime of deer coursing involved releasing the deer onto a racing track, closely pursued by grey-hounds, a "sport" intended to display the skill of the dogs and to offer opportunities for gambling. In the comfort of his elegant, classical grandstand, Dutton and his friends—and several later generations of the Sherborne family—would dine and drink and place their bets, whilst enjoying an exclusive sporting event. Today the grandstand, known as Lodge Park, is open to the public, who can view the deer course from its windows and roof.

Cricket on the Wolds

In summertime Arthur Gibbs turned his attention to cricket, although he complained that conditions were far from ideal, protesting at the state of the village pitches and the local players' lack of style. *A Cotswold Village* contains accounts of two chaotic matches. One, held at Edgeworth (near Stroud), was played in a bumpy meadow on the summit of a hill and could not begin until the players located the pitch: "It was the fat butler, I think, who, after sailing about in a sea of waving buttercups like a veritable Christopher Columbus, first discovered the stumps amongst the mowing grass." The match then proceeded cheerfully with much good-natured chaff flying about… but no fighting or squabbling, save when a boundary hit was made, when the batsman always shouted "Three runs," and the bowler "No, only one." The scores were not high; but I remember that we won by three runs, that the carpenter's son got a black eye, that we had tea in an old manor house turned into an inn, and drove home in a glorious sunset, not entirely displeased with our first experience of "prehistoric" cricket.

Another comic match took place at Bourton-on-the-Water, which Gibbs renamed "Bourton-on the bog" on account of its soggy, wasp-infested pitch. There he encountered a redoubtable local side ("on their own native 'bog' they are fairly invincible"), but the real problems began in the luncheon tent:

> What more lively scene could be imagined than a large tent with twenty-two cricketers and a few hundred wasps at work eating and drinking; then, on the tent suddenly collapsing, the said cricketers and the said wasps mixed up with chairs, tables, ham, beef, salad-dressing, and apple tart… all struggling on the floor, and striving to get out as best they can?

Despite these catastrophes Gibbs expressed his admiration for the keenness of the local players, describing the pleasure of watching "boys and men hard at work practising on sunny evenings. The rougher the

Village cricketers

ground the more they like it… They play on, long after sunset, the darker it gets, and the more dangerous to life and limb the game becomes, the happier they are."

Arthur Gibbs would be pleasantly surprised by the Cotswolds' cricket grounds today. At Swinbrook and Minster Lovell picturesque, well-rolled pitches lie close to the riverbanks, and at Ashton under Hill the ground is perfectly framed by hills. The Stanway cricket pitch is bordered by giant trees and lies close to the handsome Jacobean gateway of Stanway House. It has an unusual, thatched pavilion raised on saddle stones, a gift from James Barrie (the author of *Peter Pan*), who spent his summers at Stanway in the 1920s, and arranged many memorable matches for his literary guests. At Sheepscombe, near Stroud, the cricket pitch is dramatically sited on a hill above the village. Laurie Lee called it a "classic cricket ground with one of the best views in Gloucestershire". Laurie's uncles, grandfather and great-grandfather all played at Sheepscombe, and he sometimes took a turn there himself, running up the hill to bowl at a batsman who only gradually came into view. When Laurie Lee returned to the Cotswolds as a successful writer he became a patron of Sheepscombe Cricket Club, eventually buying the pitch outright to ensure that play could continue on Sheepscombe hill.

THE COTSWOLD OLIMPICKS

As well as the usual national sports, people in the Cotswolds indulge in some curious local pastimes. By far the most famous of these is Dover's Cotswold Olimpicks, sometimes simply known as the Cotswold Games, held every spring in Chipping Campden.

The original Cotswold Games were the brainchild of a certain Robert Dover, a local attorney known for his generosity. Dover was a fun-loving gentleman who deplored the killjoy attitudes of the Puritans, and around the year 1604 decided to inaugurate some Whitsun games for the people of Campden. On a grassy plateau close to the town (later named Dover's Hill) he organized a mixture of celebrations and traditional sports that included hare coursing, hunting, and fighting with cudgels. The first games were sponsored by two local worthies: Sir Baptist Hicks, the fabulously rich clothier of Chipping Campden, and Endymion Porter of Aston-sub-Edge, Groom of the Bedchamber to King James I. Porter was so enthusiastic about the games that he even donated "some of the King's old cloathes with a Hat and Feather and a Ruff" for Dover to wear to the grand opening ceremony.

Dover's Olimpicks proved such a success that they became an annual Campden event, and they were still thriving twenty years later, when he was presented with a volume of poems to celebrate his achievement. The frontispiece of the book shows Robert Dover presiding over the games, with a mock wooden castle perched on the hill behind him. Inside, a collection of poems pays tribute to his achievement and includes an address by Ben Johnson congratulating "my Jovial Good Friend Mr Robert Dover, on his great Instauration of his Hunting and Dancing at Cotswold." Michael Drayton also piled on the praise:

> … Lo! this is the man
> Dover, that first these noble sports began.
> Lads of the hill and lasses of the vale,
> In many a song and many a merry tale,
> Shall mention thee, and having leave to play,
> Unto thy name shall make a holiday.

Apart from a brief interruption for the Civil War the Cotswold Games continued well into the nineteenth century, when notices in the town announced that:

> The Sports will commence
> With a good match of Backswords

and listed other games such as

> Wrestling
> for belts and other prizes
> also
> Jumping in bags and Dancing
> And a Jingling Match.

By this time the Olimpicks were attracting a rowdy crowd from the industrial Midlands, swelled by workers on the railways, and in 1851 some 30,000 people poured into the town, intent on merry making, drinking and brawling. This was all too much for the Campden burgers who closed down the games on the grounds of public order. (A local cleric recorded that "Dover's Hill [had become] a meeting of the lowest characters merely for debauchery.") However, this was not the end of the games. In 1953 the Cotswold Olimpicks were re-enacted for the Festival of Britain, and ten years later they were reintroduced as an annual event. Today the Cotswolds Olimpicks are held on Dover's Hill on the Friday after the May Bank Holiday. Cannons fire from a wooden castle, bands march and play and hearty Cotswolders compete in rustic sports, such as welly-wanging, shin-kicking, sack-races and tugs-of-war. There are displays of falconry and Morris dancing, and just before 10 p.m. the May Queen lights a bonfire—the signal for a grand firework display. The evening ends with a torchlight procession down the hill and dancing in Campden Square. The following day the fun continues with the annual Scuttlebrook Wake, when the May Queen is crowned and the fair comes to Campden.

FESTIVALS, FAIRS AND MERRYMAKING

Accounts of Cotswold life in the early years of the twentieth century are filled with descriptions of merrymaking. Writing in 1924, Algernon Gissing describes some important days in his village calendar. On St. Thomas' Day (21 December) the village children "went a Thomasing" to collect money and apples. On the first day of May the May Queen was crowned with dancing round the maypole, and on Midsummer's Day the village held its annual "wake" and a travelling fair arrived for the evening. In September Harvest Home was celebrated with a village feast, and in the days leading up to Guy Fawkes' Night, the boys built a giant bonfire on the green.

Right up until the time of the First World War each Cotswold town and village had its own "wake", often held on the saint's day of the parish church. Looking back on the years before the war, Sid Knight remembered the scene at Broadway Wake:

> Excitement quickens as the crowd thickens [on Broadway Green]. The rifles on Atwell's Royal Rifle Range crack like a battalion at musketry practice, as the stolid metal figures move woodenly along their endless belt, the multicoloured celluloid balls spiral on top of the fluctuating up-and-down waterspouts as young Atwell sweats at the hand-pump

trying to keep up the pressure. "Penny a ride" shout ragged young urchins as they pummel the sorry donkeys along to China Square and back. One good thing, the poor overworked animals will have all day to lie on the green and chew the luscious grass.

Mont Abbot recalled similar scenes at Enstone Club Day, when all the villagers joined in a grand parade and dinner followed by an evening's fun at the fair. Other highlights of the Enstone year included busking on Boxing Day and the summer cross-country race. In the long summer evenings men gathered in inns to sing the old songs and children played in the village streets. Mont described their games of "holey-holey" and "jump jinny-wagtail" and remembered the day in 1915 when the local sergeant arrived with an announcement: "Children! Motors is coming. After tonight all you childern must no longer play in this 'ere road!"

CHEESE ROLLING, RIVER FOOTBALL AND OTHER STRANGE PURSUITS
The coming of motorcars, cinema and TV put an end to most traditional Cotswold games, but a few have survived into the twenty-first century. Close to the village of Brockworth (six miles south-west of Cheltenham) the precipitous Cooper's Hill is the site of a famous cheese-rolling race held every summer for the last two hundred years. On a signal from the master of ceremonies, a "guest roller" releases a giant Double Gloucester cheese at the brow of the hill and all the contestants race down after it. The first one to the bottom wins the cheese, but the extreme steepness of the hill (in places the gradient is 1 in 1) guarantees plenty of thrills and spills on the way. Nobody knows exactly how the custom began, but it may have been a way of claiming villagers' rights to graze sheep on the hill.

A rather less dangerous race takes place every May in the market town of Tetbury, where young men and women hurtle through the town carrying sacks of wool on their backs. Teams of four run in relays up and down Gumstool Hill (a street with a 1 in 4 gradient). The Tetbury woolsack races date back to the seventeenth century and probably began as a test of strength for the young wool drovers of the neighbourhood.

The origins of one local sporting custom are easy to trace. In 1902 a group of villagers in Bourton-on-the-Water chose an unusual way to celebrate the coronation of King Edward VII. Taking advantage of the famous

Bourton "water" (a shallow stretch of the River Windrush running through the village green), they set up goal posts in the river and played a riotous game of football. The tradition of "football in the river" has continued unbroken up to the present day. Every August Bank Holiday two teams of six play in knee-deep water for fifteen minutes each way. The game attracts large crowds of spectators and ends with a fair on the green.

Some other surviving customs are less boisterous, but still provide a chance for villagers to make merry. The Randwick Wap takes place in May in the village of Randwick (just north of Stroud) and involves a colourful procession of costumed villages led by a "Mop Man" wielding a wet mop to clear the crowds. A "mayor and his queen" are carried shoulder high, and the procession ends in a dunking for the mayor in the village pond. (The origins of this custom are unknown but they may have been linked to preparations for battle.) In Painswick, an annual "church clipping" ceremony is held every September. The local children wear flowers in their hair and join hands in a dance to embrace or "clip" St. Mary's Church. On Pig Face day at Avening (three miles north of Tetbury) the head of a pig is carried into church on a plate, in an obscure ceremony in memory of Queen Matilda. The service is followed by a lively banquet and fair with villagers dressed in medieval costume.

Morris Dancers (And Some Strong Reactions)

Most Cotswold festivities feature Morris dancers, especially on May Morning, when the ancient custom of dancing on the green has been revived in many villages. At least half a dozen towns and villages in the region have their own set of Morris men, and Chipping Campden is one of only four British places that can claim a continuous dancing tradition dating back at least three hundred years. Cotswold Morris men dance in teams of six, wearing distinctive white costumes decorated with ribbons and a set of bells fixed to their legs. Dances include stick dances, handkerchief dances and processionals, and are usually accompanied by fiddles and accordions. Some of the Cotswold dances act out ancient legends featuring the characters of the "fool" or the "beast". Some are believed to represent sowing and harvesting, with the sticks and handkerchiefs used to drive away evil spirits from the crops. The dances probably date to the medieval period and may have been influenced by Moorish dancing traditions.

The survival of Morris traditions in the Cotswolds is mainly due to the efforts of one man. In 1899 the scholar-musician Cecil Sharp saw a group of Morris dancers performing in the village of Headington Quarry, just outside Oxford. Realizing that he was witnessing a rare example of a dying tradition, he made careful notations and went on to record other examples, including the dances of Chipping Campden. Within a few years there was a major revival of traditional dances, especially after Sharp began to publish his *Morris Books*, and in 1911 the English Folk Dance Society was formed.

Morris dancing was all the rage among the Cotswold Arts and Crafts communities of the 1930s, but not everyone shared Sharp's enthusiasm for traditional dance. Visiting Broadway in 1937, John Moore saw it as a "refuge [for] every conceivable kind of crank from the person who plays tunes on a reed-pipe at concerts to the person who wastes his time teaching nice country boys to waste their time dancing morrises when they'd rather be playing cricket." Writing eighty years later in *The Angry Island*, A. A. Gill is even more vituperative about the "capers" of the Morris men of Stow-in-the-Wold.

LEISURE AND PLEASURE

Nowadays the Cotswolds offer an impressive range of sporting and leisure activities. As in Arthur Gibbs' time there are facilities for riding, fishing, shooting and cricket and the region has many fine golf courses. For motor racing enthusiasts there is the Castle Combe circuit and the Prescott Hill Climb, an uphill motor-racing track six miles south of Cheltenham. The Prescott Climb was first established in 1939 by the Bugatti Owners Club to test their exclusive cars. Today the club hosts events for a range of vehicles, from vintage models to state-of-the-art racing cars and bikes. The Cotswold Water Park, on the southern edge of the region, is a centre for water-sports with lakes for sailing, canoeing, water-skiing and windsurfing. The park was created in the 1960s from over 140 disused gravel pits, and includes over seventy fishing lakes. Other areas of the Water Park have been developed as nature reserves, providing habitats for some rare species of orchids, dragonflies and bats.

Lovers of wildlife can visit two major Cotswold reserves. The Cotswold Wildlife Park (just outside Burford) is set in 160 acres of parkland around a nineteenth-century manor house, and is home to mammals, birds and reptiles from all over the world, including several endangered species. The park was founded in 1970, when the house's owner decided to fill his grounds with over 200 animals and opened them up to the public. Forty years on, the Cotswold Wildlife Park has one of the largest wildlife collections in the country. It also provides its visitors with an unsual experience—the chance to see exotic animals grazing in paddocks in front of an English country house. Birdland at Bourton-on-the-Water is home to over 500 birds, including the only King Penguins in England. It has over fifty aviaries for species including parrots, falcons, pheasants, hornbills and toucans.

The Cotswolds have musical events to suit every taste. People still gather in Cotswold pubs to sing folk songs (The Fox Inn at Great Barrington even organizes an annual "Foxstock" festival) and some local singers—such as Johnny Coppin and Gwilym Davies (a transplanted Welshman)—are reviving the old folk traditions. The annual Cheltenham Festival is one of the highlights of the classical music calendar; the Cornbury Music Festival attracts international stars like Paul Simon and Blondie; and the Blenheim Battle Proms combine rousing music with battle re-enactments and air displays. In the south-west Cotswolds the fair-trade town of Nailsworth is home to Nailstock, a free music festival featuring local bands and a fancy-dress parade. In contrast, the Longborough Festival Opera (near Moreton-in-Marsh) gives the locals the chance to wear their evening dress and enjoy performances in a purpose-built opera house on the Cotswold Edge.

THE HEART OF ENGLAND: RAMBLING AND RAMBLERS

Every year, thousands of people come to the Cotswolds to walk. Many take short country walks, following the region's many footpaths and bridleways. Others tackle longer routes such as the Cotswold Way, the Windrush Way and the newly established North Cotswold Diamond Way. Of these long-distance tracks the Cotswold Way has the longest history. First established in 1970, the path was recognized as a British National Trail in 2007 and forms a continuous hundred-mile route connecting Chipping Campden and Bath. For most of its route the Cotswold Way is composed of ancient drovers' paths linking towns and villages along the Cotswold Edge, and walkers can enjoy some spectacular views from the escarpment.

One of the first enthusiasts for rambling in the Cotswolds was Algernon Gissing, For most of his career Algernon had tried—and failed—to be a bestselling novelist, but at the age of 64 he at last achieved success with *The Footpath Way in Gloucestershire* (published in 1924). Gissing drew on forty years of local knowledge to describe the tracks between Chipping Campden and Winchcombe—now part of the route of the Cotswold Way. His book is illustrated by charming pen and ink drawings and can be seen as one of the earliest, and best, ramblers' guides to the Cotswolds. Filled with observations on the history, flora and fauna of the region, it describes walks along the Cotswold Edge and the ancient Saltway, using a novelist's skill to recreate the pleasures of walking. In some startling word pictures Gissing describes the experience of being entirely covered with morning dew, the thrill of walking through mist to emerge on a sunlit summit, and the quiet pleasure of looking down on familiar villages laid out "like scrolls" on the hills below.

Since Gissing's time a host of authors have published guides for walkers in the Cotswolds. Of these, the most outstanding is Mark Richards' *The Cotswold Way: The Complete Walker's Guide*, first published by Penguin in 1984 and accompanied by the author's own maps and drawings. Richards is a keen walker who has farmed in the Cotswolds all his life and his quirky drawings and observations provide an excellent supplement to more up-to-date walkers' maps and guides. The most idiosyncratic companion to the Cotswold Way is provided by Richard Hayward, an avid Tolkien fan who interprets the route as "A Walk through Middle-Earth".

No modern guide could possibly rival Gissing in his painting of the country scene. *The Footpath Way in Gloucestershire* ends where it began with the author on the summit of Saintbury Hill (near Broadway). It is nearly midnight as he listens to the bells in the surrounding hills ringing in the New Year in the Cotswolds:

> My nearest peal chanced to be a little more than a mile away [and] I could hear six or seven others in the marvellous serenity of that night… Exquisite patches of snow-white clouds were overhead [and] we were in absolute stillness below. A few minutes before the clock struck, the bells sank to a solemn toll, and the old year was gone. Then for New Year's morning they suddenly broke again into jubilant peals. Two or three owls were hooting off and on all the time, and just before midnight came the plaintive notes of a plover in a distant field, aroused, I suppose, by the bells. Amidst such a scene, and to such a unanimity of voices, how escape thoughts of the heart of England?

Further Reading

Brill, Edith, *Life and Traditions in the Cotswolds*. Gloucester: Allan Sutton, 1987.

Burton, Anthony, *The Cotswold Way*. London: Aurum Press, 2007.

Carroll, David, *A Literary Tour of Gloucestershire and Bristol*. Stroud: Alan Sutton, 1994.

Finberg, Josceline, *The Cotswolds*. London: Eyre Methuen, 1977.

Greensted, Mary, *The Arts and Crafts Movement in the Cotswolds*. Gloucester: Allan Sutton, 1993.

Grove, Valerie, *Laurie Lee: the Well-Loved Stranger*. London: Penguin, 2000.

Hayward, Richard, *The Cotswold Way: A Walk through Middle-Earth*. Bellingham, WA: British Footpaths, 1994.

Hicks, David, *Cotswold Gardens*. London: Phoenix, 1998.

Hill, Michael and Birch, Sally, *Cotswold Stone Homes: History, Conservation, Care*. Gloucester: Alan Sutton, 1994.

Jenkins, Simon, *England's Thousand Best Houses*. London: Allen Lane, 2003.

Jenkins, Simon, *England's Thousand Best Churches*. London: Penguin, 2000.

Jones, Allan, *A Cotswold Miscellany*. Studley: Brewin Books, 2003.

MacCarthy, Fiona, *William Morris: A Life for Our Time*. London: Faber and Faber, 1994.

MacCarthy, Fiona, *The Simple Life: C. R. Ashbee in the Cotswolds*. London: Lund Humphries, 1981.

Ottewell, Gordon, *Literary Strolls around the Cotswolds and the Forest of Dean*. Wilmslow: Sigma Leisure, 2000.

Richards, Mark, *The Cotswold Way*. London: Penguin, 1984.

Sherwood, Jennifer and Pevsner, Nicholas, *Oxfordshire*. London: Penguin, 1974.

Sutton, Alan and Hudson, John, *Cotswold Images*. Gloucester: Alan Sutton, 1988.

Sutton, Alan, *The Cotswolds of One Hundred Years Ago*. Stroud: Nonsuch, 2005.

Verey, David, *Gloucestershire: The Cotswolds*. London: Penguin, 1979.

Verey, David, *Cotswold Churches*. Gloucester: Alan Sutton, 1982.

FICTION AND POETRY

Benson, E. F., *Queen Lucia* (1920). London: Heinemann, 1976.

Buchan, John, *Mr. Standfast* (1919). Ware:Wordsworth Editions, 2008.

Buchan, John, *Midwinter* (1923). Edinburgh: Black and White Publishing, 1993.

Buchan, John, *The Blanket of the Dark* (1931). Edinburgh: Polygon, 2008.

Cooper, Jilly, *The Rutshire Chronicles*. London: Bantam Press, 1986-2006.

Craik, Mrs. (Dinah Maria Mulock), *John Halifax, Gentleman* (1856). London: Collins, 1954.

Eliot, T. S., *Collected Poems 1909-1962*. London, Faber and Faber, 2002.

Fanthorpe, U. A., *Collected Poems 1978-2003*. Calstock: Peterloo Poets, 2005.

Gurney, Ivor, *Collected Poems*. Oxford: Oxford University Press, 1982.

Lee, Laurie, *Cider with Rosie* (1959). London: Vintage, 2002.

Mitford, Jessica, *Hons and Rebels* (1960). London: Phoenix, 1999.

Mitford, Nancy, *The Pursuit of Love* (1945). London: Penguin, 1976.

Morris, William, *News from Nowhere* (1890). London: Penguin Classics, 2004.

Priestley, J. B., *The Good Companions* (1929). London: Arrow Books, 2000.

Pym, Barbara, *A Few Green Leaves*. London: Macmillan, 1980.

MEMOIRS AND COMMENTARIES

Beckinsale, R. P., *Companion into Gloucestershire*. London: Methuen, 1948.

Bingley, Xandra, Bertie, *May and Mrs. Fish: Country Memories of Wartime*. London: Harper Collins, 2006.

Bryson, Bill, *Notes from a Small Island*. London: Black Swan, 1996.

Cobbett, William (ed. Ian Dyck), *Rural Rides* (1830). London: Penguin, 2001.

Gibbs, J. Arthur, *A Cotswold Village: Or Country Life and its Pursuits in Gloucestershire* (1898). London: Breslich and Foss, 1983.

Gill, A. A., *The Angry Island: Hunting the English*. London: Phoenix, 2005.

Gissing, Algernon, *The Footpath Way in Gloucestershire*. London: J.M. Dent, 1924.

Jewson, Norman, *By Chance I Did Rove* (1951). Privately published, 1973.

Knight, Sid, *A Cotswold Lad*. London: Phoenix House, 1960.

Massingham, H. J., *Cotswold Country*. London: B. T. Batsford, 1942.

Moore, John, *The Cotswolds*. London: Chapman and Hall, 1937.

Priestley, J. B., *English Journey*. London: Mandarin, 1994.

Stewart, Sheila, *Lifting the Latch: A Life on the Land* [the memoirs of Mont Abbot of Enstone]. Oxford: Oxford University Press, 1987.

Walthew, Ian, *A Place in My Country: In Search of a Rural Dream*. London: Phoenix, 2007.

Warren, C. Henry, *A Cotswold Year*. London: Hazell, Watson and Viney, 1936.

Witts, Francis, Edward (ed. David Verey), *Diary of a Cotswold Parson*, 1783-1854. Stroud: Alan Sutton, 1998.

Cotswold Places and Events

Museums and Galleries

Athelstan Museum, Malmesbury
www.athelstan-museum.org.uk

Charlbury Museum

Cheltenham Museum and Art Gallery
www.cheltenhammuseum.org.uk

Chipping Norton Museum

Corinium Museum, Cirencester
www.coriniummuseum.co.uk

Cotswold Rural Life Collection, Northleach

Court Barn Museum, Chipping Campden
www.courtbarn.org.uk

Gloucester City Museum and Art Gallery
www.gloucester.gov.uk/citymuseum

Gordon Russell Museum, Broadway
www.gordonrussellmuseum.org

Museum in the Park, Stroud
www.museuminthepark.org.uk

Oxfordshire Museum, Woodstock
www.oxfordshire.gov.uk/the_oxfordshire_museum

Tolsey Museum, Burford

Winchcombe Folk and Police Museum

Winchcombe Railway Museum and Gardens

STATELY HOMES AND HOUSES

Blenheim Palace
www.blenheimpalace.com
Broadway Tower
www.broadwaytower.co.uk
Chastleton House
www.nationaltrust.org.uk/main/w-chastleton
Chavenage House
www.chavenage.com
Dyrham Park
www.nationaltrust.org.uk/main/w-dyrhampark
Kelmscott Manor
www.kelmscottmanor.org.uk
Lodge Park
www.nationaltrust.org.uk/main/w-lodgeparkandsherborneestate
Minster Lovell Hall
Newark Park
www.nationaltrust.org.uk/main/w-newarkpark
Owlpen Manor
www.owlpen.com
Rodmarton Manor
www.rodmarton-manor.co.uk
Sezincote House
www.sezincote.co.uk
Snowshill Manor
www.nationaltrust.org.uk/snowshillmanor
Stanway House
www.stanwayfountain.co.uk
Sudeley Castle
www.sudeleycastle.co.uk
Upton House
www.nationaltrust.org.uk/main/w-uptonhouse
Woodchester Mansion
www.woodchestermansion.org.uk

VISITOR CENTRES AND ATTRACTIONS

Birdland, Bourton-on-the-Water
   www.birdland.co.uk
Castle Combe Motor Racing Circuit
   www.castlecombecircuit.co.uk
Cogges Manor Farm Museum, Witney
   www.witney.net/cogges-manor-farm-museum.htm
Cotswold Falconry Centre, Batsford Park
   www.cotswold-falconry.co.uk
Cotswold Farm Park, Guiting Power
   www.cotswoldfarmpark.co.uk
Cotswold Water Park
   www.waterpark.org
Cotswold Wildlife Park, Burford
   www.cotswoldwildlifepark.co.uk
Cotswold Woollen Weavers, Filkins
Gloucestershire and Warwickshire Steam Railway, Toddington
   www.gwsr.com
Prescott Speed Hill Climb
   www.prescott-hillclimb.com

ANCIENT MONUMENTS

Belas Knap Long Barrow, Winchcombe
Chedworth Roman Villa
   www.chedworthromanvilla.com
Great Witcombe Roman Villa
Hetty Pegler's Tump, Uley
Nympsfield Open Barrow
Rollright Stones, Long Compton
   www.rollrightstones.co.uk

CHURCHES AND ABBEYS

Ampney St. Mary (wall paintings)
Burford (Gothic "wool church" & Levellers' memorials)
Chipping Campden (Gothic "wool church")
Cirencester (Gothic "wool church")
Daglingworth (Saxon carvings)

Duntisbourne Rouse (Saxon and Norman structure)
Eastleach (twin churches, with John Keble connection)
Elkstone (Norman carvings)
Fairford (Gothic "wool church" with outstanding stained glass)
Hailes Abbey ruins
Hailes church (wall paintings)
Malmesbury Abbey (Norman carvings)
Northleach (Gothic "wool church")
Oddington (wall paintings)
Selsey (Pre-Raphaelite stained glass)
Swinbrook (Fettiplace tombs and Mitford memorials)

GARDENS AND PLANT COLLECTIONS
Batsford Arboretum
    www.batsarb.co.uk
Blenheim Palace Gardens and Grounds
    www.blenheimpalace.com/thepalace/formalgardens
Chastleton House Gardens
Edwin Wilson's Chinese Garden, Chipping Campden
Cirencester Park
Hidcote Manor Garden
    www.nationaltrust.org.uk/hidcote
Kiftsgate Court Garden
    www.kiftsgate.co.uk
Owlpen Manor Gardens
Painswick Rococo Garden
    www.rococogarden.co.uk
Rodmarton Manor Gardens
Sezincote Oriental Gardens
Snowshill Manor Gardens
Stanway Water Gardens
Sudeley Castle Gardens
Westonbirt Arboretum, Tetbury
    www.forestry.gov.uk/westonbirt

INDUSTRIAL SITES
Castle Combe village

Bibury village
Stroudwater Canal
   www.cotswoldcanals.com
Sapperton Canal Tunnel
Dunkirk Mill Centre, Nailsworth
Ruskin Mill, Nailsworth

LONG-DISTANCE WALKING PATHS
Cotswold Way
   www.nationaltrail.co.uk/Cotswold
North Cotswold Diamond Way
   www.ldwa.org.uk/ldp/members/show_path.php?path_name=Diamond
   +Way+(North+Cotswold)
Windrush Way
   www.ldwa.org.uk/ldp/members/show_path.php?path_name=
   Windrush+Way
Annual Events
Avening Pig Face Day
Badminton Horse Trials
   www.badminton-horse.co.uk
Bourton-on-the-Water Football in the River
Cheltenham Music Festival
   www.cheltenhamfestivals.co.uk
Cheltenham Racing Festival
   www.cheltenham.co.uk
Cooper's Hill Cheese Rolling
   www.cheese-rolling.co.uk
Cornbury Music Festival, Cornbury Park
   www.cornburyfestival.com
Dover's Olimpick Games, Chipping Campden
   www.olimpickgames.co.uk
Gatcombe Festival of Eventing
   www.gatcombe-horse.co.uk
Kemble Air Show
   www.kembleairday.com
Longborough Festival Opera
   www.lfo.org.uk

Painswick Clipping Ceremony
Randwick Wap
   www.randwick.org.uk/Orgs/wap.htm
Tetbury Woolsack Races
   www.tetburywoolsack.co.uk

Index of Literary, Artistic & Historical Names

Index of Places & Landmarks

.

Made in the USA
San Bernardino, CA
16 December 2019